ADVANCE PRAISE FOR

BUT I COULD NEVER GO
-VEGAN!-

"Kristy Turner's *But I Could Never Go Vegan!* is nothing short of brilliant! This isn't just a beautiful vegan cookbook; it's a resource guide that will help you excuse-proof your diet. If you have a dilemma, Kristy has the answer!"

—ANGELA LIDDON, *New York Times*–bestselling author
of *The Oh She Glows Cookbook* and creator of OhSheGlows.com

"With warmth, humor, and great recipes, Kristy Turner combats excuses people commonly use to defend their dietary status quo. Those who think they can't be satisfied without eating beef, for example, will do well to get acquainted with her plant-based fajitas, sloppy Joes, tacos, and more. *But I Could Never Go Vegan!* is guaranteed to change hearts and minds one meal at a time."

—GENE BAUR, president and cofounder of Farm Sanctuary,
author of *Farm Sanctuary: Changing Hearts and Minds About Animals and Food*

"I love the creative, whole-foods recipes in *But I Could Never Go Vegan!* Kristy Turner has heard all the excuses and has a response for each. It's true, no life is complete without the occasional calzone—but stuff 'em with Kristy's Buffalo Cauliflower and Cashew Blue Cheese and you can have calzones and be vegan too. Get ready for your taste buds to explode."

—ISA CHANDRA MOSKOWITZ, bestselling author
of *Veganomicon* and *Isa Does It*

THE EXPERIMENT

BECAUSE EVERY BOOK IS A TEST OF NEW IDEAS

"I can't imagine a vegan primer that is more humorous, welcoming, or wise than Kristy Turner's spectacular *But I Could Never Go Vegan!* If you're considering switching over to a plant-based diet—or simply eating a few more vegetarian meals—Kristy's spectacular recipes and practical guidance will give you all of the inspiration you need. Most of all, her gentle and witty voice will guide you through all of the inevitable anxieties, stumbling blocks, and mishaps that accompany a lifestyle change. This book is beautiful, creative, whimsical, and profoundly inspiring."

—GENA HAMSHAW, author of *Choosing Raw*;
www.choosingraw.com

"There's no such thing as 'can't' when it comes to compassion, and in *But I Could Never Go Vegan!*, Kristy Turner proves it with an array of inventive plant-based recipes and dazzling photographs."

—COLLEEN PATRICK-GOUDREAU, bestselling author of six books, including
The Joy of Vegan Baking and *The 30-Day Vegan Challenge*

"Kristy's book had us smiling from the moment we read the table of contents. Its lighthearted approach and delicious recipes will appeal to everyone. This is a must-read for anybody who believes life without cheese isn't possible."

—RICH LANDAU and KATE JACOBY, chefs and owners
of Vedge restaurant and coauthors of *Vedge*

"Kristy and Chris have taken everything I love about their blog and somehow upgraded it, putting together one helluva cookbook with tons of helpful information and crazy good recipes that are sure to please hard-core vegans, curious newbies, and dabbling omnivores alike. Now, if we could only figure out some way to get those Chickpea Sloppy Joes hooked up to me 24/7 through an IV . . ."

—RANDY CLEMENS, author of *The Sriracha Cookbook*, *The Veggie-Lover's
Sriracha Cookbook*, and *The Craft of Stone Brewing Co.*

BUT I COULD NEVER GO -VEGAN!-

125 RECIPES That Prove You *Can* Live Without Cheese, It's *Not* All Rabbit Food, and Your Friends *Will* Still Come Over for Dinner

by **Kristy Turner**

photographs by **CHRIS MILLER**

THE EXPERIMENT
NEW YORK

BUT I COULD NEVER GO VEGAN! *125 Recipes That Prove You* Can *Live Without Cheese, It's* Not *All Rabbit Food, and Your Friends* Will *Still Come Over for Dinner*

Copyright © 2014 Kristy Turner
Photographs copyright © 2014 Chris Miller

The Experiment, LLC
220 East 23rd Street, Suite 301
New York, NY 10010-4674
www.theexperimentpublishing.com

This book contains the opinions and ideas of its author. It is intended to provide helpful and informative material on the subjects addressed in the book. It is sold with the understanding that the author and publisher are not engaged in rendering medical, health, or any other kind of personal professional services in the book. The author and publisher specifically disclaim all responsibility for any liability, loss, or risk—personal or otherwise—that is incurred as a consequence, directly or indirectly, of the use and application of any of the contents of this book.

The Experiment's books are available at special discounts when purchased in bulk for premiums and sales promotions as well as for fund-raising or educational use. For details, contact us at info@theexperimentpublishing.com.

Library of Congress Cataloging-in-Publication Data
Turner, Kristy.
    But I could never go vegan! : 125 recipes that prove you can live without cheese, it's not all rabbit food, and your friends will still come over for dinner / by Kristy Turner.
       pages cm
    Includes index.
    ISBN 978-1-61519-210-6 (pbk.) — ISBN 978-1-61519-211-3 (ebook) 1. Vegan cooking. I. Title.
    TX837.T875 2014
    641.5'636--dc23
                        2014020051

ISBN 978-1-61519-210-6
Ebook ISBN 978-1-61519-211-3

Cover design by Mark Weddington
Cover photograph by Chris Miller
Author photograph by Chris Miller
Text design by Pauline Neuwirth, Neuwirth & Associates, Inc.

Manufactured in the United States of America
Distributed by Workman Publishing Company, Inc.
Distributed simultaneously in Canada by Thomas Allen & Son Ltd.

First printing October 2014
10 9 8 7 6 5 4

For Grandma Irene,
who not only taught me how to cook but also showed me the definition of
strength and compassion. I am who I am today because of you.

CONTENTS

MY FRIENDS WON'T WANT TO COME OVER FOR DINNER.

Fancy dinner party recipes sure to impress

NO WAY. I'M ITALIAN! (OR SOUTHERN/GERMAN/MEXICAN/FRENCH!)

Dishes inspired by not-so-vegan cuisines

BUT I HATE [INSERT VEGETABLE HERE].

Recipes to convert veggie-haters into lovers

I DON'T WANT TO BE LEFT OUT AT POTLUCKS AND FAMILY GET-TOGETHERS.

Vegan recipes that will WOW the crowds

YOU CAN'T BAKE WITHOUT BUTTER OR EGGS!

Vegan desserts that aren't missing a thing

WAIT, IS CHOCOLATE VEGAN?

Desserts that highlight chocolate—don't worry, it's vegan!

BUT I SCREAM FOR ICE CREAM!

Vegan ice cream recipes that will have you screaming for more

INTRODUCTION

IN MY PAST LIFE (OR SEVERAL YEARS AGO), I WORKED AS A FROMAGIER (CHEESE nerd) in a snooty French restaurant and in a fancy cheese shop. I had chosen to be vegetarian about five years prior to that time for health reasons, but I never even dreamed it would be possible to give up cheese or eggs. "It's how I get my protein!" I would exclaim. "You have to enjoy the little things in life, and for me that's cheese." If I ever met a vegan at a party, for example, I was always very quick to say, "Oh, I could *never* be vegan" and, probably much to that vegan's chagrin, list the many animal products I couldn't live without. Cheese was not only something I was passionate about, it was my livelihood. It was my life.

A couple of years later, I found myself working for a personal catering company, and part of my job was to go to company parties and conventions, do cooking demos, and sell our products. At one such event, when I was selling some of our energy bars, a woman came up and looked at the bars. I smiled at her and asked if she would like a sample.

"Are they vegan?" she asked.

"Oh no," I told her. "They're made with whey protein. Sorry."

She just smiled and walked away; when her back was to me, I turned to my coworker and rolled my eyes.

"Ugh, vegans!" I said. I had always considered myself a compassionate person and I loved animals, but veganism seemed really extreme. "I mean, I like vegan food and all," I said, "but I could never be that crazy-obsessive about every single thing I eat. And the whole 'No Wool' thing is just nuts."

A year later I was sitting in front of my computer, crying my eyes out. I had just watched a video about what really happens on dairy farms. For several days after, every time I thought of that mother cow's cries for her newborn baby, I cried for her. A couple of days later while in the car with my husband, Chris, I told him that I may need to go vegan. *Need.* I explained what I'd seen and told him about the other research I had done. He agreed we should try it.

So Chris and I tried veganism for a couple of weeks, and lo and behold—being vegan was not nearly as hard as I'd anticipated! I started trying different vegetables and new-to-me ingredients. The food I cooked during that time was very basic but way better than anything else I had been cooking. On top of that, my skin cleared up, my bloating went away, I lost weight, I felt more rested when I woke in the morning, and I felt *really, really* good. Then we went on our honeymoon. Not wanting to deal with trying to be vegan in another country, we decided to be vegetarian. The first few days were okay, but then the acne came back. So did the bloating and fatigue. Starting with our plane trip home, we were vegan for good.

I ended up quitting my job because I didn't want to sell products that weren't vegan. Being unemployed freed up some time to begin researching the heck out of vegan cooking. With the help of vegan bloggers, cookbook authors, and their amazing recipes, I started cooking like a madwoman; scrumptious vegan meals began to emerge from my kitchen.

Shortly after going vegan, Chris and I subscribed to a CSA (Community Supported Agriculture) delivery service to help make sure we ate a variety of fruits and vegetables. I started getting produce I wouldn't normally buy, which forced me to get a little inventive with my cooking. Trust me—any food you can think of, by now I've made a vegan version. A whole new creative side of me emerged, and I began developing my own recipes. I found a passion I had never known existed. I was enjoying creating so much that I decided to create a blog to share some of my recipes. *Keepin' It Kind* was born; in a crazy whirlwind of events, I went from passionate home cook to semiprofessional food blogger—to, now, cookbook author.

If you're reading this book, chances are that at some point in your life you've muttered the words, "I could never go vegan," too. Maybe you thought it years ago and since then actually went vegan; maybe it was yesterday in a debate with your vegan coworker. I understand how daunting it seems, and I understand there are certain things you feel you can't live without. I've been there. You have to trust me, though: becoming vegan seems most impossible *right before you make the switch*.

Once you've got a few staple vegan cheese recipes in your artillery and you realize there is such a thing as vegan chocolate, the change won't seem so scary. When you realize your brunches are going to be just as delicious, your lunches just as filling, and your dinners just as easy as in the old days, veganism will become second nature. Once you see that you don't have to give up cookies, or pizza, or Mexican food, this new lifestyle will become exciting for you. When you begin to understand that you've added much more variety to your diet than you've taken away, you'll wonder why you waited so long.

If you can eat food that is downright incredible-tasting, is good for your health, and doesn't destroy the earth or cause harm to any living creature, why would you choose anything else?

This book is for those considering the journey and for those who have already started down the path (be it yesterday or seventy years ago). In it are fun, inviting, and absolutely scrumptious recipes for everyone. All you have to do is get your butt in the kitchen!

WHERE AM I SUPPOSED TO START?

IF YOU ARE CONSIDERING TRANSITIONING TO A PLANT-BASED DIET, TAKE BABY steps. You don't have to make the change overnight. Try having just one or two vegan meals a week and work from there. Add new vegan foods to your diet, and slowly remove animal-based foods. If you make the transition at your own pace, it will be easier to stick with in the long run.

Don't be too hard on yourself if you make mistakes. Being vegan isn't about being perfect. It's about living a healthier, more compassionate life, and as long as you keep that in mind, you'll be fine.

As you begin using this book, I urge you to look over the next two sections on helpful ingredients and useful kitchen tools to help you prepare for the recipes. There are many helpful tips on how to prepare beans and grains, press tofu, and make your own vegetable broth. As you dog-ear the pages of recipes you want to try, be sure to read the headnotes, tips, and variations offered for each recipe. Keep in mind that some recipes call for components of other recipes, so you may have to prepare one ingredient beforehand. But it's worth it! For example, you'll use Pecan Parmesan (page 38) not only in Tempeh Bacon Mac 'n' Cheese (page 38) but also in Parmesan-Crusted Avocado & Kale Florentines with Smoked Paprika Hollandaise (page 122) and Pan-Fried Gnocchi & Acorn Squash with Hazelnut-Sage Pesto (page 249)—plus anywhere else you might miss a sprinkle of Parmesan.

The key to getting more comfortable with vegan cooking is just to dive right in. Rather than shying away from an ingredient you haven't heard of, embrace it. If there's a technique you haven't tried, give it a whirl. If you make a mistake, it's okay. Mistakes are the best way for you to learn and adapt to a new way of cooking.

Symbols You'll See

 GF Gluten-free or has a gluten-free option

SF Soy-free

NF Nut-free

 TG Can be made to go

PA Plan ahead—one or more ingredients must be prepared in advance

BUT VEGANS USE ALL SORTS OF CRAZY INGREDIENTS!

TRUE, THERE ARE A FEW INGREDIENTS VEGANS USE MORE THAN OMNIVORES use and vice versa, but for the most part we aren't so different. I was nervous about trying new ingredients when I first went vegan, but now they're some of the most used in my kitchen. Plus, trying new ingredients has made the variety of meals I prepare much wider than it ever was when I was an omnivore or a vegetarian.

STAPLES

Tofu/Silken Tofu—Tofu is one of most versatile ingredients you can have in your fridge. I use it all the time for making everything from hearty tofu steaks to ultra-creamy sauces. I even use silken tofu as an egg replacement in some baking. If you think you don't like the texture of tofu, then you need to try pressing it before you cook with it. Pressing helps release all the extra water so that it has a firmer texture. Pressing also increases tofu's flavor-absorbing potential by a ton.

How to Press Tofu

Lay a clean kitchen towel on top of a plate. Remove a block of firm or extra-firm tofu from its package and gently squeeze out the excess water. Place the block of tofu on top of the towel and place another clean kitchen towel on top of the tofu. Place the heaviest book you have on top of the towel-covered tofu and place 2 to 3 cans of food on top of the book. Let the tofu sit at least 30 minutes or up to 24 hours in the refrigerator.

Tempeh—Tempeh is made from fermented soy beans and is a wonderful form of vegan protein. Don't try eating it without cooking it, though. Its bitter taste will turn you off for sure (I'm speaking from experience). To remove the bitterness, it's best to marinate it, or steam it and then cook it in a flavorful sauce.

Non-Dairy Milk—A whole book could be written on the endless variety of non-dairy milk. If you tried soy milk and it didn't float your boat, don't worry—there are other options! My favorite is almond milk, but check out coconut, oat, hemp, cashew, rice, or flax milks.

Nuts & Seeds—I keep my nuts and seeds in the refrigerator because it keeps them fresher longer. I try to purchase only raw nuts and seeds as much as possible because they are easier to digest and are more versatile in terms of how you prepare and season them. We both snack on and cook with nuts and seeds, so we always have almonds, cashews, peanuts, pistachios, pecans, macadamia nuts, sunflower seeds, pepitas (pumpkin seeds), and sesame seeds on hand.

How to Make Homemade Nut Butter

Pour 2 to 3 cups of your nut of choice (peanuts, cashews, almonds, macadamia nuts, pecans, and walnuts all make really good butters) into a food processor and process until smooth. It may take a while (sometimes up to 10 minutes), and you may have to stop and scrape the sides of the food processor a few times. When it's smooth and creamy, you can eat it as is or add salt to taste and a touch of sweetener if you'd like (I always add a tiny drizzle of maple syrup). Process again until incorporated and store in an airtight container in the refrigerator (the chilled nut butter will firm up) or at room temperature (where it will stay soft and creamy).

How to Make Cashew Cream

Cashew cream is the vegan's answer to heavy cream. Soak 1 cup of raw cashews at least 3 to 4 hours or overnight. (If you forget to soak the cashews, place them in a pot with 2 cups of water and bring to a boil. Boil 10 minutes; remove from the heat.) Reserve the soaking water, drain the cashews, and place in a food processor with ½ cup of the reserved water. Process until smooth, pausing to scrape the sides as necessary. Add the reserved soaking water by the tablespoon until you have your desired consistency (the more water you add, the thinner the cream will become).

Vegetable Broth—I often rely on vegan bouillon cubes to make my broth (I like to use Edward & Sons brand, 1 bouillon cube per 4 cups of water), or if I'm really in a pinch, I purchase the boxed broth (always use the low-sodium kind when using store-bought broths). If you have time, I do recommend making your own broth because it's so easy and tastes much better.

How to Make Homemade Vegetable Broth

You'll need 2 onions (red or yellow), 5 to 6 garlic cloves, 3 carrots, 3 celery ribs, 8 ounces (225 g) cremini mushrooms, 1 red bell pepper, and 1 tomato, all roughly chopped (If you have any other "extras" lying about, such as a broccoli stalk or kale stems, throw them in, too!). Heat 2 teaspoons of extra virgin olive oil in a large stockpot and add the onions, garlic, carrots, celery, and mushrooms. Cook about 3 minutes; add the bell pepper and tomato along with 12 cups (about 3 liters) water, 2 tablespoons liquid aminos, 1 sprig fresh rosemary, 1 sprig fresh thyme, a handful of roughly chopped parsley, 2 bay leaves, 2 teaspoons salt, and pepper to taste. Bring to a boil; reduce to a simmer and simmer until it has reduced by one-third. Remove from the heat and run a strainer through the stock to remove all the solids. Taste and add more salt and pepper if needed. Transfer the broth to large jars or airtight containers, leaving about an inch at the top of each container. Let cool completely with the lids off. Once cool, cover the containers and store in the freezer for up to 2 months or in the refrigerator for 5 to 7 days.

Onions—My grandmother's favorite vegetable was onions because they are so versatile and add so much flavor to a dish. Plus, she loved the way they smelled when they cooked. I have to agree with all of the above; do you? Like my grandmother I also use them constantly and try always to keep red, yellow, sweet, and green onions on hand.

Garlic—It's always good to have a few heads of garlic handy. Roasted garlic is a great way to add garlicky flavor without the extra sharpness.

How to Roast Garlic

Preheat the oven to 400°F (200°C). Peel a head of garlic of its outer layers of skin so the cloves are exposed. Cut about ½ inch (1 cm) off the top of the bulb so the tips of the cloves are exposed. Place the entire head on a large piece of aluminum foil. Lightly drizzle with extra virgin olive oil, and use your fingers to massage the oil in. Wrap the bulb tightly in the foil and place in the oven. Bake 30 to 40 minutes, until soft when touched (carefully—don't burn yourself!). Remove from the oven and let cool until you are comfortable handling it. Squeeze  each clove out of each pod. If not using right away, refrigerate in an airtight container until ready to use.

BEANS, LENTILS & SPLIT PEAS

Beans and lentils are probably my favorite source of plant-based protein. The key is to get creative with them. For the most part, my recipes call for cooked beans. Dried beans are very easy to cook, but sometimes we don't have the forethought to cook them for a recipe. For this reason it's important to keep some canned beans stocked in your pantry. I recommend choosing organic and BPA-free brands, preferably low sodium. Always rinse and drain them well before using. If you do have time to precook your beans, here are some tips.

How to Cook Beans

Before cooking beans, soak them at least 8 hours (in the fridge if longer). Soaking makes them much more easily digestible (meaning less flatulence) and reduces cooking times. After soaking, rinse them thoroughly to remove any leftover residue. Place them in a large pot and cover with water by about 1 inch (2.5 cm)—roughly 3 to 4 cups (710 ml to 950 ml) water per 1 cup (235 ml) beans. If desired add 1 whole onion (outer layers peeled), 2 garlic cloves, and 2 bay leaves. Bring the water to a boil, reduce to a simmer, and cook until the beans are tender. You can also prepare beans in a slow cooker or a pressure cooker. Here are approximate cooking times for some common beans (older beans may require more time):

Type	Cooking Time
Black beans	90 minutes
Black-eyed peas	60 minutes
Cannellini beans	90 minutes
Chickpeas	90 minutes
Fava beans	60 minutes
Great Northern beans	60 minutes
Kidney beans (red)	60 minutes
Navy beans	90 minutes
Pinto beans	120 minutes
Red beans	90 minutes

How to Cook Lentils & Split Peas

Spread the lentils or split peas on a clean kitchen towel and pick out any shriveled or broken legumes and any stones or other debris. Rinse them well. Bring a pot of water (1½ cups/350 ml per 1 cup/235 ml lentils or peas) to a boil. Add the lentils or peas; reduce the heat to a simmer. Simmer until the legumes are tender. You can also add dry lentils and peas to soups or stews as long as there is at least 1½ cups (350 ml) of liquid per 1 cup (235 ml) lentils or peas. Here are approximate cooking times for some common lentils and peas:

Type	Cooking Time
French (Puy) lentils	30 minutes
Standard green or brown lentils	30 minutes
Green split peas	45 minutes
Red lentils	20 minutes
Yellow lentils (chana dal)	30 minutes

GRAINS

Grains are a valuable source of nutrition and are great for adding substance, flavor, and texture to your meals. I use a variety in these recipes; unless otherwise instructed, you can use this chart for guidelines on how to cook each type (including couscous— a type of pasta cooked like a grain).

How to Cook Grains

Type	Gluten-Free	Liquid per 1 cup	Cooking Method
Amaranth	Yes	3 cups	Combine the amaranth and water in a medium pot. Bring to a boil, reduce the heat, cover, and simmer until the water has been absorbed, about 25 minutes. Remove from the heat and keep covered for 10 minutes. Use a fork to fluff the grain; add salt to taste if desired.
Barley	No	3½ cups	Bring the water to a boil; add the barley. Reduce the heat, cover, and simmer for 60 minutes. Drain off excess water and add salt to taste if desired.
Brown rice (short-grain)	Yes	1½ to 2 cups	Rinse the rice in a fine-mesh strainer until the water runs clear. Bring the water to a boil; add the rice with ¼ teaspoon salt. Return to a boil, reduce the heat to low, and cover. Simmer 45 minutes or until the rice is tender. Drain off excess water and return the rice to the pot. Let the rice rest 5 minutes before serving.

Type	Gluten-Free	Liquid per 1 cup	Cooking Method
Couscous (whole wheat)	No	1½ cups	Bring the water to a boil. Add the couscous, cover, and remove from the heat. Let sit 15 minutes or until the water is absorbed. If the water is not fully absorbed, cover and let rest a few more minutes. Add salt if desired.
Farro (pearled)	No	2½ cups	Rinse the farro in a fine-mesh strainer 1 minute. Combine the farro with the water in a medium pot and bring to a boil. Stir and reduce the heat to low. Simmer uncovered 15 to 20 minutes or until the grains are tender. Drain off excess water and add salt to taste if desired.
Forbidden rice (black rice)	Yes	2 cups	Rinse the rice in a fine-mesh strainer until the water runs clear. Bring the water to a boil; add the rice with ¼ teaspoon salt. Return to a boil, reduce the heat to low, and cover. Simmer 30 minutes or until the rice is tender. Drain off excess water and return the rice to the pot, cover, and let rest 5 minutes before serving.
Millet	Yes	2 cups	For a deeper flavor, toast the millet in a medium pot 3 to 5 minutes. Add the water, bring to a boil, and reduce the heat. Simmer 20 to 35 minutes or until the millet is tender. Remove the pot from the heat, fluff with a fork, and let rest about 10 minutes before serving. Add salt to taste if desired.
Oats (rolled)	Yes (purchase certified gluten-free if necessary)	2 cups	Combine the oats and water in a medium pot; bring to a boil over medium (not high) heat. Reduce the heat to medium or medium-low and simmer 10 to 15 minutes until thickened.
Quinoa	Yes	2 cups	Unless you purchased prewashed quinoa, rinse the quinoa well before cooking. Combine with the water in a medium pot, bring to a boil, and reduce the heat. Cover and simmer 15 to 20 minutes, or until the water has been absorbed. Remove the pot from the heat and let rest, covered, 10 minutes. Uncover and fluff with a fork. Add salt to taste if desired.

Type	Gluten-Free	Liquid per 1 cup	Cooking Method
Wheat berries	No	4 cups	Soak the wheat berries at least 8 hours. Drain, combine with water in a medium pot, and bring to a boil. Reduce the heat and simmer 50 to 60 minutes or until tender. Drain off excess water and add salt to taste if desired.
Wild rice	Yes	3 cups	Rinse the rice in a mesh strainer until the water runs clear. Bring the water to a boil; add the rice with ¼ teaspoon salt. Return to a boil, reduce the heat to low, and cover. Simmer 45 minutes or until the rice is tender. Drain off excess water; return the rice to the pot to rest 5 minutes before serving.

FLOURS

When it comes to measuring flour for a recipe, many people like to use their measuring cups to scoop the flour and use their fingers or butter knives to level it off. It isn't the best way to measure flour, however, especially if you will be using it for baking. Instead, you should always gently "shake" spoonfuls of flour into your measuring cup until it is full. Gently tap the measuring cup on the counter a couple times until the flour has leveled. If necessary, use a butter knife to gently level off excess flour. If you do this over a piece of parchment paper, you can just use the paper to funnel the excess flour back into its container.

Unbleached all-purpose flour—The name says it all. It's good to always have this one around for all your standard baking needs. Be sure to get the unbleached variety, though, because it is less refined . . . and *bleach*? Really?

Whole wheat pastry flour—I like this flour because it is a little bit lighter than most whole wheat flour, good for when you want a fluffier, less dense result—like in cupcakes (see page 262 for an example).

Bread flour—Although you can use all-purpose flour to bake bread-type items, the extra gluten in bread flour really kicks it up a notch. It adds that chewy doughiness to breads that we all love. Try it in Pecan-Date Cinnamon Rolls (page 128) or pizza dough (see page 178). You'll be amazed.

Buckwheat flour—This is a heavier, more nutrient-dense flour. And it's gluten-free! It has a stronger, earthier flavor than regular flour. It's best to mix it with other flours than to use it alone.

Oat flour—You can buy it at most natural food stores, but sometimes it's easier to grind up regular ol' rolled oats in a blender until you have a fine flour. It's a great gluten-free alternative (if you use certified gluten-free oats) and adds a nice wholesome flavor to cookies, pancakes, waffles, and more.

Almond flour—This flour can be made at home by grinding raw almonds in a blender or food processor into a fine flour. I prefer unblanched (skin-on) almonds for making flour. Be sure not to overprocess because the almonds can begin to get sticky and turn into butter. Almond flour is a great gluten-free alternative (best used in combination with other gluten-free flours), but it also adds a nutty flavor to any baked good, gluten-free or not.

Chickpea flour—Also known as besan, this naturally gluten-free flour is made from ground-up dry chickpeas. You can make it at home in a high-speed blender, but it's readily available at most natural food stores, ethnic markets, and even some mainstream grocery stores. It is one of my most favorite flours because it is a great binder and egg substitute, and its high protein content makes it very filling. Whatever you do, though, do not taste it before it has been cooked—it is downright bitter and your taste buds will hate you for it.

Cornmeal—Another of my favorite secret ingredients. Not only is it a must-have for any impromptu cornbread you'll be making, but this gluten-free "flour" adds a little extra crispness to things like waffles (page 131) and pizza dough (page 181).

Vital wheat gluten—Otherwise known as wheat protein, vital wheat gluten is the protein that has been stripped from wheat, dried, and processed into powder. Though technically not a flour, it can be added to bread dough to improve its elasticity and make the bread a little chewier. It can also be used to make seitan (my main use for it), a chewy "wheat meat" that is a wonderfully tasty source of protein and a sponge for whatever flavor you want it to take on.

The starches—There are several: tapioca, potato, arrowroot, cornstarch, and the list goes on. They are all gluten-free, great for thickening sauces and binding together baked goods. I primarily use cornstarch and arrowroot powder (both flavorless or close to it), but I occasionally use tapioca as well.

SWEETENERS

Vegan sugar—My recipes call for vegan sugar, meaning unrefined, certified vegan sugar. When is sugar not vegan? Actually, most sugar is filtered through animal bone char. Whether you're vegan or not, that's gross, right? If you're sensitive to sugar, you are welcome to use a plant-based alternative such as stevia (though stevia is sweeter than sugar so you will likely need to use less), xylitol, or erythritol. There is also certified vegan brown sugar made from unrefined sugar.

Coconut sugar—This is my favorite form of dry sweetener. It is basically evaporated coconut nectar and looks very similar to brown sugar. I like it because it has a lower glycemic index, so it doesn't affect your blood sugar the way normal sugar does. It's also rich in nutrients, which is something we can't say about regular sugar at all. It's becoming more and more common, so you shouldn't have any problem finding it.

Vegan powdered sugar—This is also known as confectioners' sugar and is the key to luscious icings, frostings, and glazes. As with other sugar, look for a certified vegan version. If you are sensitive to sugar, use powdered xylitol or powdered erythritol in its place. They taste exactly the same, have a fraction of the calories, and won't affect your blood sugar. If you can't find the powdered version, purchase the regular variety and make your own powdered sugar. All you need to do is blend (in an absolutely dry blender container) 1 cup sugar or other dry sweetener with 1 teaspoon arrowroot powder or cornstarch until it's as fine as powdered sugar. Store in an airtight container.

Maple syrup—I'm not talking about that corn syrup that comes in a plastic bottle shaped like an old woman. You want to buy, as my grandpa would say, "the stuff that comes straight out of the tree." The ingredients on the bottle should say something along the lines of "100% maple syrup." This tasty sweetener is not just for topping your waffles and pancakes—it's wonderful in baked goods, too!

Agave syrup—This liquid sweetener is made from the agave plant in Mexico and South Africa and can generally be used as a replacement for honey in recipes (though, for an even better honey substitute, check out my Happy Bee Honey, page 34). It can also be used as a replacement for regular sugar, though not always 1:1.

Blackstrap molasses—Molasses is a by-product in the formation of sugar crystals. After the molasses is boiled three times, it is a much richer, stronger-flavored syrup with a low sugar content. It is also very nutrient dense and a terrific source of iron. You'll find it in several baking recipes in this book as well as in Barbecue Sauce (page 31). I also recommend trying a tablespoon in your morning oatmeal.

OILS, VINEGARS & OTHER LIQUIDS

Vinegars—My cabinet is overflowing with the various types of vinegar I keep on hand (I'm a vinegar junkie). Adding an acid such as vinegar to a dish is one of the best ways to add a little extra zing. My main go-to vinegars are balsamic, brown rice, red wine, sherry, champagne, and apple cider vinegars. Apple cider vinegar or plain distilled vinegar can be added to non-dairy milk to cause it to curdle and become a buttermilk substitute. Ume plum vinegar is another good option: It's a very strong vinegar with a powerful umami flavor (umami is a savory, meaty taste considered by many to be one of the five basic tastes alongside sweet, salty, sour, and bitter). It can be found at some markets among the soy sauces.

Extra virgin olive oil—Extra virgin olive oil is used in most of the recipes in this book. A good extra virgin olive oil ("extra virgin" meaning it is the oil from the first pressing of the olives) is an ingredient you should splurge on. Try to get one with a more robust, less acidic flavor, and opt for organic, if possible.

Olive oil spray—Many recipes call for olive oil spray to grease pans or spray over vegetables. You can purchase olive oil spray, but really, just get an oil spray bottle (I love my Misto) and fill it with your favorite oil. It's much more economical and earth friendly.

Cooking spray—I try to limit my use of aerosol spray cans, but I do suggest keeping a can of pure coconut oil or canola oil spray on hand for times when olive oil wouldn't be appropriate (like in desserts).

Coconut oil—This is one of the most versatile oils for stocking your kitchen. Refined coconut oil will give a less coconutty flavor. It can be used as a substitute for vegan butter in cooking or baking, and a teaspoon added to melted chocolate will help it set much more firmly. It will be in a jar, rather than in a bottle, in your store's oil aisle.

Canola oil—Organic is 100 percent the way to go with this oil if you're concerned about GMOs. Canola oil is a must if you plan to do any frying, but since it's flavorless, it works well in baked goods, too. Organic sunflower oil can also be used instead of canola.

Toasted sesame oil—This is a highly flavored oil that is great for sauces and dressings, occasionally for cooking.

Liquid aminos—Liquid aminos are concentrated amino acids in liquid form, usually derived from soy beans. It has a salty flavor, similar to soy sauce but less strong. For a soy-free version, coconut aminos are available.

Soy sauce, including tamari—Tamari is a particular kind of soy sauce that differs from standard varieties in its soy-to-wheat ratio. Soy sauce typically has a higher wheat content and a lower concentration of soy, making it a little mellower and saltier. Tamari is mostly or entirely wheat-free (depending on the brand) with a higher soy concentration, making it a stronger, less salty sauce. I tend to use tamari, but you can use soy sauce in its place. Either makes a good substitute for liquid aminos.

Mirin—This is a sweet rice wine found in the same aisle as the soy sauces and tamari. It has a low alcohol content, and the sugar is unrefined since it is a by-product of rice fermentation. A little goes a long way and adds a bright, sweet flavor. I add it to my sushi rice.

Vegan Worcestershire sauce—Worcestershire sauce is typically a fermented anchovy sauce (uh, gross!), but the vegan version is made without anchovies and can be used in all the same ways as standard Worcestershire sauce.

Liquid smoke—To make this great flavor enhancer, smoke from burning wood chips is collected and turned into solids, which are then dissolved in water. Then it's bottled to add an extra bit of smoky "oomph" to meals. Be sure to look for MSG-free varieties, such as Colgin's.

Extracts—You're probably most familiar with vanilla extract (and we aren't talking about those weird bottles of vanilla "flavor"), but it's good to stock your pantry with almond and chocolate extracts, too. Lemon, peppermint, maple, and hazelnut are a few others that are fun to experiment with (but not necessary for the recipes in this book). Extracts are a great way to add a stronger flavor profile to your recipe. Look for all-natural extracts with no added flavors or preservatives.

CANNED GOODS

Artichoke hearts—Sometimes you need some artichoke hearts to throw in a salad or to whip up some Artichoke Crab Cakes (page 202), and having to cook a fresh artichoke first just won't do. Canned artichoke hearts are lifesavers for this very reason. Always be sure to rinse them before you use them.

Canned tomato products—My recipes call for canned tomatoes, tomato sauce, and tomato paste quite frequently. They truly are convenient to have on hand for sauces, soups, and stews as well as for many other dishes. Look for organic, preferably BPA-free varieties.

Canned green chiles—Adding a tablespoon of diced green chiles is a great way to add a ton of flavor and just a little heat to recipes like Bean & Rice Freezer Burritos (page 91).

Jackfruit—Jackfruit is a fruit (predictably enough) that is mostly flavorless in its young, unripe form. Why do you want it? Because that flavorless fruit can take on the texture of shredded or "pulled" meat and easily absorbs whatever flavors you cook it with. You can find it at your local Asian market; many Whole Foods markets have begun carrying it in their canned fruit aisle. For savory dishes be sure to purchase the kind packed in brine or water (not syrup).

CONDIMENTS

Ketchup—There is no anger comparable to that of cooking up a batch of french fries only to discover you're out of ketchup. It's a sad time. Always keep ketchup stocked, preferably an organic variety with no preservatives, high-fructose corn syrup, or any other crazy thing.

Mustard—I'm kind of a mustard hoarder. If I'm not careful, I could fill an entire refrigerator shelf with them. For the recipes in this book, be sure to keep on hand plain yellow, spicy brown, Dijon, and my favorite: whole grain.

Miso—Typically, miso is a paste made from fermented soy beans, though soy-free varieties made from chickpeas are available. A little bit of this paste goes a long way in imparting huge umami flavor to your cooking. Recipes in this book use mellow white miso. It takes a few months to go through a tub, so it's worth the small investment.

Vegan butter—It is possible to make your own butter (and there are recipes out there if you look for them), which is very helpful if you're trying to avoid palm oil because of its implications for the earth's rainforests and the animals who live there. However, if you don't have the time or the equipment, purchase vegan butter for cooking, baking, and spreading on your toast. I prefer Earth Balance because the producer has stated that it is making efforts to use palm oil from sustainable sources.

Vegan mayonnaise—Yup, there's vegan mayonnaise, and I dare you to taste it and tell me it tastes any different from its animal-product-reliant counterpart. I like Vegenaise, Just Mayo, and Earth Balance brands.

Vegan cream cheese—If you love bagels, you'll want to keep this on hand for smearing, but it also has a place in recipes to quickly thicken a creamy sauce or to spread on a sandwich. I recommend Daiya or Trader Joe's brand.

Sriracha—Sriracha, a hot sauce made of chile peppers, garlic, and a bit of sugar, tastes amazing, and it pairs well with many flavors. Be careful when purchasing it; some brands use anchovies. I stick to the Huy Fong and Organicville brands. If sriracha isn't your thing, keep another hot sauce on hand to use interchangeably with sriracha.

OTHER GOOD STUFF

Agar agar—Agar, or agar agar, is a substance formed from algae. Its gelatinous qualities make it a great vegan gelatin substitute. It comes in flakes and powder; recipes in this book use both. The flakes can usually be found in the Japanese or Asian section of the supermarket, or at an Asian grocery store, but I've been able to find the powder only online. It may seem pricey, but a little goes a long way and it lasts forever.

Chocolate—My house is always stocked with chocolate, and I know I'm not alone, which is why this book devotes an entire chapter to it. Keep vegan chocolate chips on hand for emergency chocolate chip cookies, as well as organic, high-quality, fair trade dark chocolate bars, cocoa powder, and/or cacao powder (the less-processed, raw form).

Kelp granules—Kelp is a type of seaweed, and kelp granules are the dried, granulated form. They're a great seasoning tool for adding a seafood flavor to foods.

Medjool dates—Dates are kind of magical. They're great by themselves or stuffed with a bit of peanut butter. When pureed, they can be a great binder for pie crusts or work as an egg replacer in baking. When you blend them with a little bit of non-dairy milk, a rich caramel-like sauce results. You can usually find them in plastic containers in the produce or dried fruits section of your grocery store. Some stores will have them in their bulk foods section.

Nutritional yeast—aka nooch, aka vegan gold, aka one of the best things to happen to your kitchen. I was so hesitant to try nutritional yeast when I became vegan, but after I did I wondered what had taken me so long. It's basically an inactive yeast with a wonderfully nutty and cheesy flavor that brings umami to any dish. For those of you who truly don't care for nutritional yeast, it is often optional.

Olives & capers—These guys are always great to have on hand to brighten up a dish. The olives are a great source of healthy fat. Caper brine (the liquid from the jar) can also add a zesty, vinegary taste to a sauce or dressing. Try it in Sriracha Tartar Sauce, served with Artichoke Crab Cakes (page 202).

Salt—Every kitchen must have salt. Period. As a rule, I always have unbleached sea salt, Himalayan (pink) salt, and black salt, also known as kala namak (which is actually pink and great for adding an eggy/sulfur flavor to dishes). To switch things up, a few recipes in this book call for smoked salt, which can also be substituted for regular salt if preferred.

Spirulina—Spirulina powder is made from a type of blue-green algae. It contains many vital nutrients, making it a "superfood," and it is also a complete protein, containing every essential amino acid. It can be found in most health food stores or online, and it's good to have on hand for incorporating into other recipes, such as smoothies.

Tahini—Tahini is basically sesame seeds blended into a buttery sauce. It's absolutely necessary for making your own hummus, but you'll also find it used as the base for many a salad dressing or sauce.

Tamarind paste—It is possible to make your own tamarind paste from fresh tamarind pods, but store-bought tamarind paste or concentrate is much more convenient. It is very sour and tart, so you need only a little bit to brighten sauces, chutneys, or many other dishes. I use it to make a simple tamarind dipping sauce (page 139). You can generally find it at Asian, Indian, and many South American markets or online.

SPICES

Adding a variety of spices is a surefire way to liven up any dish. Although you don't need to stock your spice rack with all these at once, I do suggest experimenting with different spices. You may stumble across a new flavor you really like.

Allspice (ground and whole)

Ancho chile powder

Black pepper

Caraway seed

Cardamom (ground and whole)

Celery seeds

Cinnamon

Cloves (ground and whole)

Coriander

Crushed red pepper

Cumin

Curry powder

Fennel seeds

Garam masala

Garlic powder

Ginger

Mustard seeds & powder

Nutmeg

Old Bay Seasoning

Onion powder

Smoked paprika

Turmeric

HERBS

Nothing flavors a dish like fresh herbs. For those times when you've forgotten to pick up fresh herbs at the store or need only a small amount, keeping these dried herbs in your spice rack can be very helpful:

Basil	Marjoram	Rosemary	Thyme
Bay leaves	Oregano	Sage	
Dill	Parsley	Tarragon	

WON'T I NEED A BUNCH OF WEIRD APPLIANCES?

TURNS OUT THAT VEGANS, VEGETARIANS, AND OMNIVORES USE MANY OF THE same kitchen appliances! *Who knew?* The following are some tools we vegans use in the kitchen most frequently. I bought all of mine at places where omnivores shop, too, so if you're just making the switch, you may already have some.

Knives—Every cook needs three knives: a paring knife, a serrated knife, and an 8- to 10-inch chef's knife. They should feel heavy and solid in your hand. These will be your main tools, so it is important to buy the best you can afford. Have them sharpened regularly and be good to them.

Cutting board—I like a hearty wooden cutting board, but plastic ones are good, too, especially for things you don't want to stain your wooden one. No glass cutting boards, please (they ruin your knives, and the sound hurts people's ears).

Food processor—After knives and cutting boards, my food processor is probably my most used appliance. It's useful for sauces, dips, nut butters, no-bake pie crusts, and any sort of quick puree. You want one with a decent-size bowl (it should hold at least 7 quarts). A dough blade is handy for Pecan-Date Cinnamon Roll dough (page 128), and the grater attachment helps when you have a ton of vegetable grating to do. I use a Cuisinart, and I love it.

Blender—I have a Vitamix and it is used every day, whether it's just to make a smoothie or to puree something smoother than a food processor could get it (like nut cheeses or ice creams). The Vitamix is pricey and definitely an investment, but if you plan to do a lot of blending, it's totally worth it. A regular blender may work as well, but you may need to soak nuts longer or plan for a possibly less smooth consistency.

Immersion blender—Like creamy soups? Then you need one of these. Sure, you can transfer a hot soup to your blender, but it might explode and make a mess all over your kitchen. Avoid that mess by getting a very inexpensive immersion blender. Cuisinart's is inexpensive and comes in a ton of wonderful colors.

Baking sheets, baking dishes, cake pans & muffin tins—If you plan on baking, you'll need these items. Baking sheets with short rims around the edges will keep your baked goods from sliding off. When it comes to baking dishes, it's always good to have at least one 9 x 13-inch and one 8 x 8-inch for casseroles, lasagnas, brownies, and bars. A 5 x 9-inch loaf pan is good for making banana bread, pound cake, and fudge, and it can even work as a good container for homemade ice cream. Springform pans and tart pans allow you to remove the outer ring of the pan for those times when flipping the pan upside down for removal would destroy what you've made, like Savory Corn Cheesecake with Cilantro-Pepita Dressing (page 77). A regular 10-inch round cake pan is great for all the other times. A muffin tin is useful for muffins, cupcakes, and Chocolate Peanut Butter Cups (page 282).

Parchment paper or silicone baking mats—Nothing chaps my hide like when my precious cookies get stuck to the baking pan. Fortunately, it never happens when I use parchment paper or a silicone baking mat. Cut parchment paper circles in the shape of the bottom of your springform pans or tart pans so that whatever you're baking slides off the bottom piece easily. Use it when baking brownies or loaves so you can lift them cleanly out of the pan before slicing. To make the paper fit perfectly in a rectangular pan, place a large sheet under the pan you are using. Using scissors, cut a square (with one angle touching the pan's corner) out of each corner of the paper to make a cross-shaped piece of parchment paper when finished.

Spray the inside of the pan with cooking spray before placing the cross-shaped sheet inside so it sticks to the walls. Fold up the sides as you place it in the pan; there should be overhang to help you lift out the baked good later.

Spatulas—If I were talented in the musical arts, I would write a song about how much I love spatulas. Wooden ones are great for stirring food while cooking. Metal ones are great for scraping up all that flavorful stuff that sticks to the bottom of the pan. Rubber or silicone spatulas are great for getting every last bit of hummus out of a food processor or spreading brownie batter in a pan. Plastic ones have no place in the kitchen.

Biscuit cutters—These little things are used for so much more than just cutting biscuits. Try to purchase a set of different sizes so you can use them to shape burger and sausage patties, form fancy towerlike dishes such as Tofu & Avocado Tartare (page 214), and make circular ice cream cutouts for Ice Cream Sandwiches (page 292).

Microplane grater—This handy little tool is perfect for grating ginger and nutmeg and for zesting citrus fruits. It will make life easier. Promise.

Mandoline—A mandoline helps you slice things super-thin. Think paper-thin. The cheapest mandolines are plastic and work perfectly; just run whatever you're slicing over the blade repeatedly, using the safety handle or a cut-proof glove and being careful.

Salad spinner—When I went vegan, my consumption of leafy greens increased exponentially. The salad spinner makes it easy. To clean leafy greens, lettuce, or fresh herbs, fill a bowl with cold water, place the greens in the water, and move them around to release the dirt. Then drain and run them through the spinner to shake off all the water. Lay the leaves between two paper towels or clean kitchen towels and place in a sealable plastic bag. Refrigerate them and they'll stay crisp for more than a week. That's why you need a salad spinner.

Waffle iron—You probably can live without a waffle iron, but why should you? You can get one for not very much money, and the joy it will bring to you and the people you share your waffles with is immeasurable. Belgian waffle irons make thicker waffles with deeper pockets but aren't a necessity.

Ice cream maker—This is another appliance you can live without, but if you want to make your own dairy-free ice cream, having a machine that does the churning makes it so much easier. If you are worried about cost, new ones aren't terribly expensive but I have seen used ones on Craigslist for as little as $15.

ALL THOSE SPECIAL INGREDIENTS ARE WAY MORE EXPENSIVE.

Basic Condiments and Components That Don't Break the Bank

Don't let the high price tags on specialty vegan items discourage you from eating a vegan diet! Sure, some of those items might be nice to splurge on from time to time, but for the most part, you can make them all yourself. This chapter has some great basic recipes to get you started, and you will find them listed as ingredients throughout the book.

TEMPEH BACON

MAKES 16 TO 18 STRIPS

For many people, giving up bacon is one of the hardest parts of going vegan. Your body will absolutely thank you for it, however, and when you replace it with a healthier, more compassionate choice like this tempeh bacon, you'll never even miss it. Although it does not have the exact texture of bacon, that sweetly smoky flavor is still there. You can cook it in strips or crumble it for larger bacony bits.

PREP TIME: 5 minutes
COOK TIME: 10 minutes
DOWN TIME: 60 minutes

3 tablespoons liquid aminos (or tamari or soy sauce)

2 tablespoons maple syrup

1 tablespoon + 4 teaspoons extra virgin olive oil, divided

2 teaspoons liquid smoke

1½ teaspoons balsamic vinegar

½ teaspoon cumin

A few dashes of garlic powder

A few dashes of black pepper

One 8-ounce (225 g) package tempeh

1. Combine the liquid aminos, maple syrup, 1 tablespoon of the oil, liquid smoke, vinegar, cumin, garlic powder, and pepper in a shallow square baking dish.

2. Cut the block of tempeh in half to make two roughly 3 x 4-inch blocks. Slice each half lengthwise into about 8 long strips.

3. Add the tempeh strips to the marinade and toss a few times to fully coat. Arrange the strips in a single layer in the dish so every piece is in the marinade, place in the refrigerator, and marinate at least 1 hour or up to 24 hours.

4. When ready to cook, remove the dish from the refrigerator and line a plate with two paper towels. Heat 2 teaspoons of the oil in a large frying pan, preferably cast iron, over medium heat. Place 7 to 8 tempeh strips (or as many as you can fit without overlapping) in the pan and cook about 3 minutes on each side. Use the leftover marinade to deglaze the pan if necessary. After the tempeh has browned and the edges have caramelized, transfer them to the prepared plate (the paper towels will absorb the excess oil). Add the remaining 2 teaspoons of oil to the pan and repeat with the remaining strips. If you are not eating them right away, let them cool and then chill in an airtight container for 3 to 4 days.

VARIATION

▶ For bacon bits, in step 2 crumble the tempeh into small pieces and marinate according to instructions. Instead of cooking in batches, cook all the crumbles in the pan about 10 minutes, stirring as needed. Use the leftover marinade to deglaze the pan if necessary.

SUNFLOWER SAUSAGE

SERVES 4

These sausage crumbles are part of many recipes in this book, and for good reason—they taste far better than I ever remember actual sausage tasting, plus they're way better for everyone involved (you, animals, and the Earth). Another advantage: you have the choice of cooking it or eating it straight from the food processor. Both ways are terrific! You could easily make this with walnuts or pecans, but I think the mellow flavor of sunflower seeds serves as a great base.

PREP TIME: 15 minutes
COOK TIME: 5 minutes

3 to 4 teaspoons extra virgin olive oil, divided

½ medium yellow onion, chopped

1 garlic clove, minced

2 cups (280 g) raw hulled sunflower seeds

¼ cup (25 g) chopped sun-dried tomatoes (if hard, rehydrated in water until softened; oil-packed also works)

2 tablespoons liquid aminos (or tamari or soy sauce)

1½ teaspoons maple syrup

1 teaspoon liquid smoke

1 teaspoon dried sage

1 teaspoon fennel seeds

½ teaspoon cumin

½ teaspoon paprika

Salt and black pepper to taste

1. Heat 1 teaspoon of the oil in a large frying pan over medium heat. Add the onion and garlic and sauté until the onion is slightly translucent, 3 to 4 minutes. Remove from the heat.

2. In a food processor, combine the sunflower seeds, 2 teaspoons of the oil, sun-dried tomatoes, liquid aminos, maple syrup, liquid smoke, sage, fennel seeds, cumin, paprika, salt, and pepper. Pulse until broken down and combined. Add the cooked onion and garlic and pulse until the mixture is sticky and no piece is larger than a lentil, pausing to scrape the sides as necessary.

3. You can serve the sausage uncooked or cooked. To cook, heat the remaining 1 teaspoon of oil over medium heat in the same frying pan used earlier. Crumble the sausage into the pan and cook about 5 minutes, stirring and flipping as needed so it's evenly cooked. You may need to use your spatula to break up the crumbles if they begin to stick together. If you are not eating it right away, chill in an airtight container for 3 to 4 days.

VARIATIONS

▶ To make chorizo, increase the cumin and paprika to 1 teaspoon each and add ½ teaspoon cayenne. To make it extra hot, feel free to add a little bit of hot sauce.

▶ To make sausage patties, split the uncooked mixture into 6 portions. Use a biscuit cutter and your hands to form round patties; cook in the pan 2 to 3 minutes on each side, until firm.

HOMEMADE SEITAN

MAKES TWO 5- TO 6-INCH (13 TO 15 CM) PATTIES

Seitan is a hearty source of protein made from wheat gluten. It has been made for thousands of years, so I don't like to classify it as a faux meat, but its meaty texture does make it a great replacement in recipes when one might use animal protein. I mean, check out the recipe for Thai Seitan Satay with Spicy Peanut Dipping Sauce (page 101)! Store-bought seitan can be a little pricey, but it's so easy to make there's no reason to fork over those extra dollars. The awesome part is that after you pick up the ingredients, you can make several batches before needing to stock up again.

PREP TIME: 15 minutes
COOK TIME: 30 minutes

1 teaspoon + 1 tablespoon extra virgin olive oil, divided

¼ medium yellow onion, very finely diced (roughly ⅓ cup or 70 g)

2 garlic cloves, minced

Water

1½ cups (210 g) vital wheat gluten

2 tablespoons chickpea flour

2 tablespoons nutritional yeast

1 teaspoon dried marjoram

1 teaspoon dried oregano

¼ teaspoon black pepper

¾ cup (185 ml) vegetable broth

¼ cup (60 ml) liquid aminos (or tamari or soy sauce)

2 tablespoons apple cider vinegar

1. Heat 1 teaspoon of the oil in a frying pan over medium heat. Add the onion and sauté 2 to 3 minutes, until it becomes slightly translucent. Add the garlic and cook 1 or 2 minutes; remove from the heat. Set aside.

2. In a large bowl, whisk together the wheat gluten, chickpea flour, nutritional yeast, marjoram, oregano, and pepper. In a smaller bowl, mix the broth, liquid aminos, vinegar, remaining 1 tablespoon of oil, and cooked onion and garlic.

3. Add the broth mixture to the wheat gluten mixture and stir with a large spoon until mostly combined. Use your hands to knead the dough about 5 minutes, until it is fully combined and elastic. Some onions will fall out as you knead, and that's okay; you can press them back in when you form the patties in step 5. Let stand 5 minutes.

4. Fit a steamer on top of a medium or large pot of water and bring to a boil over high heat.

5. Use a knife to chop the dough in half, then use your hands to form each portion into a 5- to 6-inch (13 to 15 cm) patty at least 1 inch (2.5 cm) thick. Wrap each patty in aluminum foil.

6. When the water is boiling, place the foil-wrapped patties in the steamer basket and cover. Steam 30 minutes, flipping once halfway through to ensure even cooking. Remove the packs from the steamer basket, open the foil, and let cool. Use immediately, or store in an airtight container 1 week in the refrigerator or 2 months in the freezer.

BARBECUE SAUCE

MAKES 4 CUPS

You may be wondering, "What about BBQ sauce isn't vegan?" Well, often the sugar used in barbecue sauces (and in a majority of processed foods) is refined through bone char (charred animal bones). Some brands also use honey or other non-vegan ingredients. Several vegan BBQ sauces are out there, but if you're on a budget, a pricy bottle of vegan BBQ sauce may not make the cut. Luckily, making it at home is a snap and tastes so much better! The rich, smoky-sweet flavor of this sauce makes it a must-have staple for any vegan kitchen.

PREP TIME: 10 minutes
COOK TIME: 25 minutes

1 teaspoon extra virgin olive oil

3 garlic cloves, minced

½ medium red onion, very finely chopped

One 30-ounce can (890 ml) or two 15-ounce (445 ml) cans unsalted tomato sauce

¼ cup (40 g) + 1 tablespoon coconut sugar or vegan brown sugar

¼ cup (60 ml) apple cider vinegar

3 tablespoons blackstrap molasses

2 tablespoons liquid aminos

2 tablespoons ume plum vinegar or plain distilled vinegar

1 teaspoon cumin

1 teaspoon smoked paprika

½ teaspoon ancho chile powder

2 teaspoons Dijon mustard

1 teaspoon liquid smoke

Salt and black pepper to taste

1. Heat the oil in a medium pot over medium heat. Add the garlic and sauté until fragrant. Add the onion and sauté until just beginning to become translucent. Remove from the heat.

2. Transfer the onion mixture to a blender; add the tomato sauce, coconut sugar, apple cider vinegar, blackstrap molasses, liquid aminos, ume plum vinegar, cumin, paprika, and chile powder. Blend until smooth.

3. Transfer the mixture to the pot, bring to a boil, and quickly reduce the heat to low. Let simmer 15 to 20 minutes, stirring occasionally.

4. Add the mustard, liquid smoke, salt, and pepper. Remove the pot from the heat. Let cool before transferring to a jar or bottle. Refrigerate until ready to use, up to 10 to 14 days.

ZESTY RANCH DRESSING

MAKES 1½ CUPS

What doesn't taste good dipped into ranch dressing? What salad doesn't benefit from that cool, rich, creamy sauce? Okay, okay, there are probably a few, but *I* can't think of one. It is my belief that a ranch dressing is best when it's thick, luscious, and full of bold flavor. This recipe fits the description to a T. Raw veggies, french fries, anything BBQish—it's all taken up a notch when dipped into this stuff. It's also your salad's new BFF.

Place all ingredients in a food processor with 5 tablespoons of the reserved soaking water. Process until smooth. Chill until ready to use. It will thicken as it chills, so if you need to thin it (to drizzle on a salad, for example), you may need to stir in a couple teaspoons of water. Refrigerate in an airtight container up to 7 days.

PREP TIME: 5 minutes
DOWN TIME: 3 to 4 hours (*while cashews soak*)

½ cup (80 g) raw cashews, soaked in water 3 to 4 hours, *water reserved*

2 tablespoons apple cider vinegar

1 teaspoon agave syrup

½ teaspoon dried oregano

½ teaspoon garlic powder

½ teaspoon onion powder

½ teaspoon salt

¼ teaspoon celery seed

¼ teaspoon dried dill

TOFU SOUR CREAM

When I first went vegan, I would buy the expensive store-bought vegan sour cream whenever a recipe called for it. I would use a small bit, then the rest of the tub would go bad in my fridge. After a few times doing that, I created my own—one that's infinitely healthier and way better tasting. It's so good that I found myself using it more and more. This sour cream is sure to become one of your staples, too.

Place all ingredients in a food processor and process until smooth. Chill in an airtight container until ready to use or up to 5 days.

PREP TIME: 5 minutes

One 12-ounce (340 g) package extra-firm silken tofu (the vacuum-packed kind)

¼ cup fresh lemon juice

2 teaspoons apple cider vinegar

2 teaspoons white miso

2 teaspoons vegan mayonnaise, optional

HAPPY BEE HONEY

MAKES 1 CUP

Liquid sweeteners like agave syrup or maple syrup can be expensive. That's not to say they have no place in your pantry (because there are times when nothing but maple syrup will do), but having a homemade alternative definitely makes them last a little longer. This cruelty-free honey can be used in any recipe that calls for agave syrup or other liquid sweetener at a fraction of the cost.

PREP TIME: 2 minutes
COOK TIME: 60 minutes

6 cups (1500 ml) unfiltered apple juice
2 tablespoons coconut sugar or vegan brown sugar
1 tablespoon lemon juice

Combine the apple juice and coconut sugar in a large pot and bring to a boil. Let it boil about 10 minutes. Lower the heat and simmer until it lightly coats the back of a spoon, 60 to 70 minutes. It may seem too thin, but it will thicken as it cools. Stir in the lemon juice and remove from the heat. Transfer to a jar or bottle and let it cool completely before covering. Refrigerate up to 14 days. If it thickens, heat in the microwave 20 to 30 seconds before using.

I COULD NEVER GIVE UP CHEESE!

"Cheesy" Vegan Dishes

Cheese seems to keep a LOT of people from going vegan. As a former fromagier, it was definitely my biggest hang-up. Many vegans will admit it was one of the hardest things to give up. Another thing they will tell you, however, is that once they gave it up, their cravings ceased to exist. As easy as it is to acquire a taste for cheese, it's just as easy to lose it, especially when you have a few good vegan cheese recipes under your belt! For die-hard cheese-lovers, there are many impeccably authentic aged vegan cheese recipes out there. My cheeses are quicker but still satisfying!

TOFU CHÈVRE

MAKES ONE 8-INCH LOG

One of my biggest fears when going vegan was that I'd never have another cheese plate again. One of my favorite pastimes was eating fancy cheese and sipping wine, and I thought for sure those days were done. Luckily, I quickly discovered I could make a vegan cheese plate I liked *even more* than the old dairy stuff. Tofu Chèvre is a great go-to easy cheese to plate up with crusty bread, fruit, and nuts. It does involve several hours of down time, but it totally pays off when you pull this creamy log of vegan goodness out of the oven. It's great in any recipe when you would normally use goat cheese, including Roasted Ratatouille Tartines (page 88) and Roasted Corn, Green Chile & Tofu Chèvre Quesadillas with Avocado Crema (page 224).

PREP TIME: 10 minutes
COOK TIME: 20 minutes
DOWN TIME: 4 to 5 hours

One 14-ounce (395 g) block extra-firm tofu
1½ tablespoons white miso
1 tablespoon lemon juice
1 tablespoon extra virgin olive oil, or more as needed
1 teaspoon tahini
¼ teaspoon salt

1. Press the tofu (page 4) at least 1 hour, preferably 2.

2. After the tofu is pressed, break it into pieces and place in a food processor. Add the remaining ingredients and process until a smooth ball forms, pausing to scrape the sides as necessary. If it doesn't come together, add more oil, ½ teaspoon at a time, until it does.

3. Lay out a large piece of plastic wrap. Scoop the tofu mixture onto the plastic wrap and form it into a log about 8 inches long. Wrap completely with the plastic wrap, and roll it a little more to perfect the shape. Chill in the refrigerator 2 to 3 hours.

4. Preheat the oven to 350°F (175°C). Line a baking sheet with parchment paper or a silicone baking mat. Remove the log from the plastic wrap and place on the baking sheet. Bake 20 minutes, rolling it over once halfway through the baking time to ensure even cooking. Remove from the oven when the log is firm and slightly tan on the outside but still slightly soft to the touch. Let cool completely before serving. If not serving immediately, store in an airtight container and chill up to 3 to 4 days.

VARIATIONS

To try different flavors of chèvre, add the following ingredients to the mixture after it's fully combined in the food processor, then pulse a few times to incorporate.

▶ For Lavender Chèvre, add 1 to 2 teaspoons dried lavender.

▶ For Mixed-Herb Chèvre, add 2 to 3 teaspoons of your favorite dried herbs. (I like to use a mixture of basil, oregano, and thyme.)

▶ For Roasted Garlic Chèvre, add 2 cloves roasted garlic squeezed from their skins (page 7).

TEMPEH BACON MAC 'N' CHEESE WITH PECAN PARMESAN

SERVES 8 TO 10

Cauliflower is one of those "wonder veggies." It's so versatile that even those who claim to detest cauliflower can usually find at least one way they enjoy it. Roasting cauliflower brings out strong nutty undertones, and pureeing disguises it as a milky cream. Along with a small amount of cashews, cauliflower brings the creamy richness to this recipe. Mac 'n' cheese is definitely at the top of the list when it comes to soul-satisfying meals, and with the addition of smoky Tempeh Bacon Crumbles, this recipe becomes a complete meal, full of cheesy goodness.

1. Preheat the oven to 400°F (200°C). Line a baking sheet with parchment paper or a silicone baking mat. Spread the cauliflower florets on the baking sheet and lightly spray with olive oil. Sprinkle ¼ teaspoon of the garlic powder, the paprika, salt, and pepper over the florets. Toss to coat. Bake 20 to 25 minutes, flipping once halfway through. When the cauliflower is tender and golden, remove from the oven and let cool 2 minutes.

2. To make the cheese sauce, process the cashews and non-dairy milk in a blender or food processor until smooth and creamy. Add the cooled cauliflower, nutritional yeast, lemon juice, melted vegan butter, tomato paste, Dijon mustard, miso, onion powder, turmeric, and the remaining ½ teaspoon garlic powder. Process until smooth. Set aside.

3. Reduce the oven heat to 350°F (175°C). Lightly spray a 9 x 13-inch casserole dish with olive oil and set aside.

4. Bring the water to a boil in a large pot. Add a pinch of salt before adding the pasta to the water. Stir immediately to prevent any pasta sticking together. Cook the pasta following package instructions until al dente; remove from the heat and drain off the water. Add the cheese sauce to the pasta and mix thoroughly. Gently fold in the Tempeh Bacon Crumbles.

5. Pour the pasta mixture into the prepared casserole dish and spread evenly. Top with 1 cup of Pecan Parmesan (recipe follows) and bake until the topping is golden, 5 to 10 minutes. Remove from the oven and let sit about 5 minutes before serving.

PREP TIME: 35 minutes *(not including time to cook Tempeh Bacon)*
COOK TIME: 10 minutes
DOWN TIME: 60 minutes *(while cashews soak)*

mac 'n' cheese

½ head cauliflower, cut into florets (roughly 2½ to 3 cups/300 g)

Olive oil spray

¾ teaspoon garlic powder, divided

¼ teaspoon smoked paprika

Salt and black pepper to taste

½ cup (80 g) raw cashews, soaked in water at least 1 hour, *water discarded*

1½ (375 ml) cups non-dairy milk

½ cup (35 g) nutritional yeast

3 tablespoons lemon juice

2 tablespoons vegan butter, melted

1½ tablespoons tomato paste

½ tablespoon Dijon mustard

2 teaspoons white miso

½ teaspoon onion powder

½ teaspoon turmeric, optional

About 8 cups (2000 ml) water

16 ounces (450 g) elbow macaroni (gluten-free if necessary)

1 batch Tempeh Bacon Crumbles (page 25, see variation)

pecan parmesan

3 cups (375 g) pecan pieces

1 cup (70 g) nutritional yeast

1½ tablespoons fresh lemon juice

1 teaspoon minced garlic

to make the pecan parmesan

Combine the pecan pieces, nutritional yeast, lemon juice, and garlic in a food processor and process until the mixture resembles bread crumbs. Transfer to an airtight container and refrigerate until ready to use or up to 2 months.

‖‖‖‖‖‖‖‖‖‖‖‖‖‖‖‖‖‖‖‖‖‖‖

VARIATIONS

▶ For a quicker meal, skip the oven and serve the mac 'n' cheese straight from the pot! Pecan Parmesan is optional.

▶ For plain old-fashioned mac 'n' cheese, skip the Tempeh Bacon.

CITRUS-HERB ROASTED BEETS WITH MACADAMIA RICOTTA

SERVES 3 TO 4

You may not realize it, but beets were meant to be roasted with orange juice and paired with a creamy, tangy cheese. And not just any cheese—macadamia ricotta. It's true. Macadamia's mellow, buttery flavor makes for the richest of creamy cheeses, with a taste so subtle the flavors of whatever it's paired with really shine. What you will remember about the dish, though, is the macadamia ricotta. It's perfect for salads, sandwiches, creamy sauces, or just eating straight out of the food processor.

to make the macadamia ricotta

Combine all the ingredients and 4 teaspoons of the reserved soaking water in a food processor. Process until mostly smooth and creamy. Taste and add more salt if necessary. Chill in an airtight container up to 7 to 10 days.

to make the citrus-herb roasted beets

1. Preheat the oven to 450°F (230°C). Lightly spray a 9 x 13-inch baking dish with olive oil.

2. Place the beet medallions into the dish. Add the orange juice, vinegar, rosemary, thyme, maple syrup, oil, zest, salt, and pepper. Toss the beets to fully coat. It is okay if they overlap. Bake 30 to 40 minutes, flipping them once to ensure even cooking. When they are easily pierced with a fork, remove the pan from the oven.

3. Lay the beet slices on a large serving plate or on individual plates. Crumble the macadamia ricotta over them and garnish with orange slices. Serve immediately.

PREP TIME: 15 minutes
COOK TIME: 35 minutes
DOWN TIME: 60 minutes (*while macadamia nuts soak*)

macadamia ricotta

1 cup (140 g) raw macadamia nuts, soaked in warm water 1 hour, *water reserved*

2 tablespoons lemon juice

¾ teaspoon salt

½ teaspoon white miso

citrus-herb roasted beets

Olive oil spray

4 large red beets (5 to 6 if they are smaller), peeled, sliced into ¼-inch (1 cm) thick medallions

½ cup (125 ml) fresh orange juice

2 tablespoons apple cider vinegar

1 tablespoon chopped fresh rosemary

1 tablespoon chopped fresh thyme

1 tablespoon maple syrup

1 tablespoon extra virgin olive oil

1 teaspoon orange zest

Salt and black pepper to taste

Orange slices, optional

MUSHROOM GRILLED CHEESE SANDWICHES WITH SUNFLOWER CHEDDAR

MAKES 2 SANDWICHES, PLUS EXTRA CHEESE

You may think that if you go vegan, your days of grilled cheese sandwiches will be over. Toasted bread stuffed with warm, gooey cheese? Yeah, those days are about to be better than ever. This recipe is great for all your cheddar needs because it can be made two ways: as a cheese sauce or as a firm cheese you can slice and grate. And these sandwiches? Warm, chunky mushrooms with melty cheddar cheese, whole grain mustard, and some crusty bread? I mean, *come on!*

to make the sunflower cheddar

1. Spray an 8-inch pie pan, 8- or 9-inch loaf pan, or 6-cup muffin tin (depending on what shape you want your cheese to be) with olive oil. Set aside.

2. In a high-speed blender, combine the sunflower seeds, nutritional yeast, lemon juice, roasted red pepper, tomato paste, salt, miso, onion powder, garlic powder, mustard powder, turmeric, and 2 cups of the water. Blend into a super creamy cheese sauce. Transfer the mixture to a bowl and set aside.

3. In a medium pot, stir the agar into the remaining 1 cup water until combined. Heat the mixture over high heat until it begins to sputter, about 2 minutes. Quickly whisk in the cheese sauce until it is fully combined and smooth. Continue to whisk over high heat until it begins to boil and then reduce to a simmer. Let it simmer, whisking continuously, for 4 to 5 minutes, until very thick and hard to whisk.

4. Pour the cheese into your prepared container and refrigerate 2 to 3 hours. When it is set, serve immediately or use in any recipe that calls for cheddar cheese. To store, chill in an airtight container up to 7 to 10 days.

to make the sandwiches

1. Preheat the oven to 350°F (175°C).

2. Heat a medium frying pan over medium heat. Add the mushrooms and let them brown, stirring occasionally, 4 to 5 minutes until softened. Remove from the heat and mix in the thyme, salt, and pepper. Set aside.

PREP TIME: 25 minutes
COOK TIME: 10 minutes
DOWN TIME: 2 to 3 hours

sunflower cheddar

Olive oil spray

2 cups (280 g) sunflower seeds

½ cup (35 g) nutritional yeast

2 tablespoons lemon juice

1 tablespoon diced roasted red pepper

1 tablespoon tomato paste

2 teaspoons salt

2 teaspoons white miso

½ teaspoon onion powder

½ teaspoon garlic powder

½ teaspoon mustard powder

¼ teaspoon turmeric

2 cups (500 ml) + 1 cup (250 ml) water, divided

2 teaspoons agar agar flakes (not powder)

sandwiches

16 ounces (470 g) sliced button or cremini mushrooms

½ teaspoon dried thyme

Salt and black pepper to taste

4 slices bread (any type will do)

2 to 3 tablespoons whole grain mustard or other mustard

Olive oil spray

3. Lay out 2 slices of bread. Spread a bit of the mustard on 1 slice. Scoop about ⅓ cup of the cooked mushrooms onto a second slice and spread out evenly. Grate some of the sunflower cheddar over the top of the mushrooms. Repeat with the other slices for the next sandwich.

4. Place the two pieces of bread topped with mushrooms and cheddar on a baking sheet. Create an aluminum foil "tent" by folding a sheet in half and creasing it along the top (to keep the foil from sticking to the cheese) before placing it over the pieces of bread. Bake 4 to 5 minutes, until the cheddar begins to melt. Remove from the oven and top each with one of the mustard-covered bread slices.

5. Heat the frying pan again over medium heat. Spray one side of each sandwich with olive oil and place them in the pan, oil side down. Spray the top of each sandwich with olive oil. Cook 3 to 4 minutes on each side until golden and crisp. Remove from the heat and serve immediately.

||||||||||||||||||||||||||||||||

VARIATIONS

▶ For a smoky cheddar cheese, add 1 teaspoon liquid smoke to the sunflower seed mixture.

▶ For a nut-based cheese, replace the sunflower seeds with cashews soaked in water at least 1 hour.

▶ For a cheddar cheese sauce or instantly melted cheddar cheese, skip steps 3 and 4 and use as is.

▶ Mix it up a bit by replacing the mushrooms with seitan, tempeh bacon (page 25), BBQ Cauliflower (page 108), or even Creamy Curried Tempeh Salad (page 256).

TIPS

- Getting the sunflower seed mixture as smooth as possible before adding it to the agar mixture is very important.

- Whisking the mixture over heat for a few minutes after you add the sunflower mixture is key to having a firmer cheese. The longer it cooks, the firmer it will be.

- This cheese does not melt in the traditional sense we think of cheese melting. It does get soft and gooey, though, if heated properly. The best way to achieve gooeyness is to cover with aluminum foil (creasing along the top to keep it from sticking to the cheese), place in the oven, and bake several minutes.

TOFU FETA, SPINACH & POTATO GRATIN

SERVES 6 TO 8

PREP TIME: 25 minutes
COOK TIME: 45 minutes
DOWN TIME: 3 to 4 hours

This tofu feta is definitely the easiest cheese to make in this book, so simple there's no excuse for not making it a staple in your kitchen. It's fantastic on salads, in sandwiches, and especially in this gratin. In this recipe the tofu feta transforms a normally very heavy potato dish into a light, fresh, and spanakopita-ish gratin. If the feta is premade, this dish becomes a super-easy weeknight meal. It's so impressive, though, that no one will ever guess it's non-dairy!

to make the tofu feta

Combine the lemon juice, vinegar, water, miso, basil, and oregano in a shallow baking dish. Add the tofu and toss to combine. Cover and chill at least 3 to 4 hours.

to make the gratin

1. Preheat the oven to 375°F (190°C). Lightly spray a 9 x 13-inch baking dish with olive oil. Set aside.

2. Heat the 1 teaspoon of olive oil in a large frying pan over medium heat. Add the onion and garlic and sauté until the onion just starts to become translucent. Add the spinach and cook until heated through. Add the salt and pepper. Set aside.

3. In a small bowl, mix the non-dairy milk, yogurt, lemon juice, garlic powder, and salt and pepper. Set aside.

4. Make a layer of potato slices in the bottom of the baking dish, one overlapping the one before it. Spread half of the spinach mixture over the potatoes. Set aside ¼ cup (60 ml) of the tofu feta. Spread half of the remaining tofu feta over the spinach mixture. Add another layer of potatoes, the remaining half of the spinach, and the remaining half of the feta. Add one more layer of potatoes. Pour the milk mixture evenly over the entire top layer of potatoes.

5. Cover the dish with aluminum foil and bake 35 minutes. Remove the foil, sprinkle with the remaining ¼ cup feta, and bake for another 10 minutes. Remove from the oven and let rest 5 minutes before serving. Leftovers can be chilled in an airtight container for 4 to 5 days.

tofu feta

⅓ cup (80 ml) lemon juice

2 tablespoons rice vinegar

2 tablespoons water

2 tablespoons white miso

1 teaspoon dried basil, optional

1 teaspoon dried oregano, optional

One 14-ounce (395 g) block extra-firm tofu, crumbled

gratin

Olive oil spray

1 teaspoon extra virgin olive oil

½ medium white onion, chopped

2 to 3 garlic cloves, minced

One 16-ounce (455 g) bag frozen spinach

Salt and black pepper to taste

1 cup (250 ml) non-dairy milk

3/4 cup (170 g) plain coconut or soy yogurt

1 tablespoon fresh lemon juice

½ teaspoon garlic powder

4 to 5 large golden potatoes, thinly sliced into medallions

BALSAMIC BAKED PEARS WITH CASHEW BLUE CHEESE

SERVES 2 TO 4

Dim the lights, break open a bottle of (vegan) wine, and turn on some soft jazz (something circa 1995). It's time for some sexy balsamic-roasted pears, stuffed with cashew blue cheese and topped with "honey" and crunchy pistachios. This blue cheese gets its creaminess from cashews; its tangy bite from lemon juice, miso, and ume plum vinegar; and its little blue-green streaks from a dash of spirulina. Blue cheese has many applications: topping burgers, crumbled in salads, shown off on fancy cheese plates. It's best, however, paired with sweet and fruity things. Ladies and gents, it's about to get super classy in here!

to make the cashew blue cheese

1. Combine the cashews, lemon juice, miso, vinegar, nutritional yeast, salt, marjoram, and kelp in a food processor and process until smooth, pausing to scrape the sides with a rubber spatula as needed. When smooth, transfer the mixture to a shallow bowl. Scoop out 2 tablespoons of the cheese mixture and place in another small bowl. Spread the mixture in the first bowl along the bottom of its bowl. Set aside.

2. Add the spirulina to the small bowl with the 2 tablespoons of cheese. Mix until fully combined. Gently spread this blue-green mixture over the top of the first mixture, making sure not to mix the two together. Cut a butter knife through the cheese several times to create a marbled effect. Place in the refrigerator, uncovered (to let the cheese dry out a bit), for 3 to 4 hours. When it is a little firmer (but still soft and creamy—this is not a dry and crumbly blue cheese), use a spoon to scrape out ½ cup (120 ml) of chunks. Chill leftovers in an airtight container 7 to 10 days.

to make the balsamic baked pears

1. Preheat the oven to 400°F (200°C). Combine the vinegar, agave syrup, melted vegan butter, and salt in an 8-inch-square baking dish.

PREP TIME: 20 minutes

COOK TIME: 35 to 40 minutes

DOWN TIME: 6 to 8 hours *(partially while cashews soak)*

cashew blue cheese

1 cup (160 g) raw cashews, soaked in water for 3 to 4 hours, *water discarded*

3 tablespoons lemon juice

1 tablespoon white miso

1 tablespoon ume plum vinegar

1 teaspoon nutritional yeast

½ teaspoon salt

⅛ teaspoon dried marjoram

⅛ teaspoon kelp granules

⅛ teaspoon spirulina powder (see tip)

balsamic baked pears

½ cup (125 ml) balsamic vinegar

2 tablespoons agave syrup

1 tablespoon melted vegan butter

Pinch of salt

2 not-quite-ripe pears (preferably Bosc, but any will do)

Happy Bee Honey (page 34), for drizzling

⅓ cup (130 g) chopped pistachios

2. Slice the pears in half lengthwise and use a spoon or melon-baller to cut out the pits and create a small "stuffing hole." Place the pear halves in the dish, cut side down. Use a pastry brush to brush the vinegar mixture over the pears. Bake for 25 minutes, brushing the pears with the cooking liquid halfway through. Flip each pear over so it is cut side up, brush with cooking liquid again, and bake 10 to 15 minutes, until the tops are golden and caramelized.

3. Plate the pears and stuff the holes with the blue cheese chunks. Drizzle with Happy Bee Honey and sprinkle with the pistachios. Serve immediately.

TIP

- If you are unable to find spirulina, use spinach powder (also at some health food stores) or grind dried bay leaves into a powder using a food processor or spice grinder (though this will affect the taste somewhat). If you don't need that blue-green streak through your blue cheese, feel free to leave it out—the flavor of the cheese will not be changed.

CAPRESE FARROTTO WITH MACARELLA (MACADAMIA MOZZARELLA)

SERVES 4, PLUS EXTRA CHEESE

Fresh. Creamy. Mild. Ooey. Gooey. Yes, I am talking about mozzarella. And not just any mozzarella—this macadamia-nut mozzarella! *Macarella*, if you will. When heated in a sandwich, on a pizza, or all over your favorite lasagna, it does that steamy, melty thing we all know and love. It's also perfect in a salad, especially when combined with tomato and basil. Caprese Farrotto celebrates that trio of flavors in a risotto-style dish. Farro, a nutty-tasting grain, gives it a chewy, toothsome texture. Quit missing mozzarella and get your macarella on!

to make the macarella

1. Lightly coat 5 wells of a muffin tin with olive oil spray. Set aside.

2. Combine the macadamia nuts, non-dairy milk, arrowroot powder, lemon juice, nutritional yeast, and salt in a blender and blend until completely smooth. Pour into a medium pot. Add the agar and whisk until dissolved. Place the pot over medium-high heat and heat, whisking constantly. Bring to a boil, then quickly reduce the heat to a simmer, still whisking.

3. After 3 to 5 minutes, when the mixture is very thick, glossy, and hard to stir, remove from the heat and pour quickly into the wells of the prepared muffin tin, filling each well almost to the top. (You should be able to fill 4 to 5 wells.)

4. Place the tin in the refrigerator and chill until completely set, 2 to 3 hours. When the cheese rounds are firm, transfer them to an airtight container and refrigerate until ready to use.

to make the basil pistou

Combine the basil, oil, garlic, and broth in a blender or food processor and pulse until smooth. Add the salt and pepper. Set aside until ready to use.

to make the farrotto

1. Heat the oil in a large shallow saucepan over medium heat. Add the garlic and sauté for 2 minutes, or until fragrant. Add the onion and sauté until just translucent.

{ RECIPE CONTINUES }

PREP TIME: 20 minutes
COOK TIME: 25 minutes
DOWN TIME: 4 to 6 hours *(partially while macadamia nuts soak)*

macarella

Olive oil spray

1 cup (140 g) macadamia nuts, soaked in water 2 to 3 hours, *water discarded*

1½ cups (375 ml) unsweetened non-dairy milk

1 tablespoon arrowroot powder

1 tablespoon lemon juice

1½ teaspoons nutritional yeast

½ teaspoon salt

1½ teaspoons agar powder (not flakes)

basil pistou

2 cups (60 g) roughly chopped basil

1½ tablespoons extra virgin olive oil

2 garlic cloves

2 tablespoons vegetable broth

Salt and black pepper to taste

farrotto

1 teaspoon extra virgin olive oil

2 to 3 garlic cloves, minced

½ medium yellow onion, chopped

1½ cups (270 g) uncooked farro, rinsed

1½ teaspoons dried basil

1 teaspoon dried oregano

4 cups (1,000 ml) vegetable broth, divided

2 cups (310 g) halved cherry tomatoes

½ cup (35 g) nutritional yeast

Juice of ½ lemon

Salt and black pepper to taste

2. Add the farro, basil, oregano, and ¼ cup of the broth. Cook for 1 to 2 minutes, until most of the liquid has been absorbed.

3. Add 1¼ cups of the broth, stir, and cover. Cook for about 5 minutes, or until the liquid has been absorbed. Add another ½ cup of broth and the tomatoes, stir, and cover. Cook until the liquid has been absorbed. Continue the pattern, adding ½ cup of broth at a time, until all the broth has been added and absorbed.

4. Add the nutritional yeast, lemon juice, salt, and pepper. Thinly slice 1 to 2 macarella rounds. Serve the farrotto topped with the macarella slices and basil pistou.

||||||||||||||||||||||||||

VARIATION

▶ To make this dish gluten-free, replace the farro with arborio rice or your rice of choice.

 TIPS

- For the macarella, it is vital that the mixture be as smooth as possible before transferring to the pot (before cooking).

- It's also very important to whisk the mixture at least 3 to 5 minutes. The longer you let it cook, the firmer your cheese will be.

- This cheese will not melt on the farrotto, but if you prefer your cheese soft and gooey, follow the instructions for melting Sunflower Cheddar (page 43). Plus, check out the Roasted Veggie Deep Dish Pizza (page 184).

WHERE WOULD I GET MY PROTEIN?

Satisfying Ways to Pack In the Protein

No one cares about your protein intake until you become vegan. It's true! Even when I tell people that a) nearly everything has some protein; b) I get protein from several sources but the majority from beans, nuts, seeds, and leafy greens; and c) my muscles haven't atrophied so I must be doing something right, they still think vegans are lacking in protein. Well, I have news for you: There is protein in every recipe in this book (some more than others). This chapter is focused specifically on protein—found where you'd least expect it.

BROCCOLI & QUINOA TABBOULEH WITH TAHINI-HERB DRESSING

SERVES 6

Would you believe that broccoli has almost 3 grams of protein per cup? When you combine it with quinoa, a protein powerhouse (it has a whopping 8 grams per cup), you get 11 grams of protein per 1 cup of zesty, fresh tabbouleh. But that's not all! Top that tabbouleh with a rich, creamy herbal dressing made with tahini to get an extra 3 grams per tablespoon. Twenty grams of protein per serving? Not too shabby for a light salad, right?

1. Combine the tahini, lemon juice, water, basil, parsley, and agave syrup in a food processor and process until smooth. Add the dill and pulse a few times until incorporated. Transfer to an airtight container; if not using right away, refrigerate until ready to use.

2. Place the broccoli in the food processor and pulse until broken into pieces about the size of the tip of your pinkie finger. Transfer to a large bowl.

3. Add the quinoa, parsley, mint, tomato, cucumber, red onion, and radishes to the broccoli and toss together. Mix in the lemon juice. Add salt and pepper if desired. Serve drizzled with the tahini-herb dressing (or serve it alongside the salad). Chill leftovers in an airtight container up to 3 days.

PREP TIME: 30 minutes (*not including time to cook quinoa*)

tahini-herb dressing

½ cup (120 g) tahini

⅓ cup (80 ml) lemon juice

⅓ cup (80 ml) water

⅓ cup (15 g) chopped fresh basil

⅓ cup (15 g) chopped fresh parsley

½ to 1 tablespoon agave syrup

2 teaspoons dried dill

Salt to taste

tabbouleh

3 cups (225 g) broccoli florets and stem slices

2 cups (320 g) cooled cooked quinoa (see page 10)

1 cup (40 g) chopped fresh parsley

½ cup (20 g) chopped fresh mint

¾ cup (120 g) chopped tomato

¾ cup (120 g) diced cucumber

½ cup (135 g) diced red onion

6 radishes, very thinly sliced

½ cup (125 ml) lemon juice

Salt and black pepper to taste, optional

SPINACH EDAMAME HUMMUS

SERVES 4 TO 6

Popeye the Sailor Man was onto something when he claimed to get his bulging muscles from spinach: one bunch contains about 10 grams of protein! I, however, find that mixing some fresh spinach into a dip is much more palatable than downing cans of it. Make that dip a hummus with protein-packed edamame and tahini and you'll be all set to be a fighting sailor! (All you need are some cute anchor tattoos for your forearms.) Serve with raw veggies, chips, or pita bread, or spread on your favorite sandwich.

Combine the edamame, spinach, and garlic in the bowl of a food processor and process until broken down and combined. Add the parsley, lemon juice, tahini, broth, oil, tamari, onion powder, and paprika; process until smooth. Add salt and pepper and garnish with the remaining edamame. Chill in an airtight container until ready to serve, up to 4 days.

PREP TIME: 5 minutes

2 cups (280 g) shelled edamame, plus more for garnish

1 cup (30 g) spinach leaves

2 garlic cloves

¼ cup (10 g) chopped fresh parsley

¼ cup (60 ml) lemon juice

¼ cup (60 g) tahini

¼ cup (60 ml) vegetable broth or water

2 tablespoons sesame oil (or extra virgin olive oil)

½ teaspoon tamari (or soy sauce or liquid aminos)

½ teaspoon onion powder

A few dashes of smoked paprika

Salt and black pepper to taste

CHICKPEA "FRIES"

SERVES 2 TO 4

These aren't your typical fries. First, they're not even fried. Second, they're not made with potatoes, or any type of vegetable. They're made from chickpea flour (also known as besan), an incredible source of protein and a versatile ingredient for any vegan kitchen (which is featured in several recipes throughout this book). Third, if you split them between two people, each would get more than 20 grams of protein. They do have a couple things in common with ordinary fries, however, besides their shape: they taste just as amazing when dipped into ketchup, and they're a great companion to a sandwich!

PREP TIME: 15 minutes
COOK TIME: 40 to 50 minutes
DOWN TIME: 2 to 3 hours

2 cups (220 g) chickpea flour

1 teaspoon black salt (kala namak) or regular salt

¾ teaspoon garlic powder

¾ teaspoon onion powder

½ teaspoon cumin

½ teaspoon smoked paprika

Dash of cayenne pepper

4 cups (1,000 ml) water

2 tablespoons extra virgin olive oil

Olive oil spray

Salt and black pepper to taste

Vegan ketchup, Barbecue Sauce (page 31), or Zesty Ranch Dressing (page 32)

1. Line a 9 x 13-inch baking dish with parchment paper. Set aside.

2. In a large bowl, combine the chickpea flour, black salt, garlic powder, onion powder, cumin, paprika, and cayenne. In a medium pot, bring the water to a rolling boil. Whisk in the chickpea flour mixture until mostly smooth (a few bumps are okay). Add the oil and continue to whisk for about 3 minutes, until it has the texture of thick pudding. Remove from the heat.

3. Pour into the prepared baking dish. Refrigerate overnight or at least 2 to 3 hours, until the chickpea mixture is hardened.

4. Preheat the oven to 400°F (200°C). Use the parchment paper to lift the hardened chickpea mixture out of the dish. Keeping the mixture on the parchment paper, use a knife to cut ½- to ¾-inch (1 to 2 cm) strips along the shorter way. Then cut those strips in half lengthwise. Move the parchment paper, with the fries, onto a baking sheet. Spread the fries so they are not touching. Lightly spray with olive oil and, if desired, add a dash of salt and/or pepper.

5. Bake for 40 minutes, flipping the fries every 10 minutes so all four sides get 10 minutes each. If they are still a little soft, bake for 10 more minutes, flipping over once halfway through. Remove from the oven and serve immediately with your choice of dipping sauces.

||||||||||||||||||||||||||||||

VARIATIONS

▶ Try different spice blends in place of the cumin, paprika, and cayenne: 1½ teaspoons garam masala is great, or try 1 teaspoon each of dried basil, oregano, and thyme.

TIP

You can fry the fries instead of baking them. Coat the bottom of a large frying pan, preferably cast iron, with olive oil and heat over medium heat. Add in batches and cook 3 to 4 minutes on each side. Line a plate with paper towels. Remove the fries from the pan and place them on the prepared plate to absorb excess oil. Serve immediately.

LOADED MEXICAN STUFFED BAKED POTATOES

SERVES 2 TO 4

The era of the Atkins diet gave the potato a bad rap. They were panned as starchy and high in carbohydrates, and in those carb-shunning days, that was enough to put people off potatoes forever. Yes, potatoes are rich in complex carbohydrates, but let's not ignore that they have 5 to 7 grams of protein each. If that's not enough for you potato haters, though, let's bake those potatoes and fill them with spicy black beans to add a mere *15 grams of protein* per cup! With stats like that, don't be surprised if, while eating this meal, your shirt begins to rip to make way for your new bulging biceps.

PREP TIME: 15 minutes
COOK TIME: 1 hour *(mostly inactive)*

2 large russet potatoes, scrubbed clean and dried

1 teaspoon extra virgin olive oil

½ medium yellow onion, chopped

2 to 3 garlic cloves, minced

3 cups (525 g) cooked black beans (see page 8) or two 15-ounce (425 g) cans, rinsed and drained

1 cup (250 ml) vegetable broth, divided

3 tablespoons diced canned green chiles

1 teaspoon cumin

½ teaspoon smoked paprika

¼ teaspoon ancho chile powder

2 tablespoons nutritional yeast, optional

4 tablespoons (60 ml) fresh lime juice, divided

Salt and black pepper to taste

1 cup (160 g) diced tomatoes

1 cup (140 g) corn kernels

Tofu Sour Cream (page 33)

Peasamole (page 240) or Guacamole (page 105)

Chopped green onions

1. Preheat the oven to 400°F (200°C). Place the potatoes on a baking sheet and bake for 1 hour, or until easily pierced with a fork.

2. While the potatoes are baking, cook the beans. Heat the oil in a frying pan over medium heat. Add the onion and garlic and sauté until the onion starts to become translucent. Add the beans, ½ cup (120 ml) of the broth, green chiles, cumin, paprika, and chile powder. Cover, leaving a small crack open, and simmer for 5 minutes, or until the broth has mostly cooked away. Add another ¼ cup (60 ml) of broth and repeat. Add the remaining ¼ cup of broth and mash the beans with a potato masher. Cook for 2 to 3 minutes. Add the nutritional yeast, 2 tablespoons of the lime juice, salt, and pepper. Remove from the heat.

3. In a medium bowl, combine the tomatoes, corn, the remaining 2 tablespoons of lime juice, and salt.

4. When the potatoes are done baking, slice them lengthwise almost all the way through the center, leaving the two halves connected. Place the potatoes on plates. Use a spoon to break the potato flesh into pieces, but leave the potatoes in their skins.

5. Scoop some beans into the center of each potato, letting it overflow onto the plate just a bit. Top with a few spoonfuls of the tomato mixture, a couple dollops of sour cream, a spoonful of the Peasamole or Guacamole, and a sprinkle of green onions. Serve immediately. Leftovers can be chilled in an airtight container for 3 to 4 days.

FALAFEL TACOS WITH SRIRACHA-TAHINI SAUCE

SERVES 4

page 51

You know those times when you need a filling meal that is either falafel or tacos? Happens to me *all the time*. Well, these falafel tacos are just as you would imagine—tacos filled with delightfully healthy baked falafel. And that's not all: You also get a creamy, tangy, hot, and spicy sriracha-tahini sauce to make every bite just a little more awesome. Each taco is packed with more than 8 grams of protein from the chickpeas, chickpea flour, tortillas, and tahini. If you are in need of a really protein-heavy meal, though, skip the tacos and serve the falafel with Broccoli & Quinoa Tabbouleh (page 52) or Spinach Edamame Hummus (page 55).

1. Combine all the sriracha-tahini sauce ingredients in a food processor. Process until smooth. Chill until ready to use.

2. Preheat the oven to 350°F (175°C). Line a baking sheet with parchment paper or a silicone baking mat. Set aside.

3. Combine all the falafel ingredients in a food processor and process until you have a mostly smooth ball of "dough." If the mixture gets too dry, add water by the teaspoon until it forms a ball.

4. Use a tablespoon or ice cream scoop to scoop the dough and use your hands to roll it into a ball. Flatten it slightly and place on the prepared baking sheet. Repeat with the rest of the dough. You should have 18 to 20 falafel.

5. Bake for about 20 minutes, flipping them halfway through to ensure even cooking. Remove from the oven.

6. To assemble the tacos, stuff a little lettuce into each taco shell, then add 2 to 3 patties to each (breaking them up if desired). Top with the tomatoes and any other taco fillings. Drizzle with the sriracha-tahini sauce and serve.

PREP TIME: 15 minutes
COOK TIME: 20 minutes

sriracha-tahini sauce
¼ cup (60 g) tahini
¼ cup (60 ml) water
1 to 2 tablespoons sriracha
1 tablespoon capers
Juice of 1 lemon
1 garlic clove, minced
1 teaspoon dried dill

falafel
1½ cups (255 g) cooked chickpeas (see page 8) or one 15-ounce (425 g) can, rinsed and drained
½ cup (20 g) loosely packed fresh cilantro (or mixture of parsley and cilantro)
¼ medium red onion, chopped
2 to 3 garlic cloves
Juice of ½ lemon
3 tablespoons chickpea flour
1½ teaspoons dried dill
1½ teaspoons dried oregano
1 teaspoon smoked paprika
1 teaspoon cumin
1 teaspoon nutritional yeast, optional
Several dashes of black pepper
Salt to taste

tacos
8 taco shells (see page 121 to make your own)
1 to 2 cups (30 to 60 g) chopped lettuce
2 to 3 Roma tomatoes, sliced
Other fillings (e.g., cucumber, avocado, bell pepper)

"HONEY" MUSTARD KALE SLAW

SERVES 2 TO 4

For those who think greens are just rabbit food, here's some food for thought: One bunch of kale has roughly 15 to 18 grams of protein. Half a head of red cabbage has roughly 6 grams of protein. That means this entire dish has more than 20 grams of protein just from the leaves. Add some carrots and a lovely dressing made from whole grain mustard and Happy Bee Honey (page 34) and you have a very healthy, filling, and delicious salad you won't be giving to any rabbits.

PREP TIME: 20 minutes
DOWN TIME: 1 to 4 hours

slaw

1 bunch lacinato (dino) kale, stems removed

2 cups (220 g) grated carrots (about 2 to 3 medium)

½ head red cabbage

dressing

2 tablespoons Happy Bee Honey (page 34) or agave syrup

2 tablespoons fresh lemon juice

1 tablespoon extra virgin olive oil

4 teaspoons whole grain mustard

Sesame seeds, for sprinkling

1. Stack 4 to 5 kale leaves on top of each other and slice into thin strips on a bias (diagonally). Repeat with the rest of the kale. Combine the sliced kale and grated carrots in a large bowl.

2. Cut the halved cabbage head in half (into quarters). Cut out the core. Slice each quarter into very thin strips, or shred using a box grater. You should have roughly 2 cups of shreds. Place the cabbage in the bowl with the kale and carrots.

3. Combine the dressing ingredients in a cup and use a fork to whisk together. Pour over the slaw and toss to fully combine. Chill 1 to 4 hours before serving. Serve cold or at room temperature, sprinkled with the sesame seeds.

||||||||||||||||||||||||||||||

VARIATIONS

▶ If you don't care for red cabbage, try using green cabbage instead.

▶ For a more traditional, less crunchy kale salad, massage the dressing into the chopped kale for about 5 minutes before adding the rest of the ingredients. (And if you think you could never massage a vegetable, think again. Trust me, it's worth it.)

TOFU DOESN'T TASTE LIKE ANYTHING.

Tofu Prepared with All the Flavor You Can Handle

Tofu gets a bad rap as being plain and boring. I admit, I bought into this idea for many years. One tofu scramble, however, changed all that. The correct preparation can turn an unimaginative white block of soy into something addictively tasty and quite magical. These recipes will surely have you re-thinking tofu and the huge variety of things you can do with it. Boring ol' tofu is a thing of the past!

MEDITERRANEAN TOFU SCRAMBLE

SERVES 4

The tofu scramble not only changed my view of tofu forever but also became both a breakfast and dinner staple for months after I went vegan. Its simplicity, its versatility, and the fact that it's almost foolproof make it a great recipe for new vegans and a tried-and-true favorite for longtime vegans. Black salt is great for giving your scramble a sulfuric, eggy taste; nutritional yeast adds just the right amount of nutty cheesiness. This recipe is my favorite scramble with a Mediterranean twist. Serve it with pita bread and a side of olives and dolmas for a platter you won't soon forget.

PREP TIME: 10 minutes
COOK TIME: 20 minutes

1 teaspoon extra virgin olive oil

4 shallots, sliced

One 14-ounce (395 g) block extra-firm tofu

2 tablespoons vegetable broth, or more as needed

2 teaspoons dried basil

1½ teaspoons dried oregano

1 teaspoon cumin

1 teaspoon black salt (kala namak) or regular salt

½ teaspoon smoked paprika

¼ teaspoon turmeric, optional

¼ cup (20 g) nutritional yeast, optional

2 tablespoons lemon juice

2 cups (60 g) roughly chopped fresh spinach

6 canned artichoke hearts (about one 14-ounce/395 g can), rinsed, drained, and quartered

⅓ cup (35 g) sliced sun-dried tomatoes (if hard, rehydrated in water until softened)

⅓ cup (60 g) assorted sliced olives

2 tablespoons capers

1. Heat the oil in a large frying pan over medium heat. Add the shallots and sauté for 3 to 4 minutes. Crumble the tofu into the pan. Cook, stirring gently, until the tofu is not releasing any water and is beginning to brown on the edges, about 10 minutes.

2. Meanwhile, in a small cup combine the broth, basil, oregano, cumin, black salt, paprika, and turmeric. When the tofu has stopped releasing water, add the broth mixture. Cook for about 5 more minutes, until the tofu has absorbed the liquid. If it begins to stick, add another tablespoon of broth to deglaze the pan and reduce the heat.

3. Add the nutritional yeast and lemon juice. Fold in the spinach, artichoke hearts, and sun-dried tomatoes. Cook until the spinach just begins to wilt. Remove from the heat, mix in the olives and capers, and serve warm.

|||||||||||||||||||||||||||||

VARIATIONS

You can make a different scramble every time:

▶ Try using half an onion instead of the shallots or replacing the veggies with different ones. You can add 2 to 3 cups of sliced mushrooms, bell peppers, broccoli, or another vegetable with the tofu, nix the artichoke hearts, and replace the spinach with kale or another green.

▶ Try replacing the dried basil and oregano with different herbs. Play around until you find your favorite combo.

▶ Serve the scramble inside a pita for a tofu scramble pocket or between two slices of bread for a scramble sandwich.

TOFU "BRAVAS"

SERVES 2

So, Spain came up with this little dish you may have heard of: *patatas bravas.* It's fried or roasted potatoes smothered in a tomato-based bravas sauce. It's their version of french fries and ketchup, and they do it *way, way better.* You could make a whole meal out of the stuff, but eating a whole bowl of potatoes doesn't always make you feel very healthy. Enter tofu. It's so simple: just sub some pan-fried tofu cubes and smother them with that awesome bravas sauce. It's a little lighter, a little less starchy, but still strong on flavor. Now we can enjoy a whole bowl and still feel like we did our bodies good.

1. Slice the tofu in half lengthwise into 2 large rectangles. Lay one flat on the cutting board and place the other one directly on top. Slice the 2 rectangles four times widthwise and four times lengthwise to make 32 cubes.

2. Place the cubes in a shallow bowl. Cover with the lemon juice, garlic powder, onion powder, salt, and pepper. Gently toss until fully coated. Let sit about 10 minutes.

3. While the tofu is resting, make the bravas sauce. Heat the olive oil in a small frying pan over medium heat. Add the onion and sauté until translucent. Transfer to a blender, add the rest of the bravas sauce ingredients, and blend until smooth. Set aside.

4. Line a plate with paper towels. Pour enough oil into a large frying pan, preferably cast iron, to coat the bottom; heat over medium heat 3 to 4 minutes. Add about one third of the tofu cubes and fry on each side for 2 to 3 minutes, until crispy and golden brown. Remove and place on the paper towels to absorb the extra oil. Repeat with the remaining two thirds of the tofu cubes until all are cooked.

5. Serve warm with the bravas sauce either drizzled over the tofu cubes or on the side as a dip. Chill leftovers in an airtight container up to 3 to 4 days.

PREP TIME: 15 minutes
COOK TIME: 15 minutes
DOWN TIME: 60 minutes (*while tofu presses*)

One 14-ounce (395 g) block extra-firm tofu, pressed for at least 1 hour (see page 4)

2 tablespoons fresh lemon juice

½ teaspoon garlic powder

½ teaspoon onion powder

½ teaspoon salt

¼ teaspoon black pepper

bravas sauce

1 teaspoon extra virgin olive oil

½ medium sweet onion, roughly chopped

One 15-ounce (425 g) can unsalted diced tomatoes, with liquid

1 tablespoon vegan mayonnaise

2 to 3 teaspoons sherry vinegar

1 teaspoon ground paprika

¼ teaspoon cayenne pepper

½ teaspoon agave syrup

Salt and black pepper to taste

Olive oil or canola oil for frying

CREAMY MUSHROOM FETTUCCINE ALFREDO

SERVES 4

Decadent fettuccine Alfredo may seem like a big no-no after you go vegan, but quite the contrary, my friend! Silken tofu is wonderful for creating thick, creamy sauces without any dairy (and it's much healthier to boot!). In this recipe, tofu helps to create an über-rich sauce that coats each noodle perfectly. The mushrooms are completely optional but add a little extra flavor and texture. Either way, you'll feel like you're indulging—even without the dairy.

PREP TIME: 5 minutes
COOK TIME: 20 minutes

One 12-ounce (340 g) package extra-firm silken tofu (the vacuum-packed kind)

1½ cups (375 g) non-dairy milk

¼ cup (60 ml) white wine

¼ cup (20 g) nutritional yeast

1 tablespoon extra virgin olive oil

2 teaspoons garlic powder

2 teaspoons onion powder

¼ teaspoon nutmeg

2 tablespoons arrowroot powder (or cornstarch)

Water

Salt

16 ounces (450 g) fettuccine (make sure it is eggless pasta)

8 ounces (225 g) sliced cremini mushrooms, optional

Additional salt and black pepper to taste

1. To make the Alfredo sauce, combine the silken tofu, non-dairy milk, wine, nutritional yeast, oil, garlic powder, onion powder, nutmeg, and arrowroot powder in a blender and blend until smooth and creamy. Set aside.

2. Bring a large pot of water to a boil. Add a pinch of salt, then add the pasta. Cook, following package instructions, until al dente. Drain off the water and set aside.

3. While the pasta is cooking, cook the mushrooms in a large shallow saucepan over medium heat, stirring occasionally until they have browned and reduced but haven't gotten mushy. Pour in the sauce and cook until fully heated. Add salt and pepper.

4. Top the pasta with the sauce and serve. Leftovers can be chilled in an airtight container 2 to 3 days.

TIP

For an even thicker and creamier sauce, add a couple tablespoons of vegan cream cheese to the sauce before blending.

BBQ BAKED TOFU

SERVES 2

Sometimes you just need something warm, chewy, and coated in sticky barbecue sauce, am I right? To satisfy that craving, tofu fits the bill perfectly. Pressing it removes the water, resulting in a much denser, chewier tofu. When it bakes in the sweet and smoky Barbecue Sauce, it fully absorbs the flavor and the sauce forms a thick and almost caramelized coating. Serve it up with corn on the cob and "Honey" Mustard Kale Slaw (page 63) or a side of Frites (page 80) if you prefer, and you'll feel like you're right smack dab in the middle of a vegan backyard BBQ party!

PREP TIME: 10 minutes

COOK TIME: 35 minutes

DOWN TIME: 60 minutes *(while tofu presses)*

Olive oil spray

One 14-ounce (395 g) block extra-firm tofu, pressed for at least 1 hour (see page 4)

½ cup (125 g) + 2 tablespoons Barbecue Sauce (page 31), divided

2 tablespoons balsamic vinegar

2 tablespoons liquid aminos (or tamari or soy sauce)

1. Preheat the oven to 375°F (190°C). Lightly spray an 8 x 8-inch baking dish with olive oil. Combine ½ cup of the Barbecue Sauce, the vinegar, and the liquid aminos in the dish and mix well.

2. Slice the pressed tofu in half widthwise. Slice each half in half, creating 4 flat rectangles. You can keep them this size or slice each rectangle diagonally to create 8 triangles.

3. Place the tofu pieces in the prepared baking dish and fully coat each side with the marinade. Bake for 30 minutes, flipping once halfway through to ensure even cooking.

4. After the tofu has cooked for 30 minutes, flip the pieces one more time and brush the remaining 2 tablespoons of Barbecue Sauce on top. Bake for 5 more minutes. Remove and serve immediately. Leftovers can be chilled in an airtight container up to 7 days.

SESAME-SRIRACHA TOFU SANDWICHES

SERVES 4

Freezing tofu allows for maximum flavor absorbency. It also makes the texture slightly chewier. This procedure gets a great response from meat-lovers, and when you cook it in a spicy sesame-sriracha sauce and scoop it into a sandwich with some kimchi, you may have a riot on your hands when everyone runs to the kitchen for seconds.

1. Combine the broth, liquid aminos, sriracha, maple syrup, tomato paste, liquid smoke, chile powder, paprika, and cumin and mix well. Set aside.

2. In a large frying pan, heat the oil over medium heat. Add the onion and sauté for 2 to 3 minutes. Add the garlic and ginger; sauté for 1 minute. Crumble the tofu into the pan. Add the broth mixture and mix well. Let it simmer, stirring occasionally, until all the liquid has been absorbed, about 10 minutes. Lower the heat and continue to cook, stirring occasionally, for 10 minutes. Add the salt and pepper; remove from the heat. Stir in the fresh parsley.

3. While the tofu is simmering, place the sesame seeds in a small frying pan and toast over medium heat, stirring frequently to prevent burning. When they begin to smell nutty and look toasted, they are done. Remove from the heat, add to the finished tofu mixture, and toss to coat.

4. Split open the sandwich buns and spread a layer of Tofu Sour Cream on the bottom half of each. Scoop the tofu mixture on top and add a couple spoonfuls of kimchi. Top each with the green onions and the top half of the bun. Serve immediately. The tofu mixture can be cooked ahead of time and will keep, chilled in an airtight container, 4 to 5 days.

PREP TIME: 20 minutes
COOK TIME: 25 minutes
DOWN TIME: 24 hours (*while tofu presses, freezes, and defrosts*)

¼ cup (60 ml) vegetable broth

¼ cup (60 ml) liquid aminos (or tamari or soy sauce)

¼ cup (60 ml) sriracha

1 tablespoon maple syrup

1 tablespoon tomato paste

1 teaspoon liquid smoke

1 teaspoon ancho chile powder

1 teaspoon smoked paprika

½ teaspoon cumin

2 teaspoons toasted sesame oil

½ red onion, diced

2 garlic cloves, minced

1 inch (2.5 cm) fresh ginger, peeled and grated

One 14-ounce (395 g) block extra-firm tofu, pressed, frozen, and thawed (see tips)

Salt and black pepper to taste

¼ cup (10 g) chopped fresh parsley

⅓ cup (40 g) sesame seeds

4 large rolls/buns (gluten-free, if necessary)

Tofu Sour Cream (page 33) or vegan mayonnaise

1 cup (185 g) kimchi (see tips)

Chopped green onions

TIPS

- For super flavor absorbency, press the tofu for 1 hour. Wrap it in plastic wrap, place in an airtight container, and freeze. The day before you use it, defrost in the refrigerator for at least 8 hours.

- Be careful when purchasing kimchi—sometimes it can contain fish oil.

SAVORY CORN CHEESECAKE WITH CILANTRO-PEPITA DRESSING

SERVES 6 TO 8 AS AN APPETIZER, 3 TO 4 AS A MEAL

Eons ago, in my pre-vegan days, I had a savory corn cheesecake at a Super Bowl party. (Or was it a Cinco de Mayo party? I don't know. Either way, there were margaritas.) I was so enamored of that cheesecake! I forgot to ask for the recipe (because *margaritas*!), and I've spent the last several years dreaming of that magical dish: its crispy blue corn tortilla chip crust; rich, cheesy corn filling; and cilantro dressing that found its way into every bite. Now this savory cheesecake has manifested itself in vegan form and is waiting for you and me to devour it. I'll bring the margaritas.

1. Preheat the oven to 350°F (175°C). Spray a 7- or 8-inch springform pan with olive oil. Place a round piece of parchment paper in the bottom.

2. Combine the tortilla chips and almonds in a food processor and process into a coarse flour. Add the vegan butter and pulse just until combined. Transfer to the prepared pan and use your fingers to press into a flat layer on the bottom. Set aside.

3. Gently squeeze the tofu to remove excess water. Combine the tofu, cream cheese, lime juice, onion powder, garlic powder, and paprika in the food processor and process until smooth. Add the corn and bell pepper and pulse until combined and mostly smooth (some corn or bell pepper pieces are good). Add salt.

4. Pour the corn mixture onto the prepared crust. Use a rubber spatula to smooth the top. Bake for 40 to 45 minutes, until completely set and a toothpick inserted into the center comes out clean. Remove from the oven and cool in the pan for about 10 minutes.

5. To make the dressing, combine the cilantro, pepitas, vinegar, garlic, chiles, nutritional yeast, mayonnaise, lime juice, and oil in the food processor. Process until smooth. Add water, 1 tablespoon at a time, to thin it to your desired consistency. Add salt.

PREP TIME: 20 minutes
COOK TIME: 45 minutes
DOWN TIME: 10 to 60 minutes (*while cheesecake cools*)

crust

Olive oil spray

1½ cups (115 g) crumbled blue corn tortilla chips

1 cup (150 g) raw almonds

¼ cup (55 g) vegan butter

filling

Half a 14-ounce block (about 200 g) extra-firm tofu

¾ cup (190 g) vegan cream cheese

1 tablespoon lime juice

½ teaspoon onion powder

½ teaspoon garlic powder

¼ teaspoon smoked paprika

1½ cups (210 g) corn kernels (fresh or frozen and defrosted)

½ cup (70 g) diced red bell pepper

Salt to taste

dressing

½ bunch fresh cilantro, no stems

¼ cup (40 g) raw pepitas (pumpkin seeds)

¼ cup (60 ml) sherry vinegar

2 garlic cloves

2 tablespoons diced canned green chiles

2 tablespoons nutritional yeast

2 tablespoons vegan mayonnaise

1 tablespoon lime juice

1 tablespoon extra virgin olive oil

1 to 2 tablespoons water

Salt to taste

toppings

1 cup (155 g) chopped cherry tomatoes

Chopped chives

{ RECIPE CONTINUES }

6. After 10 minutes, remove the outer ring of the springform pan and use the parchment paper to slide the cake onto a cooling rack. Let cool completely before serving (you can refrigerate it after you've removed the outer ring if you're in a hurry). It will still feel a little soft in the center and the crust will be a little crumbly. That's okay.

7. Drizzle with the dressing, top with the tomatoes, garnish with the chives, and serve. Leftovers can be chilled in an airtight container 2 to 3 days.

||||||||||||||||||||||||||||

VARIATION

▶ If you want more of a warm, gooey, cheesy sort of dip that you eat with a fork, slice and serve after it's cooled for 10 to 15 minutes.

VEGAN COOKING IS TOO HARD.

Easy Recipes to Whip Up in 35 Minutes or Less

One of the leading excuses for eating animal products is the mere convenience of it. I get it. The idea of preparing something with only plants can seem intimidating and time consuming; grabbing a quick burger sounds much easier. The truth is, it's very possible to create a quick and simple meal, and you don't have to be a whiz in the kitchen to accomplish it. Here are some of my favorite recipes for when I don't have time to cook or need to take something to go.

PORTOBELLO STEAK FRITES

SERVES 2

French fries, or *frites*, as we fancy people like to call them, are a favorite for many. Lucky for us—they're naturally vegan! So are portobello steaks, which are incredibly tasty and satisfying, not to mention ridiculously easy to make. And the frites? Just as easy. The hardest part about this new classic is waiting for it to come out of the oven. According to one of my recipe testers, it's a "quick-and-dirty weeknight meal that makes you get out the tablecloths."

PREP TIME: 15 minutes
COOK TIME: 25 minutes

portobello steaks

- 2 tablespoons liquid aminos (or tamari or soy sauce)
- 1 tablespoon balsamic vinegar
- 1 teaspoon liquid smoke
- 1 teaspoon dried thyme
- ½ teaspoon dried basil
- Black pepper to taste
- 2 large portobello mushroom caps (about 6 ounces/170 g each), cleaned, stems removed
- Olive oil spray

frites

- 2 to 3 large red or russet potatoes
- Olive oil spray
- ½ teaspoon garlic powder
- Salt and black pepper to taste

Zesty Ranch Dressing (page 32) or vegan ketchup, optional

1. Move one oven rack to the top and one to the middle of the oven and preheat to 400°F (200°C). Line two baking sheets with parchment paper or silicone baking mats.
2. In a small bowl, mix the liquid aminos, vinegar, liquid smoke, thyme, basil, and pepper. Set aside.
3. Lightly spray the mushroom caps with olive oil (top and bottom). Place them on one of the baking sheets, gill side up. Drizzle with the liquid aminos mixture. Let them marinate about 10 minutes.
4. Slice the potatoes in half lengthwise, lay the cut side flat on the cutting board, and slice each into 4 to 5 strips. If you want skinnier fries, slice the strips in half lengthwise. Try to keep them about the same size so they cook evenly.
5. Spread the fries on the second baking sheet. Lightly spray with olive oil, sprinkle the garlic powder over them, and add salt and pepper. Toss the fries to fully coat each piece; spread them out again, being careful not to crowd them.
6. Place the baking sheet with the potatoes on the top rack and bake for 20 to 25 minutes, flipping once halfway through to ensure even cooking. When the potatoes have about 12 minutes left to bake, place the baking sheet with the mushrooms in the oven on the middle rack.
7. When the frites are soft with a crisp exterior and the mushrooms have cooked for about 12 minutes, remove both from the oven. Transfer the frites to two plates and add a mushroom to each. Serve immediately with Zesty Ranch Dressing or ketchup, if desired.

AVOCADO & WHITE BEAN SALAD WRAPS

SERVES 2

"After a long, hard day at work, what I love most is to come home and cook an elaborate meal," said no one *ever*. My kitchen is my happy place, but there are times when even I don't feel like making dinner. My go-to recipe when I haven't the energy to do anything but collapse on the couch and watch *Downton Abbey* is to combine mashed avocado with mashed white beans and a few other ingredients and roll it up in lavash or stuff it into tacos or a sandwich. I've also been known to eat it with a spoon. The whole thing comes together really quickly and, including the time it takes to put on your sweats and slippers, dinner is on the coffee table in 20 minutes.

PREP TIME: 20 minutes
COOK TIME: 5 minutes

1 teaspoon extra virgin olive oil

1½ cups (265 g) cooked great Northern beans (see page 8) or one 15-ounce (425 g) can, rinsed and drained

1 tablespoon liquid aminos (or tamari or soy sauce)

1 tablespoon white balsamic vinegar

1 large or 2 small avocados, halved and pitted

2 tablespoons lime juice

2 tablespoons fresh parsley or cilantro

1 tablespoon diced canned green chiles

1 teaspoon garlic powder

1 teaspoon smoked paprika

½ teaspoon onion powder

Salt and black pepper to taste

2 lavash wraps or large tortillas

1 to 2 Roma tomatoes, thinly sliced

2 big handfuls of baby spinach

1. Heat the oil in a large frying pan over medium heat. Add the beans and sauté until warm. Add the liquid aminos and cook, stirring occasionally, until it has cooked away. Add the vinegar and cook, stirring once or twice, until the liquid has cooked away. Remove from the heat and use a fork to mash the beans.

2. Scoop the avocado flesh into a large bowl and mash until there are no chunks. Add the mashed beans, lime juice, parsley, green chiles, garlic powder, paprika, and onion powder. Mix until combined. Add salt and pepper.

3. Lay out one lavash wrap and spread half of the avocado mixture on it. Going widthwise, or the shortest distance across the lavash, add a row of tomato slices, a row of spinach next to it, another row of tomatoes, and another row of spinach. Start rolling the wrap over the first row of tomatoes and continue until it is completely rolled up. Chop into 3 to 4 sections. Repeat with the second wrap and remaining ingredients and serve. Leftovers can be chilled in an airtight container 2 to 3 days.

‖‖‖‖‖‖‖‖‖‖‖‖‖‖‖‖‖‖‖‖‖‖

VARIATIONS

▶ Chickpeas can be used instead of white beans.
▶ Try serving the filling as a dip for chips!

CHICKPEA OMELETS

SERVES 2

I really can't take credit for this recipe. It's inspired by the hundreds of versions I've found online since I became vegan. When considering veganism, Chris and I actually said to each other, "Well, we can still occasionally have an omelet, right?" But the more we researched the horrific way egg farms work, the more sure we were that we would never have another egg-based omelet again. A quick online search for "vegan omelets" turned up a bazillion recipes for *pudla* or *chilla*, both of which mean "chickpea flour pancakes." When chickpea flour is mixed with a liquid, it forms a perfect pancake batter, and when cooked, it tastes remarkably eggy. Add black salt and you have a dead ringer. If you've ever thought you couldn't give up eggs, try this one out.

PREP TIME: 5 minutes
COOK TIME: 20 minutes

- 1 cup (110 g) chickpea flour
- 1 tablespoon nutritional yeast, optional
- 1 teaspoon black salt (kala namak) or regular salt
- ½ teaspoon cumin
- ½ teaspoon dried thyme
- ¼ teaspoon garlic powder
- ¼ teaspoon smoked paprika
- ¼ teaspoon turmeric
- ⅛ teaspoon black pepper
- ½ cup + 2 tablespoons (155 ml) water, divided
- 1 teaspoon extra virgin olive oil
- 2 cups (140 g) sliced mushrooms
- 2 cups (60 g) chopped kale or other greens
- ½ cup (50 g) chopped sun-dried tomatoes (if hard, rehydrated in water until softened)
- ¼ cup (25 g) chopped green onion (white part only)
- Olive oil spray

1. In a large bowl, combine the chickpea flour, nutritional yeast, black salt, cumin, thyme, garlic powder, paprika, turmeric, and pepper. Stir in ½ cup of the water until mostly smooth (it will still be a little lumpy) with a pancake batter consistency. If it is too thick, add water 1 tablespoon at a time until it thins out to the desired consistency. Set aside while you cook the vegetables.

2. Heat the oil in a large frying pan over medium heat. Add the mushrooms and sauté until just beginning to release water, 3 to 4 minutes. Add the kale, sun-dried tomatoes, and green onion and sauté just until the kale is wilted. Remove from the heat and add to the chickpea flour batter. Mix until combined.

3. Carefully clean out the frying pan, spray generously with olive oil, and heat over medium heat. If you want two large omelets, spoon half of the batter into the pan. If you want 4 smaller omelets, scoop out one quarter of the batter. Cover the pan and cook for 3 to 4 minutes, until the edges are lifting from the pan and it is beginning to firm up. Use a spatula to gently flip the omelet over (this may take some practice) and cook for 2 to 3 minutes on that side. Repeat with the remaining batter, spraying the pan with olive oil between omelets. Serve warm. The omelets can be made ahead of time and chilled in an airtight container for a day or two.

|||||||||||||||||||||||||||||||

VARIATIONS

▶ The omelets are good cold too, but if you'd like to reheat them, it takes only about 30 seconds in the microwave.

▶ Do you have leftover veggies in the fridge? Throw those into the batter instead of cooking up new veggies. Use whatever you have—get creative!

▶ If you make smaller omelets, try putting one in a sandwich with some lettuce, fresh tomato, avocado, and mustard. Take it to lunch and make your coworkers jealous.

SAVORY OVERNIGHT QUINOA OATMEAL

SERVES 1

I love being that chick making the office smell awesome with the lunch I'm heating up in the microwave. This quinoa oatmeal is one of those quick and easy lunches you can throw in the fridge the night before and take to work the next day. Pack some fresh veggies to stir in after you nuke it, and you too can make your coworkers' mouths water (whether they're vegan or not). It also makes a great breakfast on the go or the perfect simple dinner waiting for you when you get home.

1. Put the quinoa in a large canning jar or airtight container. Add the oats, chickpeas, non-dairy milk, broth, nutritional yeast, roasted red pepper, sun-dried tomatoes, olives, liquid aminos, basil, oregano, and pepper. Cover the jar and shake until combined. Refrigerate until ready to serve, at least 3 to 4 hours.

2. To heat, pour the jar's contents into a medium pot and cook over medium heat, stirring occasionally, for 5 to 7 minutes, until heated through and thickened. If it gets too thick and sticky, add a couple tablespoons of broth or water. Alternatively, microwave for 3 to 4 minutes, until heated through and thickened, stirring once halfway through. Stir in the greens, if using, and top with the tomatoes, avocado, and green onions, if using.

||||||||||||||||||||||||||||||

VARIATION

▶ For a more traditional, sweet overnight quinoa "oatmeal," replace the vegetable broth with more non-dairy milk or apple juice. Replace the remaining ingredients with dried or fresh fruits of choice, ¼ cup (about 30 g) chopped nuts, 2 teaspoons maple syrup or Happy Bee Honey (page 34), ½ teaspoon cinnamon, ½ teaspoon ground ginger, and a pinch of salt.

PREP TIME: 10 minutes *(not including time to cook quinoa)*
COOK TIME: 5 minutes
DOWN TIME: 3 to 4 hours

⅓ cup (55 g) cooked quinoa (see page 9)

⅓ cup (35 g) uncooked rolled oats (gluten-free if necessary)

⅓ cup (55 g) cooked chickpeas (or canned chickpeas, rinsed and drained)

½ cup (125 ml) non-dairy milk

½ cup (125 ml) vegetable broth or water, plus more if needed

2 tablespoons nutritional yeast

2 tablespoons chopped roasted red pepper

2 tablespoons chopped sun-dried tomatoes (if hard, rehydrated in water until softened)

2 tablespoons chopped pitted olives (any kind)

1 tablespoon liquid aminos (or tamari or soy sauce)

½ teaspoon dried basil

½ teaspoon dried oregano

Black pepper to taste

optional add-ins

Greens such as spinach, chard, or kale

Chopped cherry tomatoes

Chopped avocado

Chopped green onions

TIP This recipe is a great way to use up leftover quinoa, but if you don't have any, you can cook 1 cup dried quinoa (page 9) to make roughly 3 cups cooked. That is more than enough to provide you with lunches for a whole week! You could even double, triple, or septuple the recipe and cook it all together. Once cooked, divide it into individual servings to serve right away or reheat later.

ROASTED RATATOUILLE TARTINES

SERVES 4 TO 6

*T*artine is a really pretty word for "open-faced sandwich." It is also a very simple, convenient, satisfying meal that is perfect for vegans. I have them a few times a week, stacking whatever fruits or vegetables I have in my fridge on top of toast or fresh bread. Sometimes a batch of these quick, enticing, admittedly inauthentic tartines will provide lunches for an entire week! The luscious and tangy Tofu Chèvre spread on a slice of French bread makes the perfect stage to let the robust, tomatoey ratatouille shine.

1. Preheat the oven to 400°F (200°C). Line two baking sheets with parchment paper or silicone baking mats.
2. Spread the eggplant, squash, bell pepper, and onion across both sheets. Lightly spray with olive oil. Evenly sprinkle the oregano, basil, thyme, salt, and pepper over the vegetables and toss to coat. Roast for 20 minutes, or until tender, flipping once halfway through to ensure even cooking.
3. When the vegetables are tender, remove from the oven and transfer to a large bowl. Mix in the tomatoes.
4. To serve, spread a bit of the Tofu Chèvre on each slice of bread. Top with the ratatouille. Serve immediately. Chill leftover ratatouille in an airtight container 3 to 4 days.

PREP TIME: 15 minutes *(not including time to prepare Tofu Chèvre)*
COOK TIME: 20 minutes

roasted ratatouille

1 medium eggplant, chopped into 1-inch (2.5 cm) pieces

3 yellow squash or zucchini, halved lengthwise, thickly sliced

1 large red bell pepper, chopped into 1-inch (2.5 cm) pieces

½ large red onion, thinly sliced

Olive oil spray

2 teaspoons dried oregano

1 teaspoon dried basil

1 teaspoon dried thyme

Salt and black pepper to taste

One 15-ounce (425 g) can unsalted diced fire-roasted tomatoes, with liquid

tartines

½ batch Tofu Chèvre (page 36)

2 slices French bread per person (gluten-free if necessary)

BEAN & RICE FREEZER BURRITOS

SERVES 6

Don't you love it when you find something you'd stored in your freezer months earlier and forgotten about? Like that awesome soup or that little bit of leftover pesto? Wouldn't it be lovely, when you're super hungry and standing in front of your refrigerator, staring blankly, with both the fridge and the freezer doors open, to suddenly spot those crazy-tasty and satisfying bean and rice burritos that you planted there a couple months before? You should get on that now—future you is going to be so thankful!

PREP TIME: 15 minutes *(not including time to cook rice)*
COOK TIME: 20 minutes

1 teaspoon extra virgin olive oil

½ medium yellow onion, chopped

2 to 3 garlic cloves, minced

3 cups (525 g) cooked pinto beans (see page 8) or two 15-ounce (425 g) cans, rinsed and drained

1 cup (250 ml) vegetable broth, divided

3 tablespoons diced canned green chiles

1 teaspoon cumin

½ teaspoon smoked paprika

¼ teaspoon ancho chile powder

2 tablespoons nutritional yeast, optional

Juice of ½ lime

Salt and black pepper to taste

6 large flour tortillas

2 cups (320 g) cooked brown rice (see page 9)

1. Heat the oil in a frying pan over medium heat. Add the onion and garlic and sauté until the onion starts to become translucent. Add the beans, ½ cup of broth, green chiles, cumin, paprika, and chile powder. Cover, leaving a small crack open, and simmer for 5 minutes, or until the broth has mostly cooked away. Add ¼ cup broth and repeat. Add the final ¼ cup broth and use a potato masher to mash the beans. Cook for 2 to 3 minutes, then add the nutritional yeast, lime juice, salt, and pepper. Remove from the heat.

2. Wrap the flour tortillas in a damp kitchen towel and microwave for 30 seconds. Spread about ⅓ cup of rice in a strip down the middle of a tortilla. Top with about ½ cup cooked

{ RECIPE CONTINUES }

beans. Fold the ends over the rice and beans and roll up the burrito. Place on a plate seam side down and repeat with the remaining ingredients.

3. You can serve the burritos now, or you can freeze them for a meal later. To freeze, wait until the burritos have cooled. Roll each individual burrito in parchment paper followed by plastic wrap or a resealable plastic bag. Place the wrapped burritos in an airtight container. Freeze up to 1 month.

4. Remove the plastic wrap, but not the parchment paper, from a burrito. Reheat in the microwave for 2 to 3 minutes, or until warm and soft. Alternatively, preheat the oven to 350°F (175°C) and bake the parchment-wrapped burrito(s) for 10 minutes, or until heated through. Serve hot with Guacamole (page 105), Tofu Sour Cream (page 33), salsa, or all three.

||||||||||||||||||||||||||||||||

VARIATIONS

▶ For cheesy bean and rice burritos (as pictured), add a bit of grated Sunflower Cheddar (page 42) to the burrito before rolling up.

▶ To spice it up, add a splash of hot sauce to the beans while cooking.

▶ For breakfast burritos, use the fillings for Chickpea Scramble Breakfast Tacos (page 120).

WHERE'S THE BEEF?

"Meaty" Food, Minus the Meat

If you claim to be a hard-core carnivore, ask yourself: Is it meat that you can't live without, or is it the way the meat is prepared, the flavors it is cooked with, and the aromas it wafts at you? If you replace the meat in your favorite dishes, you'll most likely find it's not the animal you're crazy about eating, but the meal. Here are healthier, kinder, vegan spins on traditionally meat-heavy meals. After trying a few of these recipes, no one will be asking, "Where's the beef?"

PORTOBELLO POT PIE

SERVES 6

PREP TIME: 50 minutes
COOK TIME: 20 minutes

1 batch Southern Biscuits (page 233), prepared through step 3

Olive oil spray

2 pounds (907 g) portobello mushrooms (about 8)

1 tablespoon arrowroot powder

1 cup (250 ml) vegetable broth

2 teaspoons extra virgin olive oil

2 leeks (white part only), halved lengthwise and thinly sliced (see tip on page 189)

1 carrot, peeled and diced small

1 celery rib, thinly sliced

1 tablespoon chopped fresh rosemary

1 tablespoon chopped fresh sage

1 tablespoon chopped fresh thyme

2 tablespoons liquid aminos (or tamari or soy sauce)

½ cup (125 ml) dry white wine

Salt and black pepper to taste

1 cup (140 g) frozen green peas, thawed

2 tablespoons nutritional yeast, optional

Many of us have had a frozen pot pie in our lives—the kind you cook in the microwave. The insides are always pretty good, but the crust is chewy and burnt around the edges. A real, homemade pot pie, on the other hand, is the sort of meal that inspires cravings. In this meat-free version, the flaky biscuit crust atop a personal serving of portobello mushroom strips, loads of veggies, and a decadent white wine broth will leave you wanting more for years to come.

1. Set out six 8-ounce ramekins. Using a biscuit cutter the same size as the ramekins (or the rim of one of the ramekins), cut out the biscuits. When you cannot cut out any more, roll the dough, flatten it out, and use the cutter to cut out a couple more. Place the biscuits on parchment paper until ready to use. If you cut out more than 6 biscuits, you can bake them according to their instructions (page 233) after the pot pies have baked.

2. Preheat the oven to 400°F (200°C). Lightly spray the ramekins with olive oil and place them on a baking sheet. Set aside.

3. Remove the stems from the portobellos and chop the stems into ½-inch (1 cm) chunks. Slice each mushroom cap on the bias (diagonally) into ½-inch (1 cm) strips. Slice those strips into ½-inch (1 cm) chunks.

4. Add the arrowroot powder to the broth and mix to combine. Set aside.

5. Heat the 2 teaspoons olive oil in a large shallow saucepan over medium heat. Add the leeks and sauté for 2 to 3 minutes, until soft. Add the carrot, celery, and portobello stems and caps; mix to combine. Cook for 3 to 4 minutes to let the mushrooms release some of their water.

6. When the mushrooms have softened, add the rosemary, sage, thyme, liquid aminos, wine, salt, and pepper. Mix to combine and cook until the liquid has been absorbed. Add ½ cup of the broth mixture and cook until it has been absorbed.

Add the remaining ½ cup of broth and the peas and cook for about 2 minutes, letting the liquid reduce barely by half.

7. Add the nutritional yeast (if using), taste, and add more salt and pepper if desired. Remove from the heat.

8. Divide the mixture among the prepared ramekins and top each with one uncooked biscuit. Brush the tops of the biscuits with the non-dairy milk/melted butter mixture from the Southern Biscuits recipe. Place the baking sheet with the ramekins in the oven and bake for 15 to 20 minutes, until the biscuits are golden. Serve immediately.

||||||||||||||||||||||||||||

VARIATION

▶ If you don't want to do individual servings, lightly grease a 9 x 13 inch baking dish and fill it with the filling. Cut out the biscuits, distribute them on top of the filling, and bake as directed in step 8.

LENTIL-MUSHROOM MEATLOAF WITH KETCHUP GLAZE

SERVES 4 TO 6

Every mom has her *one recipe* she's known for. For my mom it was meatloaf—the ol' fashioned kind covered in ketchup. A couple times, she tried to get me to help her make it, but I was grossed out by the raw meat and preferred not to look at the meatloaf until it was finished cooking. *This* meatloaf is a whole other story! Made from lentils, vegetables, and oats, it's a cinch—and that classic ketchup glaze will make you feel like you're eating Mom's signature dish.

1. Preheat the oven to 375°F (190°C). Line a baking sheet with parchment paper.

2. Mix the glaze ingredients in a small bowl and set aside.

3. Whisk the flaxseed meal and water together in a cup and set aside.

4. Heat the oil in a frying pan over medium heat. Add the onion and garlic and sauté for 2 to 3 minutes. Add the mushrooms, carrot, and celery and sauté until the carrot is tender. Remove from the heat and transfer to a food processor. Add about 1¼ cups of the lentils and the nutritional yeast, tomato paste, liquid aminos, Worcestershire sauce (if using), parsley, thyme, sage, fennel seeds, and ½ cup of the oats. Pulse until fully combined and everything is similar in size. Add salt and pepper.

5. Transfer the mixture to a large bowl. Add the almond flour, flaxseed mixture, and the remaining ¾ cup lentils and ½ cup oats; mix until a thick dough is formed. If it is too liquidy, add more oats. If it is too dry (not forming a ball), add water by the tablespoon until no longer crumbly.

6. Turn the mixture out onto the prepared baking sheet. Use your hands to shape it into a loaf. Brush half of the glaze on the top and sides and bake for 30 minutes. Brush the remaining glaze on top and bake for another 10 to 15 minutes, until a toothpick inserted into the center comes out mostly clean. Let it cool on the sheet for about 5 minutes, then use the parchment paper to lift the loaf onto a cooling rack. Cool for another 5 minutes, then serve warm. Leftovers can be chilled in an airtight container 3 to 4 days.

PREP TIME: 20 minutes (*not including time to cook lentils*)
COOK TIME: 45 minutes

ketchup glaze

½ cup (125 ml) vegan ketchup

2 tablespoons coconut sugar or vegan brown sugar

1 tablespoon apple cider vinegar

¼ teaspoon mustard powder

meatloaf

1 tablespoon flaxseed meal

3 tablespoons warm water

1 teaspoon extra virgin olive oil

½ medium sweet onion, chopped

2 to 3 garlic cloves, minced

8 ounces (225 g) sliced cremini mushrooms

½ cup (80 g) diced carrot

⅓ cup (40 g) diced celery

2 cups (320 g) cooked lentils (see page 8), divided

2 tablespoons nutritional yeast, optional

2 heaping tablespoons tomato paste

2 tablespoons liquid aminos (or tamari or soy sauce)

1 tablespoon vegan Worcestershire sauce, optional

1½ teaspoons dried parsley

1½ teaspoons dried thyme

1 teaspoon dried sage

1 teaspoon fennel seeds

1 cup (100 g) rolled oats (certified gluten-free if necessary), divided, plus more if needed

½ teaspoon salt

Several dashes of black pepper

½ cup (50 g) almond flour

CHICKPEA SLOPPY JOES

SERVES 6 TO 8

PREP TIME: 5 minutes
COOK TIME: 20 minutes

Didn't it always seem like Sloppy Joes were the one recipe your elementary school got right? Everything else usually ended up in the garbage (like those hockey pucks they called chicken nuggets? Blech). When you got older, Sloppy Joes were the one meal you kinda, sorta wished someone would cook for you, even though you're supposed to want more "grown-up" foods like *salads*. Well, here you go: a Sloppy Joe sandwich that tastes better than your old cafeteria's, and it happens to be vegan! Mashed chickpeas are a surprisingly good substitute for ground meat, and the flavor of these sandwiches is so addictive, both children and adults will be asking for seconds. To really impress, serve them up with Frites (page 80) or onion rings (page 153).

4 cups (510 g) cooked chickpeas (page 8) or two 15-ounce (425 g) cans, rinsed and drained

Vegan hamburger buns (gluten-free, if necessary)

1 teaspoon extra virgin olive oil

½ medium red onion, diced

2 to 3 garlic cloves, minced

½ red bell pepper, diced

One 15-ounce (425 g) can unsalted, diced fire-roasted tomatoes, with liquid

¼ cup (60 g) tomato paste

3 tablespoons liquid aminos (or tamari or soy sauce)

2 tablespoons sriracha

1 tablespoon maple syrup

2 teaspoons dried oregano

1½ teaspoons cumin

1 teaspoon smoked paprika

1 teaspoon dried thyme

1 teaspoon liquid smoke

1 tablespoon nutritional yeast, optional

Salt and black pepper to taste

Tofu Sour Cream (page 33) or vegan mayonnaise, optional

1. In a medium bowl, mash the chickpeas with a fork into small chunks or shreds. Set aside.

2. Preheat the oven to its lowest temperature. Open the buns and heat the halves, cut side up, on the center rack (or on a baking sheet) for 10 to 15 minutes.

3. Meanwhile, heat the olive oil in a large shallow saucepan over medium heat. Add the onion and garlic and sauté until the onions are translucent and the garlic is fragrant. Add the bell pepper and mashed chickpeas; sauté about 2 minutes. Add the tomatoes, tomato paste, liquid aminos, sriracha, maple syrup, oregano, cumin, paprika, thyme, liquid smoke, nutritional yeast (if using), salt, and pepper; simmer, stirring occasionally, for 10 to 15 minutes, until heated through and slightly thickened. If it sticks, add a little water to deglaze the pan and lower the heat a bit.

4. Scoop the chickpea mixture onto the warmed buns and top with a dollop of Tofu Sour Cream or vegan mayonnaise (if using). Serve immediately. Leftover filling can be chilled in an airtight container 3 to 4 days.

THAI SEITAN SATAY WITH SPICY PEANUT DIPPING SAUCE

SERVES 2 TO 4

Seitan is a great food in and of itself, not just a meat substitute. However, if you're looking to replicate the taste and mouthfeel of beef, seitan is your best bet. The similarity is uncanny, especially if you cook the seitan in a cast-iron grill pan to get those lovely grill marks. In this dish, a coconut milk marinade with bold flavors from lime, lemongrass, and ginger turns this satay from ordinary to absolutely incredible. The spicy peanut dipping sauce is a winner, too. Don't be surprised if you find yourself dipping everything in it (especially the Rainbow Millet-Hummus Collard Summer Rolls, page 147).

PREP TIME: 15 minutes (*not including time to make Homemade Seitan*)
COOK TIME: 15 minutes
DOWN TIME: 60 minutes

satay

½ cup (125 ml) coconut milk

2 garlic cloves, minced

2 tablespoons diced fresh lemongrass (see tip, page 137)

2 tablespoons lime juice

2 tablespoons tamari or soy sauce (or liquid aminos)

1 tablespoon coconut sugar or vegan brown sugar

1 teaspoon grated fresh ginger

½ teaspoon curry powder

1 batch Homemade Seitan (page 28) or store-bought

Fresh cilantro

spicy peanut dipping sauce

½ cup (130 g) smooth peanut butter

2 tablespoons lime juice

2 tablespoons tamari or soy sauce (or liquid aminos)

2 tablespoons vegetable broth, or more to taste

1½ tablespoons maple syrup

2 teaspoons hot sauce

1 teaspoon grated fresh ginger

8 skewers, soaked for 15 minutes if wooden

Olive oil spray

1. In an 8 x 8-inch baking dish, combine the coconut milk, garlic, lemongrass, lime juice, tamari, coconut sugar, ginger, and curry powder. Slice the seitan into 1-inch (2.5 cm) wide strips and place in the baking dish. Toss to coat in the marinade. Cover and marinate for 1 hour, flipping the strips halfway through.

2. In a small bowl, whisk together the dipping sauce ingredients. If you like a thinner sauce, add more broth to reach your desired consistency. If needed, the sauce can be made a day in advance.

3. Skewer the seitan strips. Heat a grill pan, preferably cast iron, over medium heat and lightly spray with olive oil. Grill the satays 3 to 5 minutes on each side, until they are browned with grill marks. Serve warm with the dipping sauce.

BLT & AVOCADO SOFT TACOS

SERVES 3 TO 4

It doesn't get much better than a vegan BLT with avocado. Crisp, smoky tempeh bacon with the simple, clean flavors of tomato and lettuce and the creaminess of avocado? It's clearly one of the best vegan sandwiches in existence. However, if you turn that sandwich into a soft taco, you'll encounter a whole new level of tastiness. Tempeh bacon is the star here, easily relieving any bacon cravings you may be experiencing. Going vegan doesn't mean you'll miss out on BLTs—they just get better!

PREP TIME: 10 minutes (*not including time to make Tempeh Bacon*)

Olive oil spray

1 batch Tempeh Bacon (page 25)

6 to 8 small flour tortillas (gluten-free, if necessary)

2 cups (60 g) chopped lettuce or baby greens

3 to 4 Roma tomatoes, diced

1 avocado, pitted, peeled, and sliced into strips

1. Prepare the Tempeh Bacon through step 3. While it is cooking (step 4), heat a frying pan over medium heat. Lightly spray each side of a tortilla with olive oil and cook for about 1 minute on each side. Repeat for the remaining tortillas. To keep them warm, place on a plate and cover with a warm, lightly damp towel. Alternatively, wrap the tortillas in a damp kitchen towel and microwave for 30 seconds.

2. To serve, place some lettuce down the middle of a tortilla and top with a few slices of bacon, some tomato chunks, and avocado slices.

VARIATIONS

▶ Switch out the soft tortillas for crunchy taco shells (see page 121), ditch the tortillas and serve with more lettuce and Zesty Ranch Dressing (page 32) for a salad, or grab some bread and have classic BLT sandwiches.

BBQ JACKFRUIT FAJITAS WITH GUACAMOLE

SERVES 4

At first, putting fruit in a fajita just sounds wrong. Jackfruit, however, is not your ordinary fruit. When shredded, it takes on the appearance and texture of shredded "pulled" meat, and its mild flavor makes it a perfect substitute. Now imagine it cooked in BBQ sauce along with bell peppers and onions—sounds perfect, right? When you serve it up in a cast-iron pan with warm tortillas and guacamole, the crowd will go wild. Neither you nor your family will miss the plain ol' grilled meat!

to make the guacamole

In a large bowl, mash the avocados using a potato masher or fork until creamy with only small chunks left. Add the remaining guacamole ingredients and mix until combined. Cover and chill until ready to use. This can be made a couple hours ahead, if needed.

to make the fajitas

1. Rinse the jackfruit thoroughly in a colander. Use two forks or your fingers to tear into shreds (see page 106). Set aside.

2. Mix the Barbecue Sauce, tomato paste, hot sauce, salt, and pepper in a small bowl. Set aside.

3. Heat the oil in a large frying pan over medium heat. Add the onion and sauté until translucent.

4. Add the jackfruit and bell pepper and sauté until most of the liquid released from the jackfruit is gone. Stir in the sauce mixture, reduce the heat to medium-low, cover the pan, and cook for 10 to 15 minutes, stirring occasionally. Add more salt and pepper, if desired, and remove from the heat.

5. While the jackfruit is cooking, heat a second frying pan over medium heat. Lightly spray each side of a tortilla with olive oil and cook in the frying pan, 30 to 60 seconds on each side. Repeat with the remaining tortillas. To keep them warm, place them on a plate and cover with a warm, lightly damp towel. Alternatively, wrap the tortillas in a damp kitchen towel and microwave for 30 seconds.

PREP TIME: 15 minutes
COOK TIME: 30 minutes

guacamole

2 avocados, halved, pitted, and peeled

¼ cup (10 g) chopped cilantro

1½ tablespoons lime juice

1 garlic clove, minced

½ teaspoon cumin

Salt to taste

fajitas

Two 20-ounce cans (1,130 g) jackfruit, packed in brine (not syrup)

1½ cups (375 ml) Barbecue Sauce (page 31) or store-bought vegan barbecue sauce

2 tablespoons tomato paste

1 tablespoon hot sauce

Salt and black pepper to taste

1 teaspoon extra virgin olive oil

1 medium yellow onion, sliced

2 red bell peppers, sliced

6 to 8 small flour tortillas (or corn or other gluten-free tortillas, if necessary)

Olive oil spray

Tofu Sour Cream (page 33), optional

{ RECIPE CONTINUES }

6. To serve, pile some BBQ jackfruit onto a tortilla and top with Guacamole and Tofu Sour Cream, if using. Repeat with the remaining ingredients. Leftovers can be chilled in an air-tight container 3 to 4 days.

||||||||||||||||||||||||||||

VARIATION

▶ Try serving this BBQ jackfruit in a sandwich or wrap, or even on top of a salad. Leftovers are perfect to pack for lunch the next day.

JUST THINKING ABOUT SALAD MAKES ME YAWN.

Entrée Salads That Demand Your Attention

Vegans don't always eat salads, but when we do, we go all out: no limp iceberg lettuce or stale carrot shreds. We fill our bowls with mounds of vegetables, fruits, grains, legumes, nuts, and *sometimes* lettuce. Dressings range from thick and creamy to light and tangy. Some salads are cold, some are warm, and some are *both*! Occasionally, our salads are appetizers, but when they're done right—like the ones in this chapter—they're the main event.

BBQ CAULIFLOWER SALAD WITH ZESTY RANCH DRESSING

SERVES 4

You know those big BBQ sandwiches stuffed with onion rings? Imagine taking away the bread, dumping everything else into a bowl with some lettuce, and dousing it with ranch dressing. That's what this salad is all about. Roasted cauliflower coated in Barbecue Sauce (page 31) makes an unforgettable replacement for meat and is an instant favorite of all who try it (even cauliflower-phobes). Topped with corn, tomatoes, and Crispy Baked Onion Rings (page 153), this salad is for everyone who thinks a salad can't be hearty, satisfying, and downright mouthwatering. All that, *and* it's vegan!

1. Preheat the oven to 400°F (200°C). Line a baking sheet with parchment paper or a silicone baking mat.
2. Spread the cauliflower florets on the sheet. Lightly spray with olive oil. Drizzle with the liquid aminos and liquid smoke and sprinkle with the cumin, garlic powder, onion powder, paprika, salt, and pepper. Squeeze the lemon juice over them. Toss to fully coat each piece. Roast for 20 minutes, tossing once halfway through to ensure even cooking.
3. Mix the Barbecue Sauce and cornstarch in a cup. After 20 minutes, remove the cauliflower from the oven, add the sauce, and toss. Bake 5 to 10 minutes more, until most of the BBQ sauce has dried.
4. Toss together the greens, corn, tomatoes, and avocado in a bowl. Divide the salad among four bowls, top with the BBQ cauliflower, drizzle with the dressing, and top with the onion rings. Serve immediately.

PREP TIME: 15 minutes (*not including time to prepare Onion Rings and Zesty Ranch Dressing*)
COOK TIME: 30 minutes

BBQ cauliflower

1 head cauliflower, broken into small florets

Olive oil spray

1 tablespoon liquid aminos

½ teaspoon liquid smoke

½ teaspoon cumin

½ teaspoon garlic powder

½ teaspoon onion powder

½ teaspoon smoked paprika

Salt and black pepper to taste

Juice of ½ lemon

1 cup (250 ml) Barbecue Sauce (page 31) or store-bought

1 tablespoon cornstarch

salad

4 cups (120 g) mixed greens or lettuce

1½ cups (210 g) corn kernels

1½ cups (240 g) diced tomatoes

1 avocado, pitted, peeled, and chopped into chunks

Zesty Ranch Dressing (page 32)

Crispy Baked Onion Rings (page 153)

ROASTED ROOT VEGGIE & KALE SALAD WITH CASHEW BLUE CHEESE

SERVES 4

Come autumn, I just want to roast all of the vegetables, especially root vegetables. Roasting brings out their sweetness and depth, and when you throw them in a kale salad with creamy cashew blue cheese and bright, citrusy tangerines, the combination is amazing! The balsamic reduction adds one more velvety sweet layer of flavor. Massaging kale with lemon juice breaks down the fibers, making the pieces softer and easier to chew (and stab with your fork). It may sound weird, but all the cool vegans are doing it.

1. Preheat the oven to 400°F (200°C). Line two baking sheets with parchment paper or silicone baking mats.

2. Spread the beets and sweet potatoes on one baking sheet, keeping them separated so the beets don't bleed onto the sweet potatoes. On the other sheet, spread the celery root. Drizzle the liquid aminos over the celery root. Spray all the vegetables with olive oil and evenly distribute the thyme, nutmeg, salt, and pepper across them.

3. Roast for 15 minutes, then toss to ensure even cooking (keeping the beets as separate from the sweet potatoes as possible). Scoot the celery root toward one side and lay the carrots on that baking sheet. Lightly spray the carrots with olive oil, sprinkle with salt and pepper, return both sheets to the oven, and roast for 15 minutes.

4. Meanwhile, place the kale in a large bowl. Add the lemon juice and oil. "Massage" with your hands for 2 to 3 minutes, rubbing the lemon juice and oil into the leaves. Set aside.

5. In a medium pot, bring the vinegar to a boil over medium heat (*not* high heat); reduce the heat and simmer for 10 minutes, or until reduced by at least half, if not two-thirds (the longer it cooks, the thicker it will be). Remove from the heat and pour into a bowl or cup to cool.

6. When the vegetables are fork-tender, remove to cool for about 5 minutes. Add to the kale with the tangerines and toss. Serve with Cashew Blue Cheese and the balsamic reduction.

PREP TIME: 30 minutes *(not including time to prepare Cashew Blue Cheese)*
COOK TIME: 30 minutes

3 medium beets, peeled and chopped into 1-inch (2.5 cm) pieces

1 large or 2 small sweet potatoes, peeled and chopped into 1-inch (2.5 cm) pieces

1 small celery root (celeriac), peeled and chopped into 1-inch (2.5 cm) pieces

1 tablespoon liquid aminos (or tamari or soy sauce)

Olive oil spray

2 teaspoons dried thyme

Several dashes of ground nutmeg

Salt and black pepper to taste

8 to 10 small rainbow carrots, peeled, or 1 cup (160 g) chopped carrots

1 bunch kale (12 to 16 ounces), stems removed, chopped

3 tablespoons lemon juice

1½ teaspoons extra virgin olive oil

1 cup (250 ml) balsamic vinegar

2 to 3 tangerines, peeled and separated into wedges

Cashew Blue Cheese (page 46)

||||||||||||||||||||||||||||

VARIATIONS

▶ Try adding different root vegetables or even winter squash.

▶ If sweet salads are not your thing, replace the reduction with Lemon-Tahini Dressing (page 117) or Dijon-Thyme Vinaigrette (page 255).

THREE PEA & ORZO PISTACHIO PESTO SALAD

SERVES 4 TO 6

Whether you've never had an orzo and pesto salad or have been known to buy it in quart-size containers and eat half with a plastic spork on your way home, you'll love my veganized recreation. This version of that classic deli salad features three types of peas for added protein. The pesto is made with pistachios rather than with pine nuts, which makes for a less bitter, more buttery flavor. The addition of Tofu Feta and sun-dried tomatoes will take you right back to the deli days. I'm sure you'll eat it with a normal utensil, though.

1. To make the pesto, place the pistachios and garlic in a food processor and process until crumbled. Add the nutritional yeast, lemon juice, basil, and oil and process until smooth. Add the broth by the tablespoon to thin the sauce to your desired thickness. Taste and add the salt and pepper. Set aside.

2. Bring the water to a boil in a medium pot. Add the orzo and cook until lightly tender, 8 to 9 minutes. Drain off the water, rinse the orzo in cold water, and drain again.

3. Combine the orzo with the peas, chickpeas, black-eyed peas, and sun-dried tomatoes. Toss with the pesto. Serve at room temperature or chill until ready to serve. Serve topped with Tofu Feta.

|||||||||||||||||||||||||||

VARIATION

▶ To make this gluten-free, replace the orzo with quinoa, millet, or rice.

PREP TIME: 10 minutes *(not including time to prepare Tofu Feta)*
COOK TIME: 10 minutes

pesto
⅓ cup (130 g) pistachios
2 to 3 garlic cloves
2 tablespoons nutritional yeast
1 tablespoon lemon juice
2 cups (60 g) packed fresh basil
2 tablespoons extra virgin olive oil
3 to 4 tablespoons vegetable broth, divided
Salt and black pepper to taste

salad
4 cups water
1½ cups dry orzo
1 cup (140 g) green peas (defrosted if frozen)
1½ cups (255 g) cooked chickpeas (see page 8) or one 15-ounce (425 g) can, rinsed and drained
1½ cups (265 g) cooked black-eyed peas or one 15-ounce (425 g) can, rinsed and drained
1 cup (100 g) sliced sun-dried tomatoes (if hard, rehydrated in water until softened)
½ batch Tofu Feta (page 44)

BELUGA LENTIL & COUSCOUS SALAD WITH ORANGE-CHAMPAGNE VINAIGRETTE

SERVES 4 TO 6

Luncheons. They're basically lunch but with tablecloths and too many forks. If you find yourself hosting one, or if you just like to tuck your napkin into your collar when you're eating alone, this is one gorgeous salad that is sure to impress. Beluga lentils are the stars here, named for the way they resemble the caviar of the same name. An orange-champagne vinaigrette and chopped parsley bring this dish to life while keeping it perfectly balanced. When you tell your guests that you are serving the vegan salad equivalent of champagne and caviar, you will be guaranteed a spot in the Luncheon Host Hall of Fame (I'm pretty sure it's a thing).

1. Combine the lentils and 3 cups of the water in a medium pot and bring to a boil. Reduce the heat and simmer 15 to 20 minutes, until tender. Do not overcook because they will fall apart and get mushy. When tender, remove from the heat, drain off the water, and lightly season with salt and pepper. Pour into a large bowl to cool.

2. While the lentils are cooking, bring the remaining ¾ cup of water to a boil in a small pot. Add the couscous, stir, cover, and remove from the heat. Let it sit for about 10 minutes. If it's still a little dry or hasn't absorbed the water, cover again and let it sit for a few more minutes. Otherwise, fluff with a fork and pour into the bowl with the lentils.

3. Meanwhile, to prepare the mushrooms, heat the oil in a large frying pan over medium heat. Add the shiitake mushrooms and sauté for about 5 minutes. Add the bunapi mushrooms and sauté for another 3 minutes, or until both are tender. Add salt and pepper. Remove from the heat and add to the lentils and couscous. Add the radicchio and parsley to the bowl.

4. With a fork, mix the dressing ingredients in a cup or small bowl. Add the dressing to the bowl and toss until combined. Serve at room temperature or chill until ready to serve.

PREP TIME: 15 minutes
COOK TIME: 30 minutes

1½ cups (315 g) beluga lentils, rinsed and picked through

3 cups + ¾ cup water, divided

Salt and black pepper to taste

¾ cup (270 g) dry couscous (gluten-free if necessary), rinsed

1 teaspoon extra virgin olive oil

2 heaping cups (120 g) sliced shiitake mushrooms

1½ cups (85 g) bunapi mushrooms (see tip)

Salt and pepper to taste

1½ cups (75 g) shredded radicchio

½ cup (20 g) chopped fresh parsley

orange-champagne vinaigrette

¼ cup (60 ml) champagne vinegar

¼ cup (60 ml) orange juice

1 tablespoon agave syrup

1 tablespoon extra virgin olive oil

1 tablespoon whole grain mustard

TIP

Bunapi mushrooms (also known as shimeji or white beech mushrooms) are Japanese mushrooms grown in small clusters. One cluster has a bunch of tiny mushrooms with small, round caps and thin stems that share one base. They're usually packaged in small plastic bags in the mushroom section of the produce department. If you can't find them, 2 cups of sliced button mushrooms will work just fine.

ROASTED BROCCOLI & APPLE SALAD WITH LEMON-TAHINI DRESSING

The best salads include a large variety of textures and a balance of savory and sweet flavors. I like to combine cooked ingredients with raw and add fresh fruit for sweetness, dried fruit for something tart and chewy, and nuts or seeds for some extra crunch. Cheesy tamari-and-maple-roasted broccoli pairs with chunks of apple for the perfect balance of savory and sweet; raw celery, dried cherries, and almonds add a circus of textures; and a light, creamy, tangy dressing ties it all together. Topping it with crumbled tempeh bacon adds one more smoky layer of flavor that takes this salad over the top!

1. Preheat the oven to 400°F (200°C). Line two baking sheets with parchment paper or silicone baking mats.

2. Chop the broccoli into small florets and slice the stems thinly. Place in a bowl and toss with the tamari and maple syrup. Add the nutritional yeast and toss again. Spread the broccoli on the prepared baking sheets. Bake for 20 minutes, tossing once halfway through to ensure even cooking. Remove from the oven and let cool for about 5 minutes.

3. Meanwhile, in a small bowl or cup, use a fork to whisk together the dressing ingredients. Set aside. If you are using the Tempeh Bacon, cook the crumbles now.

4. Place the cooled broccoli in a large bowl and add the spinach, apples, celery, onion, dried cherries, and almonds. Toss until fully combined.

5. Divide the salad among serving bowls. Drizzle with the dressing and sprinkle the Tempeh Bacon on top, if using.

||||||||||||||||||||||||||||||

VARIATIONS

▶ To jazz up the salad a bit, try marcona almonds (a sweeter, plumper type of Spanish almond).

▶ If you're in a rush or want to lighten up the salad, skip roasting the broccoli. Instead, steam for about 5 minutes and rinse in ice-cold water. Dry it off and it's ready to use!

PREP TIME: 20 minutes (not including time to prepare Tempeh Bacon)
COOK TIME: 20 minutes

roasted broccoli

2 medium bundles broccoli (roughly 2 pounds or 1,000 g)

2 tablespoons tamari (or soy sauce or liquid aminos)

1 tablespoon maple syrup

2 tablespoons nutritional yeast

dressing

3½ tablespoons lemon juice

2 tablespoons tahini

2 tablespoons apple cider vinegar

1½ tablespoons maple syrup

2 teaspoons Dijon mustard

A couple dashes of garlic powder

salad

Up to 1 batch Tempeh Bacon crumbles, marinated for at least 1 hour (page 25, see variation), optional

2 to 3 cups (60 to 90 g) baby spinach

1½ to 2 apples, cored and diced (choose a tart but sweet variety, like Pink Lady or Honeycrisp)

3 celery ribs, sliced

½ medium red onion, very thinly sliced

⅔ cup (95 g) dried cherries

½ cup (75 g) roughly chopped almonds (preferably roasted, but raw will also work)

WARM LEMONY OLIVE POTATO SALAD

SERVES 4 TO 6

page 107

PREP TIME: 10 minutes
COOK TIME: 20 minutes

20 to 24 tiny golden or fingerling potatoes (about 455 g), halved

1 tablespoon extra virgin olive oil

1 to 2 teaspoons dried rosemary

Salt and black pepper to taste

4 to 5 cups (120 to 150 g) baby greens (I use a mixture of baby kale, spinach, and chard)

1½ cups (270 g) sliced olives (I use both black and green)

Juice of 1 lemon

Don't get me wrong—I still love the creamy potato salads you find at many a summer get-together, but this version is a little lighter. The olives and lemon juice give it a salty and briny but bright and zesty flavor. The rosemary-roasted potatoes melt in your mouth, and you also get a serving of greens, just slightly wilted from the heat of the potatoes. It's wonderful warm or at room temperature, but it's also great when it has been chilled overnight. Plus, this salad is so easy to make that it is great for a quick weeknight meal or last-minute dinner party, served alongside BBQ Baked Tofu (page 73) or Artichoke Crab Cakes (page 202).

1. Preheat the oven to 400°F (200°C). Line a baking sheet with parchment paper or a silicone baking mat.

2. Spread the potato halves on the sheet. Drizzle on the oil; add the rosemary, salt, and pepper. Toss to fully coat.

3. Roast the potatoes for 20 minutes, flipping them once halfway through.

4. Meanwhile, combine the greens and olives in a large bowl.

5. As soon as the potatoes are done, transfer them to the bowl with the greens. The greens will wilt a bit, which is okay, but if you want to keep them crisp, let the potatoes cool a bit before adding them. Add the lemon juice and toss to fully combine. Serve immediately or chill until ready to serve.

WHAT ABOUT BRUNCH?

Vegan Breakfasts That Will Wake You Right Up

Lazy mornings spent eating waffles while reading in your pajamas. Sunny mornings when you grab a quick bite on your way out to face the day. Special mornings when you cook something fancy for the one you love. They're all about to get a delicious makeover. It may seem like breakfast will disappear without eggs and bacon, but the best brunches of my life have happened AV (after veganism), and the same can be true for you. Get ready to start your days off right!

CHICKPEA SCRAMBLE BREAKFAST TACOS

SERVES 3 TO 4

B reakfast tacos. Have two words ever sounded so good together (with the exception of *peanut* and *butter*)? This breakfast taco is stuffed with roasted sweet potato hash and a chickpea scramble, which is similar to a tofu scramble (see page 66) but based on soy-free "tofu" made from cooking chickpea flour in water, letting it thicken, and chilling it until firm. It's then scrambled just as you would scramble tofu (or eggs, BV—before veganism). Stuff that scramble inside tortillas, and the rest is history. Beautiful, scrumptious history.

PREP TIME: 15 minutes
COOK TIME: 30 minutes
DOWN TIME: 1 hour

chickpea scramble

1 cup (110 g) chickpea flour

½ teaspoon black salt (kala namak) or regular salt

½ teaspoon garlic powder

½ teaspoon onion powder

¼ teaspoon smoked paprika

¼ teaspoon turmeric

2 cups (500 ml) water

2 tablespoons extra virgin olive oil, divided

tacos

2 medium sweet potatoes, peeled and diced

1 red bell pepper, chopped

½ medium red onion, diced

1 teaspoon cumin

½ teaspoon smoked paprika

A couple dashes of cinnamon

Salt and black pepper to taste

Olive oil spray

6 to 8 corn tortillas

½ avocado, peeled, pitted, and sliced

Fresh cilantro

Hot sauce, optional

1. Line an 8 x 8-inch baking dish with parchment paper. Set aside.

2. In a medium bowl, combine the chickpea flour, black salt, garlic powder, onion powder, paprika, and turmeric. In a medium pot, bring the water to a rolling boil, then reduce the heat to medium-high. Slowly whisk in the chickpea flour mixture until the texture is lumpy-smooth. It will bubble up and pop and spray at first, so you need to whisk quickly. Whisk in 1 tablespoon of the oil and continue to whisk for 3 to 4 minutes, until the mixture has the consistency of a thick pudding and your arm hurts from all that whisking. Pour into the prepared baking dish. Cover the dish and refrigerate at least 1 hour.

3. When the chickpea mixture is firm, preheat the oven to 400°F (200°C). Line a baking sheet with parchment paper or a silicone baking mat. Spread the sweet potato, bell pepper, and onion on the sheet and top with the cumin, paprika, cinnamon, salt, and pepper. Spray with olive oil and toss to coat. Roast for 25 minutes, flipping once halfway through to ensure even cooking.

4. While the sweet potatoes are in the oven, prepare the chickpea scramble. Slice the chickpea mixture into about 25 squares. Heat the remaining 1 tablespoon of oil in a large frying pan. Scoop the chickpea squares into the pan and use a spatula to crush them a bit. Continue to cook for 7 to 8 minutes, stirring frequently to prevent sticking. If they do stick,

deglaze the pan with a tiny bit of water and reduce the heat. When the chickpea scramble is heated through and slightly browned in parts, remove from the heat.

5. Reduce the heat to 375°F (190°C). Wrap the tortillas in a slightly damp kitchen towel and microwave for 30 seconds. Spray both sides of one tortilla with olive oil and drape over two rungs of your oven rack so it looks like a folded taco shell. Repeat with the remaining tortillas. Bake for 6 minutes, remove from the oven, and let cool (they will get crispier as they cool).

6. Pack each taco shell with the sweet potatoes, chickpea scramble, and avocado. Top with the cilantro and hot sauce, if using, and serve.

PARMESAN-CRUSTED AVOCADO & KALE FLORENTINE WITH SMOKED PAPRIKA HOLLANDAISE

SERVES 2

PREP TIME: 20 minutes
COOK TIME: 15 minutes
DOWN TIME: 1 hour *(while cashews soak)*

Afraid you'll miss the feeling of being oh-so-fancy when you order eggs Florentine at brunch? No worries—you can feel fancy all the time with these super-easy vegan Florentines you can make at home! Avocado replaces the egg, and yes, you could serve it with some fresh, cold avocado and be totally content, but it's even better to coat the avocado slices in panko bread crumbs and Pecan Parmesan and bake them briefly so the coating gets nice and crispy. Then just add English muffins, kale, and a smoked paprika hollandaise sauce and you can go on being your fancy self.

1. Preheat the oven to 400°F (200°C). Line a baking sheet with parchment paper or a silicone baking sheet.

2. Combine the Pecan Parmesan and bread crumbs in a small shallow bowl. Pour the lemon juice into another small shallow bowl.

3. Cut the avocado in half and remove the pit. Without removing the peel, slice each half into 4 quarters. Use a spoon to carefully scoop each slice out of its peel. One at a time, place an avocado quarter in the lemon juice and, using one hand, turn to coat on all sides. Using your *other* hand, place the slice in the bowl of crumbs and gently turn to coat all sides. Place each slice on the prepared baking sheet. Lightly spray the slices with olive oil and sprinkle with salt and pepper. Bake for 15 minutes, or until the exterior is golden and crisp.

4. Meanwhile, heat the 1 teaspoon of oil in a large shallow saucepan over medium heat. Add the garlic and sauté until golden and fragrant. Add the kale and keep stirring until just beginning to wilt. Remove from the heat and add salt and pepper.

5. To prepare the hollandaise sauce, combine the cashews, vinegar, lemon juice, nutritional yeast, mustard, turmeric, and 6 tablespoons of the reserved soaking water in a blender or food processor and process until smooth. Add more soaking water as needed to thin the sauce. Add salt and pepper. You

avocado & kale

¼ cup (40 g) Pecan Parmesan (page 38)

¼ cup (20 g) panko bread crumbs

Juice of 1 lemon

1 large avocado

Olive oil spray

1 teaspoon extra virgin olive oil

Salt and black pepper to taste

1 garlic clove, minced

4 cups (160 g) tightly packed destemmed chopped kale

hollandaise

½ cup (80 g) raw cashews, soaked in water at least 1 hour, *water reserved*

1 tablespoon apple cider vinegar

1 tablespoon lemon juice

1 tablespoon nutritional yeast

1 teaspoon whole grain mustard

½ teaspoon turmeric

½ teaspoon smoked paprika

Salt and black pepper to taste

2 English muffins

Sliced tomato, optional

can make the sauce up to 2 days in advance; if so, you may need to add more water later to thin it out.

6. Split the English muffins in half and toast them. Place halves on each plate, cut side up. Place a tomato slice on each, if using. Divide the kale among the muffin halves. Top each half with two crispy avocado slices. Drizzle hollandaise sauce over the top and serve immediately.

BUCKWHEAT BANANA BREAD PANCAKES WITH PEANUT BUTTER SYRUP

SERVES 4

You know those times when you can't decide whether you want to have banana bread or pancakes for breakfast? You can't make up your mind but all you know is that whatever you choose is going to be doused in peanut butter syrup? It's a tough spot. Luckily, this recipe combines banana bread with buckwheat pancakes for a vegan and gluten-free breakfast everyone can enjoy! It's topped with a luscious blend of peanut butter and maple syrup. The only tricky decision left is whether or not to share.

1. In a small bowl, combine the peanut butter syrup ingredients. Heat in the microwave for 30 seconds, stir, and set aside until ready to use. This can also be made up to 4 days in advance and chilled, but you may need to reheat when ready to use.

2. In a small bowl, combine the non-dairy milk and vinegar and set aside to curdle for 5 to 10 minutes.

3. In a large bowl, combine the mashed bananas, oil, maple syrup, and vanilla. Add the milk mixture. In another bowl, combine the buckwheat flour, oat flour, flaxseed meal, baking powder, salt, ginger, cloves, and nutmeg. Add the dry ingredients to the wet and stir until just combined.

4. Heat a large frying pan or griddle over medium heat. Generously spray with cooking spray. Use a ⅓-cup (80 ml) measuring cup to scoop batter onto the pan (about 2 or 3 pancakes at a time, depending on the pan size). Cook for about 4 minutes, or until the edges of the pancakes begin to lift and look golden. Flip with a spatula and cook for 2 to 3 more minutes. Transfer the pancakes to a plate and cover with a kitchen towel until ready to serve. Repeat, spraying the pan before each batch, until all the batter is used.

5. Serve the pancakes warm, topped with banana slices, nuts, chocolate chips (if using), and the peanut butter syrup.

PREP TIME: 15 minutes
COOK TIME: 20 minutes

peanut butter syrup
¾ cup (180 ml) maple syrup
½ cup (130 g) smooth peanut butter
1 teaspoon vanilla extract
Pinch of salt, optional

pancakes
1½ cups (375 ml) non-dairy milk
1 tablespoon apple cider vinegar
3 very ripe bananas, mashed
¼ cup (60 ml) canola oil
1½ tablespoons maple syrup
1 teaspoon vanilla extract
¾ cup (85 g) buckwheat flour
¾ cup (85 g) oat flour (certified gluten-free if necessary)
1 tablespoon flaxseed meal
1½ tablespoons baking powder
1 teaspoon ground cinnamon
½ teaspoon salt
½ teaspoon ground ginger
¼ teaspoon ground cloves
¼ teaspoon ground nutmeg
Cooking spray

extra toppings
Sliced banana, optional
Chopped nuts (walnuts, pecans, or peanuts would all be nice), optional
Chocolate chips, optional

||||||||||||||||||||||

VARIATION

▶ If you don't have buckwheat or oat flour, use an equal amount of whole wheat or all-purpose flour, or a gluten-free flour blend of your choice.

THE BEST BREAKFAST SANDWICH OF ALL TIME

MAKES 3 SANDWICHES

I settled on the title of this recipe because "The Breakfast Sandwich of the Gods" sounded a little pretentious, even though it is probably the best breakfast sandwich that has ever existed, vegan or not. With hash browns, a sunflower sausage patty, chickpea scramble, a ketchup-sriracha concoction, and mashed cheesy avocado all smushed into a toasted bagel, this is the kind of meal that could make a god say, "Oh man!" It's messy in the best possible way and so satisfying it will fuel you for hours.

PREP TIME: 10 minutes *(not including time to prepare Chickpea Scramble and Sunflower Sausage)*
COOK TIME: 15 minutes

1 potato, peeled and grated

Cold water

3 tablespoons vegan ketchup

1 tablespoon sriracha

1 avocado, pitted and peeled

2 teaspoons nutritional yeast

2 teaspoons lemon juice

Salt and black pepper to taste

Olive oil

3 bagels, sliced in half (gluten-free if necessary)

3 Sunflower Sausage patties (page 26, see variation on making patties)

½ batch Chickpea Scramble (page 120)

12 to 15 baby spinach leaves

1. Place the potato in a large bowl. Cover with cold water and use your hands to mix until the water gets cloudy. (The cloudiness is the starch being released, and you want to get rid of as much of it as possible.) Drain in a fine-mesh strainer, return the potato to the bowl, and repeat three to four times, until the water no longer gets cloudy.

2. Drain again and squeeze the grated potato a few times to release as much water as possible. Transfer to a kitchen towel and place another kitchen towel on top. Gently dry by patting and rubbing the top towel. Remove the top towel and let the potato air-dry for 3 to 5 minutes while you prepare other ingredients.

3. In a small cup, mix the ketchup and sriracha. Set aside. Combine the avocado, nutritional yeast, and lemon juice in a small bowl and mash together. Add salt and pepper.

4. Pour a thin layer of oil into the bottom of a large frying pan and heat over medium heat 2 to 3 minutes. Add the potato and flatten with a spatula into a thin layer. Cook, without touching, for 6 to 7 minutes, until the bottom is crisp. Sprinkle salt over the hash browns, then gently flip over sections. Cook until fully crisp, 3 to 5 minutes. Remove from the heat.

5. Toast each half of both bagels. Spread the ketchup mixture on the bottom halves and the avocado mixture on the top halves. Scoop some hash browns onto the ketchup mixture. Top with the Sunflower Sausage and a scoop of the Chickpea Scramble. Sprinkle a few spinach leaves on top of the chickpea scramble and add the bagel tops.

6. Serve immediately or wrap in aluminum foil to eat on the go. Be sure to have some napkins handy—this is about to get messy!

TIPS

- Most bagels are vegan, but always read the ingredients. Sometimes an egg wash is used or honey sneaks in.
- Make the Chickpea Scramble and Sunflower Sausage in advance so the sandwich can come together quickly. If you're short on time, no one will judge you for using frozen hash browns, cooked according to the package instructions.

VARIATIONS

▶ Instead of bagels, try English muffins or even Southern Biscuits (page 233).

▶ Replace the Chickpea Scramble with Tofu Scramble (page 66) and the Sunflower Sausage with Tempeh Bacon (page 25).

▶ Spice it up a bit more by adding some crushed red pepper to the mashed avocado.

PECAN-DATE CINNAMON ROLLS

MAKES 8 ROLLS

These are The Rolls. The Rolls that will make your house smell like heaven. The Rolls that are meant to be eaten while wearing pajamas. The Rolls that will be eaten in silence because no one will be able to focus on anything else but the sticky, chewy, nutty, cinnamony, buttery doughiness of every bite. The Rolls that will make you crave cozy Sunday mornings all week long. If you have any left over, you are not doing life right.

1. In a small bowl, combine the non-dairy milk, yeast, and sugar. Let sit for 10 minutes to activate the yeast. You will know it's working when the milk gets foamy.

2. In a food processor fitted with a dough blade (see tips), combine the milk mixture with 3 tablespoons of the melted vegan butter, 1 cup of the flour, salt, cinnamon, and ginger. Process until combined. Add more flour ¼ cup at a time until a ball forms (you may not use it all). If the dough gets too dry, add melted butter by the teaspoon until the dough is moist. You want it to be soft and pliable; when you touch it, it should show a dent but not stick to your finger.

3. Lightly grease a large bowl and transfer the ball of dough to the bowl. Loosely cover with a damp kitchen towel and place in a warm area. (If your kitchen is cold, turn the oven to its lowest temperature and set the bowl on top of or near it.) Let the dough rise for 1 hour, or until it has doubled in size.

4. In a food processor, combine the pecans, sugar, and cinnamon. Pulse until it resembles a coarse flour. Set aside.

5. After the dough has risen, gently punch it down a couple times. Transfer to a floured surface. Stretch and/or roll the dough into a roughly 10 x 16-inch (25 x 40 cm) rectangle. Use a pastry brush to spread 2 tablespoons of the melted vegan butter over the dough. Sprinkle the pecan mixture over it, then spread the chopped dates on top. Roll the long edge closest to you over the filling to form a log. Carefully press the seam closed with your fingers. Use a serrated knife to cut the log in half. Cut the two halves in half, then cut them in half to make 8 rolls.

PREP TIME: 40 minutes
COOK TIME: 20 minutes
DOWN TIME: 60 minutes

dough

1 cup (250 ml) non-dairy milk, heated to 110°F (45°C)

2¼ teaspoons instant yeast

1 tablespoon coconut sugar

3 tablespoons melted vegan butter, or more if needed

2 to 3 cups (260 to 390 g) bread flour, divided

½ teaspoon salt

¼ teaspoon ground cinnamon

¼ teaspoon ground ginger

filling

⅓ cup (40 g) pecans

2 tablespoons coconut sugar or vegan brown sugar

1 tablespoon ground cinnamon

4 tablespoons melted vegan butter, divided

⅓ cup (55 g) pitted and finely diced Medjool dates (see tips)

Cooking spray, optional

icing

1 cup (120 g) vegan powdered sugar or powdered xylitol

1 to 2 tablespoons non-dairy milk

1 teaspoon vanilla extract

6. Lightly spray an 8- or 10-inch cake pan with cooking spray or brush with a little more melted butter. Place the rolls in the pan cut side up, spacing them as evenly as possible. Preheat the oven to 350°F (175°C) and place the pan on or near the oven. When the oven is preheated, brush the rolls with the remaining 2 tablespoons melted butter and bake for 20 to 25 minutes, until set and golden.

7. Whisk together the icing ingredients, starting with 1 tablespoon of the non-dairy milk and adding more if too thick, and pour about half over the rolls. Serve the rolls warm, each drizzled with another generous spoonful of icing.

||||||||||||||||||||||||||||

VARIATION

▶ Unbleached all-purpose flour can be used in place of bread flour, but the rolls will not be as light and doughy.

TIPS

- A food processor fitted with a dough blade is best for this recipe. A stand mixer also works, but the food processor yields fluffier dough. You can also stir by hand if you don't have either appliance.

- To keep the dates from getting sticky and clumping, chop them on a lightly floured surface and toss them in a tiny bit of flour as you go.

LEMON CORNMEAL WAFFLES WITH BLUEBERRY SAUCE

SERVES 4

The best thing about waffles is all the nooks and crannies for toppings to nestle into. In these waffles lemon brings a subtle punch of flavor and the cornmeal adds extra crispness that keeps them from getting soggy under the pile of toppings. And speaking of which, how about a big scoop of blueberry sauce? Use fresh blueberries in the summer and frozen in the winter, and this classic brunch will keep you happy all year round.

to make the waffles

1. In a small bowl, combine the non-dairy milk and lemon juice. Set aside to curdle for 5 to 10 minutes, then add the coconut oil, honey, lemon zest, and vanilla; whisk together.

2. In a large bowl, whisk together the flour, cornmeal, baking powder, salt, and cinnamon. Add the milk mixture and use a wooden spoon to mix until just combined.

3. Cook the waffles according to your waffle iron's instructions. Serve warm, topped with blueberry sauce (see below). If not serving immediately, place them on a wire rack and cover with a kitchen towel to keep them warm.

to make the blueberry sauce

Combine the blueberry sauce ingredients in a small pot and bring to a boil. Reduce the heat and simmer, stirring frequently, for 3 to 5 minutes, until thickened. Remove from the heat and serve warm.

PREP TIME: 15 minutes
COOK TIME: 25 minutes

2 cups (500 ml) non-dairy milk

⅓ cup (80 ml) lemon juice

⅓ cup (80 ml) coconut oil, melted

¼ cup (60 ml) Happy Bee Honey (page 34) or agave syrup

2 tablespoons lemon zest

1 teaspoon vanilla extract

1½ (195 g) cups unbleached all-purpose flour

¾ cup (105 g) fine-ground cornmeal

1½ tablespoons baking powder

½ teaspoon salt

¼ teaspoon cinnamon

blueberry sauce

4 cups (600 g) blueberries (fresh or frozen)

1 tablespoon cornstarch

1 to 2 tablespoons agave syrup (depending on sweetness preference)

1 tablespoon lemon juice

1 tablespoon water

CARAMEL APPLE-STUFFED FRENCH TOAST

SERVES 4 TO 6

French toast on its own is a normal weekend breakfast, and chickpea flour and non-dairy milk make for a simple vegan version. When you stuff a delicious filling inside, you've got more of a special-occasion meal on your hands (or plate)—especially when that filling is warm, caramelized apples tossed in a rich, date-based caramel sauce, and *even more especially* when the French toast is dusted with powdered sugar and drizzled with extra sauce. One of my recipe testers made it for her husband on Valentine's Day, and they thought it was the perfect celebration meal. Breakfast in bed, anyone?

1. In a food processor, combine the caramel sauce ingredients. Process until completely smooth, scraping the sides as necessary.

2. Melt the vegan butter in a large frying pan over medium heat. Add the apple slices and coconut sugar; stir to combine. Simmer, stirring occasionally, until the liquid is gone and the apples are softened and golden. Stir in the lemon juice and remove from the heat. Stir in 2 tablespoons of the caramel sauce.

3. In a large shallow bowl or baking dish, mix the non-dairy milk, coconut milk, chickpea flour, maple syrup, cornstarch, vanilla, cinnamon, nutmeg, and salt. Slice the bread into four to six 2-inch (5 cm) slices. Use a bread knife to make a slit in the top of each slice, keeping the sides and bottom intact, creating a pocket.

4. Carefully spread the cream cheese inside one side of each pocket, then stuff it with about ⅓ cup (80 ml) of apples.

5. Preheat the oven to its lowest setting. Line a baking sheet with parchment paper or a silicone baking mat. Set aside.

6. Heat a large frying pan or griddle over medium heat. Spray generously with cooking spray. Take one "sandwich" and soak in the milk mixture, 15 to 20 seconds on each side. Place the

PREP TIME: 30 minutes
COOK TIME: 20 minutes

caramel sauce

10 Medjool dates, pitted
⅔ cup (160 ml) non-dairy milk
¼ cup (60 ml) water
½ teaspoon vanilla extract
Salt to taste

apples

1 tablespoon vegan butter
2 Granny Smith apples, cored and thinly sliced
2 tablespoons coconut sugar or vegan brown sugar
1 tablespoon lemon juice

French toast

1 cup (250 ml) non-dairy milk
½ cup (125 ml) canned coconut milk or vegan creamer
½ cup (55 g) chickpea flour
2 tablespoons maple syrup
1½ tablespoons cornstarch
1 teaspoon vanilla extract
½ teaspoon cinnamon
Dash of nutmeg
Dash of salt
1 large loaf of French bread, about 4 to 5 inches wide (not a baguette)
Vegan cream cheese
Cooking spray
Maple syrup, for drizzling
Vegan powdered sugar or powdered xylitol, for dusting, optional

{ RECIPE CONTINUES }

soaked sandwich on the heated pan and cook until golden and crisp, 3 to 4 minutes on each side. Transfer to the prepared baking sheet and place in the oven. Repeat with the remaining sandwiches, spraying the pan again before each. Serve warm, topped with maple syrup, the remaining caramel sauce, or both. Dust with powdered sugar if desired.

||||||||||||||||||||||||||||||

VARIATIONS

▶ Simplify the recipe by leaving out the caramel sauce and replacing the apples with uncooked strawberries, blueberries, blackberries, or even mango!

▶ Make plain French toast by slicing regular-size slices of bread and leaving out the fruit and caramel altogether.

FAKE "FOODS" FREAK ME OUT.

Solid Vegan Recipes That Aren't Imitating Meat, Dairy, or Anything Else

Don't like the idea of eating mock meats or non-dairy cheeses? I totally get it. Though there are tons of great options in those departments (including in this book), sometimes you just want real food made from plants. These recipes aren't trying to imitate a dish normally made with animal products. They are delicious meals that allow the plants to truly shine in their own right.

CORN FRITTERS WITH CREAMY CHILE-LIME SAUCE

SERVES 2 TO 4

Corn and quinoa join together in this recipe to form the most delectable little fritters. Corn flour works as a binder to hold these little balls together as they fry. Lemongrass, parsley, and coriander make these the zestiest little corn fritters you've ever tried. The bright and tangy yogurt-based chile-lime sauce is the perfect pairing.

1. Combine the chile-lime sauce ingredients in a food processor or blender and process until smooth. To meld the flavors, chill until ready to use.

2. In a large bowl, combine the quinoa, corn, corn flour, green onions, non-dairy milk, mayonnaise, lemongrass, tamari, nutritional yeast (if using), parsley, cumin, coriander, paprika, and cayenne; mix until fully combined. It should be moist enough to hold together when squeezed, but not wet like a batter. If it is too wet, add corn flour by the tablespoon until you have the right consistency. Add salt and pepper.

3. Line a baking sheet with parchment paper or a silicone baking mat. Use your hands to form the dough into balls just smaller than a golf ball and place them on the prepared sheet.

4. Heat a large frying pan, preferably cast iron, over medium heat. Pour in enough oil to coat the bottom and heat for 2 to 3 minutes. Line a plate with paper towels.

5. Carefully place 5 to 6 fritters in the pan and cook for 3 to 4 minutes, moving them around every 30 seconds or so to allow them to cook on all sides, until golden and firm. Use a slotted spoon to scoop them up and transfer them to the plate, placing more paper towels on top to absorb the excess oil. Repeat with the remaining fritters, adding more oil to the pan as needed. Serve warm, topped with the creamy chile-lime sauce and sprinkled with chopped green onions.

VARIATION

▶ If you do not wish to fry the fritters, preheat the oven to 350°F (175°C). Spray the fritters lightly with olive oil and bake for 20 to 25 minutes, until firm and golden, flipping once halfway through to ensure even cooking.

PREP TIME: 15 minutes (*not including time to cook quinoa*)
COOK TIME: 15 minutes

creamy chile-lime sauce

1 cup (225 g) plain coconut yogurt

3 tablespoons lime juice

2 tablespoons diced Anaheim pepper

1 teaspoon onion powder

1 teaspoon garlic powder

fritters

2 cups (320 g) cooked quinoa (see page 9)

1½ cups (210 g) corn kernels (fresh, or defrosted if frozen)

1 cup (130 g) corn flour (not cornmeal or masa harina)

¼ cup (25 g) chopped green onions (white part only), plus extra for garnish

¼ cup plus 2 tablespoons (90 ml) non-dairy milk

2 tablespoons vegan mayonnaise

2 tablespoons chopped lemongrass (see tip)

1 tablespoon tamari (or soy sauce or liquid aminos)

2 teaspoons nutritional yeast, optional

1 teaspoon dried parsley

½ teaspoon cumin

½ teaspoon ground coriander

½ teaspoon smoked paprika

A few dashes of cayenne pepper

Salt and black pepper to taste

Canola oil for frying

TIP

You must remove the outer, woodier layers of lemongrass prior to slicing. Run your knife down the stalk, leaving a small slice all the way down. Peel away the outer layers and now you're good to go!

POTATO & PEA SAMOSA CAKES WITH TAMARIND SAUCE

MAKES 15 CAKES

page 135

Samosas are a traditional savory Indian pastry, usually stuffed with spiced potatoes and other vegetables. These cakes are basically samosa filling without the pastry. The tart and sassy tamarind sauce makes the perfect accompaniment. The patties would be well received as finger food or as a side to Lentil, Chard & Sweet Potato Curry (page 143), but you could also pile four or five (or nine) on your plate for an unforgettable main course.

1. Combine the tamarind sauce ingredients in a small bowl and whisk together. Chill until ready to use.

2. Mix the broth, curry powder, cumin, ginger, paprika, cardamom, and cayenne in a small bowl. Set aside.

3. Combine the oil and mustard seeds in a large shallow saucepan and heat over medium heat until the seeds begin to pop. Add the onion and garlic and sauté until the onion is almost translucent. Add the potatoes, bell pepper, carrot, and broth mixture; sauté until the potatoes and carrots are soft. If the liquid absorbs too quickly or the potatoes begin to stick, add a bit more broth to deglaze the pan and lower the heat.

4. When the vegetables are fork-tender, remove from the heat. Use a potato masher to very lightly mash the potatoes and vegetables (leaving big chunks). Add salt and pepper. Let cool for 5 to 10 minutes.

5. Preheat the oven to 375°F (190°C). Line a baking sheet with parchment paper or a silicone baking mat.

6. When the vegetables have cooled enough to touch, mix in the chickpea flour and fold in the peas. Spray a 2½-inch (6.5 cm) round biscuit cutter with olive oil and place on the prepared baking sheet. Scoop 2 heaping tablespoons of the mixture into the biscuit cutter and use your fingers to press it into a flat patty. Carefully lift the biscuit cutter, leaving the cake on the sheet. Repeat with the rest of the samosa mixture.

7. Bake for 20 minutes, or until the cakes are firm and golden brown. Remove from the oven and cool for about 5 minutes on the sheet. Serve with the tamarind sauce.

PREP TIME: 25 minutes
COOK TIME: 35 minutes

tamarind sauce

3 tablespoons tamarind paste (from a jar, not a block)

⅓ cup (80 ml) water

¼ cup (60 ml) agave syrup

1 tablespoon tamari (or soy sauce or liquid aminos)

1 tablespoon grated fresh ginger

Salt to taste

samosa cakes

½ cup (125 ml) vegetable broth, plus additional if needed

2 teaspoons curry powder

1 teaspoon cumin

1 teaspoon ground ginger

½ teaspoon paprika

½ teaspoon ground cardamom

¼ to ½ teaspoon cayenne pepper

2 teaspoons extra virgin olive oil

1 teaspoon mustard seeds

½ medium red onion, chopped small

2 garlic cloves, minced

1 pound (455 g) small golden potatoes, chopped small

½ red bell pepper, chopped small

1 carrot, chopped small

Salt and black pepper to taste

½ cup (55 g) chickpea flour

½ cup (70 g) green peas (fresh or defrosted if frozen)

Olive oil spray

MEXICAN BOWL WITH QUINOA, FARRO & AMARANTH TRIO

SERVES 2 TO 4

The Bowl is one of the most revered dishes in vegan cuisine. It consists of several elements—such as beans, grains, greens, vegetables, dips, sauces, and nuts or seeds—thrown together in a bowl to create one super meal. In Portland, Oregon, it's practically a separate food group. This Bowl does not stray far from the basic recipe, containing a trio of quinoa, farro, and amaranth along with beans, guacamole, and cheese. It's a celebration of the best of Mexican cuisine, and it's happening in your bowl—so stop reading and get munching!

PREP TIME: 25 minutes (*not including soaking cashews or quinoa*)
COOK TIME: 20 minutes

cashew queso

- ½ cup (80 g) raw cashews, soaked in water for at least 1 hour, *water reserved*
- 1½ tablespoons fresh lemon juice
- 2 tablespoons nutritional yeast
- 1 teaspoon white miso
- ½ teaspoon garlic powder
- Salt to taste

tomato, corn & zucchini salad

- 2 large or 3 small Roma tomatoes, diced small
- 1 zucchini, diced small
- ⅔ cup (95 g) corn kernels (fresh or defrosted if frozen)
- 1 green onion (white part only), finely chopped
- ¼ cup (10 g) cilantro
- Juice of 1 lime
- Several dashes of cayenne pepper
- Salt to taste

quinoa, amaranth & farro trio

- ¼ cup (45 g) quinoa, soaked in water for 1 hour, *water discarded*
- ¼ cup (50 g) amaranth
- ¼ cup (45 g) farro (or brown rice for gluten-free)
- 2 cups (500 ml) vegetable broth
- ¼ cup (60 ml) water

1. Combine all the cashew queso ingredients, including 6 tablespoons of the reserved soaking water, in a food processor and process until smooth. Chill in an airtight container until ready to use. This can be made a few days in advance, if needed.

2. Combine the salad ingredients in a bowl and mix until combined. Cover and chill until ready to use. This can be made a day in advance, if needed.

3. Combine the quinoa, amaranth, farro, broth, and water in a medium pot. Cover and bring to a boil, then crack the lid just a hair and reduce the heat. Simmer until all liquid has been absorbed, about 20 minutes. Remove from the heat and fluff with a fork. Cover again and let rest until ready to use.

4. During the last 10 minutes of cooking, prepare the beans. Heat the oil in a frying pan over medium heat. Add the onion and sauté until translucent. Add the garlic and the beans and mix to combine. Add the broth, liquid aminos, cumin, paprika, and chile powder; mix to combine. Cook until the liquid is absorbed, stirring occasionally to prevent sticking. Remove from the heat and stir in the lime juice. Add salt and pepper.

5. Divide the greens among the serving bowls; top with the cooked grains, beans, and salad. Top each with a generous dollop of guacamole and a drizzle of cashew queso. Sprinkle toasted pepitas and chopped cilantro over all. Serve immediately, with hot sauce, if desired.

beans

1 teaspoon extra virgin olive oil

½ medium red onion, diced

2 garlic cloves, minced

1½ cups (265 g) cooked black beans (see page 8) or one 15-ounce (425 g) can, rinsed and drained

½ cup (125 ml) vegetable broth

½ tablespoon liquid aminos (or tamari or soy sauce)

1 teaspoon cumin

½ teaspoon smoked paprika

½ teaspoon ancho chile powder

Juice of ½ lime

Salt and black pepper to taste

the bowl

2 cups (60 g) chopped greens (e.g., spinach, kale, chard, or romaine)

Guacamole (page 105)

⅓ cup (55 g) toasted pepitas

Chopped cilantro

Hot sauce, optional

LENTIL, CHARD & SWEET POTATO CURRY

SERVES 4

One sure sign you're cooking something really tasty is when the aroma fills your house and makes it smell magical. This is one of those recipes. Onions, garlic, fresh ginger, curry powder, and garam masala (a smoky, peppery blend of spices often found in Indian cooking) become incredibly fragrant while cooking. By the time you finally get to serve yourself a bowl, your nose won't be able to handle the teasing any longer! Serve on top of rice or quinoa, or alongside a piece of vegan chapatti, naan, or crusty French bread.

1. Heat the oil in a large shallow saucepan over medium heat for about 30 seconds. Add the onion and sauté until translucent. Add the garlic and continue to sauté for about 1 minute. Add the jalapeño and sauté for about 2 minutes. Add the ginger, curry powder, garam masala, and turmeric (if using). Stir to fully combine and cook for about 2 minutes.

2. Add the broth, sweet potatoes, and lentils; stir to combine. Cover and bring to a boil, then reduce the heat and cover again, this time leaving the lid open a crack. Simmer for about 20 minutes.

3. When the lentils are tender and the liquid has decreased, add the yogurt, lime juice, and chard; cook until the chard is just starting to wilt. Add the black salt and pepper, mix to combine, and remove from the heat. Serve warm.

PREP TIME: 15 minutes
COOK TIME: 30 minutes

1 teaspoon extra virgin olive oil

1 small onion, chopped

3 to 4 garlic cloves, finely minced

½ jalapeño pepper, finely chopped

1 inch (2.5 cm) fresh ginger, peeled and grated

1 tablespoon curry powder

1½ teaspoons garam masala

½ teaspoon turmeric (optional)

4 cups (1,000 ml) vegetable broth

3 cups (375 g) peeled and chopped sweet potatoes (about 2 medium)

1½ cups (315 g) yellow lentils (toor dal), rinsed and picked through

¾ cup (170 g) plain vegan coconut or soy yogurt

Juice of ½ lime

1 bunch chard, center stems removed, leaves roughly chopped

1 teaspoon black salt (kala namak) or regular salt

Black pepper to taste

LEMONY GREEN VEGGIE PASTA

SERVES 3 TO 4

Springtime is all about wearing sandals, soaking up the sun, and buying all the beautiful green veggies that begin to appear at your local farmers market. There's nothing like coming home with a tote bag full of the season's freshest gifts. Naturally, you want to dive in and use them all at once, so lightly cook the snap peas and asparagus with a leek and a few handfuls of spinach. Then add that beautiful mess of green vegetables to pasta with a simple lemon sauce and top with fresh pea shoots. Hello, spring!

PREP TIME: 10 minutes
COOK TIME: 15 minutes

½ cup (125 ml) lemon juice

2 teaspoons Dijon mustard

1 tablespoon + 1 teaspoon extra virgin olive oil, divided

Water

Salt

4 cups (280 g) pasta of choice (gluten-free if necessary)

1 leek (white part only), halved lengthwise and thinly sliced (see tip, page 137)

1 garlic clove, minced

2½ cups (200 g) snap peas

½ bundle asparagus, cut into 1-inch (2.5 cm) segments

1 teaspoon dried basil

1 teaspoon dried thyme

4 to 5 handfuls baby spinach

Black pepper to taste

1 cup (25 g) pea shoots or microgreens

1. In a small bowl, whisk together the lemon juice, mustard, and 1 tablespoon of the oil. Set aside.

2. Bring a large pot of water to a boil. Add a pinch of salt and the pasta. Cook, following the package instructions, until al dente. Remove from the heat and drain the water.

3. Meanwhile, heat the remaining 1 teaspoon of oil in a frying pan over medium heat. Add the leek and sauté for 2 to 3 minutes. Add the garlic and sauté for about 2 minutes. Add the snap peas, asparagus, basil, and thyme, and sauté until the snap peas become tender, about 5 minutes. If the vegetables begin to stick, add a few tablespoons of water to deglaze the pan, and lower the heat. When tender, remove from the heat and stir in the spinach.

4. Add the vegetables to the pasta in the pot. Stir in the lemon juice mixture and add salt and pepper to taste. Serve warm with pea shoots piled on top.

RAINBOW MILLET-HUMMUS COLLARD SUMMER ROLLS

SERVES 2 TO 3

It's a collard wrap. It's a summer roll. The jury is in: it's a collard wrap inside a summer roll and pretty much the perfect lunch. Millet is a seed that is often classified as a grain (much like quinoa), and it is packed with protein, which makes these rolls very filling. They come together in a jiff, and the rice paper snugly holding the collard wraps together makes them much more portable (no toothpicks for these rolls, my friend!).

PREP TIME: 30 minutes
COOK TIME: 20 minutes

½ cup (180 g) dry millet
1½ cups (375 ml) water

hummus

1½ cups (255 g) cooked chickpeas (see page 8) or one 15-ounce (425 g) can, rinsed and drained
2 to 3 garlic cloves, chopped
3 tablespoons tahini
3 tablespoons lemon juice
1 to 2 tablespoons extra virgin olive oil
½ teaspoon cumin
½ teaspoon smoked paprika
Salt and black pepper to taste

4 to 6 large collard leaves
Warm water
Four to six 8-inch (20 cm) round rice paper sheets
2 to 3 carrots, cut into 3-inch (8 cm) long matchsticks
1 red bell pepper, thinly sliced
¼ head red cabbage, sliced into strips

Spicy Peanut Dipping Sauce (page 101), optional

1. Toast the millet in a medium pot over medium heat for about 3 to 4 minutes. Be sure to stir several times to prevent burning. When the millet is golden and nutty smelling, add the water and bring to a boil. Reduce the heat, cover, and simmer (no peeking) for 10 minutes. Remove from the heat and let sit, still covered, for 10 minutes. Remove the lid and fluff with a fork.

2. While the millet is simmering, combine the hummus ingredients in a food processor and process until smooth and creamy (see tips). Add 1 cup of the hummus to the millet. Stir until combined. Set aside. This portion can be made in advance and chilled in an airtight container 2 to 3 days.

3. Lay a collard leaf on the cutting board, underside up. Chop off the bottom of the stem. Run a knife parallel to the leaf surface along the thick, woody center stem, shaving it off. Repeat with the remaining leaves. If they are large, trim the top, bottom, and sides of each leaf to form a 4-inch (10 cm) square and reserve the trimmings from the top and sides (the bottom and stems can be discarded).

4. Fill a wide bowl with warm water. Submerge 1 rice paper sheet in the water and promptly remove. It's okay if it's still slightly stiff; it will continue to absorb the water and get softer and clingier. Lay it on a dry surface, preferably not wood. Place 1 collard leaf square on the rice paper, underside of the leaf up, with one edge close to the edge of the rice paper closest to you (the corners should touch the edge of the circle but not hang over).

{ RECIPE CONTINUES }

5. Spread a scant ¼ cup of the millet mixture in a row down the center of the leaf along the main vein, not extending past the edges of the leaf. On top of the millet mixture, lay a couple carrot sticks, then a couple bell pepper slices, then a few strips of red cabbage. Top with a few collard leaf trimmings, if you have them.

6. Starting with the edge closest to you, begin to roll the rice paper over the fillings. Fold the sides over the fillings and continue to roll, using your fingers to tuck in the fillings as you go. Set aside, seam side down. Repeat with the remaining ingredients. Serve immediately with Spicy Peanut Sauce (if using). If you wish to serve them later, wrap each roll individually in plastic wrap and chill 1 to 5 hours.

IIIIIIIIIIIIIIIIIIIIIIIIIII

VARIATION

▶ If you're feeling lazy, ditch the rice paper and don't trim the collard leaves into squares (but do still remove the center stems). Lay out a strip of the millet mixture down the middle of the leaf and top with the carrots, red bell pepper, and red cabbage. Fold the leaf and eat it like you would a taco. Easy peasy.

TIPS

- Heating the chickpeas prior to putting them in the food processor will result in a creamier hummus.

- If you're in a time crunch, use store-bought hummus.

- The tricks to rolling summer rolls are to not soak the rice paper in the warm water, not overstuff, and always be tucking the fillings in as you roll. If you've never done it before, hang in there. You'll get it.

IT'S ALL RABBIT FOOD.

Vegan Food That Isn't Exactly "Healthy"

Vegan and *healthy* are not synonymous. I do believe a vegan diet is the healthiest diet, as long as you eat nutrient-dense whole foods such as vegetables and fruits. It is possible, though, to create vegan renditions of typically unhealthy foods that are a bit healthier than the originals but don't taste like it. Craving nachos? I got your vegan nacho supreme right here. Onion rings and chili fries aren't far behind. No need to deprive yourself—just enjoy indulgences in moderation. It's all about balance!

JACKFRUIT NACHO SUPREME

SERVES 6

Are you afraid your friends won't come over to watch the game after you go vegan? When you serve up these nachos, you won't be able to keep them away! What makes these nachos "supreme" is the whole layer of spicy shredded jackfruit hiding beneath black bean and corn salsa, sour cream, guacamole, and, of course, super-creamy cashew-based nacho cheese. It creates a mountain of nachos that no group of armchair quarterbacks can resist devouring.

1. Toss the salsa ingredients together in a large bowl, cover, and chill until ready to use. The longer it sits, the tastier it gets.

2. Combine the nacho cheese ingredients, including ½ cup of the reserved soaking water, in a food processor or blender and process until smooth. Cover until ready to serve.

3. Place the jackfruit in a colander and rinse thoroughly. Use two forks or your fingers to tear it into shreds. Set aside.

4. Heat the oil in a large shallow saucepan over medium heat. Add the garlic and sauté for 1 minute. Add the onion and sauté until translucent. Add the bell pepper and green chiles and sauté until the bell pepper is tender, about 5 minutes. Meanwhile, mix the liquid aminos, tomato paste, liquid smoke, cumin, paprika, and chile powder in a cup. Add the shredded jackfruit to the pan and sauté for a couple more minutes before adding the tomato paste mixture. Stir to combine and simmer for about 10 minutes, until heated through and the sauce has thickened. Add smoked salt and pepper; remove from the heat.

5. Spread the tortilla chips on a large plate or platter. Top with the jackfruit. Add the black bean and corn salsa. Drizzle the nacho cheese over the top. Top with Tofu Sour Cream and/or Guacamole, if using. Sprinkle with the green onions. Serve immediately.

PREP TIME: 30 minutes
COOK TIME: 25 minutes

black bean and corn salsa

1½ cups (265 g) cooked black beans (see page 8) or one 15-ounce (425 g) can, rinsed and drained

1½ cups (210 g) corn kernels (fresh, or defrosted if frozen)

1 cup (160 g) chopped Roma tomato

½ cup (20 g) chopped fresh cilantro

2 tablespoons fresh lime juice

1 tablespoon chopped jalapeño

Salt to taste

nacho cheese

¾ cup (120 g) raw cashews, soaked for at least 1 hour, *water reserved*

¼ cup (35 g) nutritional yeast

2 tablespoons chopped canned green chiles

2 tablespoons lime juice

2 teaspoons white miso

1 teaspoon garlic powder

1 teaspoon cumin

½ teaspoon turmeric, optional

Salt to taste

nachos

Two 20-ounce cans (1130 g) jackfruit packed in brine (not syrup)

1 teaspoon extra virgin olive oil

3 garlic cloves, minced

½ large onion, chopped

1 red bell pepper, chopped

2 tablespoons diced canned green chiles

¼ cup (60 ml) liquid aminos

¼ cup (60 g) tomato paste

2 teaspoons liquid smoke

1½ teaspoons cumin

VARIATION

▶ If you prefer hot nacho sauce, transfer it to a medium pot and warm over medium-low heat, stirring occasionally while the jackfruit is cooking.

1 teaspoon smoked paprika

½ teaspoon dried ancho chile powder

Smoked salt or regular salt to taste

Black pepper to taste

6 to 8 handfuls tortilla chips

Tofu Sour Cream (page 33), optional

Guacamole (page 105), optional

¼ cup (25 g) chopped green onions (white and green parts)

CRISPY BAKED ONION RINGS

SERVES 2 TO 3

PREP TIME: 30 minutes
COOK TIME: 20 minutes

"*Baked onion rings?*," you may be exclaiming. "*For shame!*" Now, before you go slamming this book shut, listen up. It is possible to get crisp baked onion rings with a crunchy, crumbly exterior and a soft interior. It is possible for said baked onion rings to satisfy your greasy, fast-food-style onion ring craving. It is possible for these onion rings to be just as delectable as the fried version while being healthier for you. It's called having your onion rings and eating them, too.

1 large sweet onion

1 cup (250 ml) unsweetened non-dairy milk

Juice of 1 lemon

1 cup (140 g) arrowroot powder or cornstarch

2 cups (80 g) panko bread crumbs (gluten-free if necessary)

1 teaspoon salt

1 teaspoon garlic powder

½ teaspoon smoked paprika

Olive oil spray

Vegan ketchup, Barbecue Sauce (page 31), or Zesty Ranch Dressing (page 32), optional

1. Preheat the oven to 400°F (200°C). Line two baking sheets with parchment paper or silicone baking mats.
2. Slice the onion into almost ½-inch (1 cm) slices. Separate into rings.
3. In one shallow bowl, combine the non-dairy milk and lemon juice. Pour the arrowroot powder into another shallow bowl. In a third, larger shallow bowl, combine the bread crumbs, salt, garlic powder, and paprika. (You may have to stir a few more times during the coating process.)
4. One at a time, place an onion ring in the milk mixture, coating it completely (see tips). Then dredge it in the arrowroot powder, coating it completely. Tap off the excess powder before dipping it quickly back into the milk. Dredge the ring through the bread crumbs, making sure to coat each one well. Place on one of the prepared baking sheets. Continue with the remaining rings.
5. Spray the onion rings with olive oil and bake for 15 to 20 minutes, until crisp and golden. Serve immediately with ketchup or other dip of choice.

TIPS

- To prevent your fingers from becoming sticky messes, use one hand for dipping in the milk and the other hand for dipping in the arrowroot powder and bread crumbs.
- It's very important to tap the excess arrowroot powder off the onion ring before transferring it back to the milk. Too much arrowroot will make the onion rings dry.
- To maximize baking sheet space, place smaller onion rings inside the larger ones.

CHOCOLATE STOUT CHILI FRIES

SERVES 2, WITH EXTRA CHILI

After a long week, there's no meal that screams "Screw it!" like chili fries and beer. After the things you've put up with—your car breaking down, your dog chewing up your shoes *again*, and having to work late every night—you absolutely deserve to dig into an indulgent meal that tells the world you *just don't care anymore!* This chili recipe has taken your week into consideration and has a dark stout and chocolate added right in for flavor depth and intensity as well as for a little more stress relief. Served atop a pile of Frites, this meal is ready to help you *let it all go.*

1. Heat the oil in a large pot over medium heat. Add the onion and garlic and sauté until the onion just starts to become translucent. Add the carrots, celery, bell pepper, Anaheim pepper, and green chiles and cook for 3 to 4 minutes. Add the tomatoes with liquid, tomato sauce, beer, beans, liquid aminos, maple syrup, cocoa powder, tomato paste, chile powder, cumin, paprika, parsley, thyme, and cayenne. Stir to combine and bring to a boil. Reduce the heat and simmer for about 30 minutes (see tip).

2. Add the liquid smoke, salt, and pepper to the chili. Serve on top of the Frites, garnished with Tofu Sour Cream and your preferred additional toppings.

||||||||||||||||||||||||||||

VARIATION

▶ If you want to make the chili gluten-free or don't want to use beer, use ½ cup coffee or more tomato sauce.

▶ Use a 15-ounce (425 g) can of each bean for extra simplicity.

TIP

For best time management, bake the Frites while the chili simmers.

PREP TIME: 20 minutes
COOK TIME: 40 minutes

1 tablespoon extra virgin olive oil

1 small sweet onion, chopped

3 garlic cloves, minced

2 carrots, chopped

1 celery rib, chopped

1 red bell pepper, chopped

1 small Anaheim pepper, finely diced

2 tablespoons diced canned green chiles

Two 15-ounce cans (850 g) unsalted diced fire-roasted tomatoes

One 15-ounce can (445 ml) unsalted tomato sauce

½ cup (125 ml) vegan stout-style beer (such as Lagunitas Imperial Stout)

1½ cups (265 g) cooked kidney beans (see page 8)

1½ cups (265 g) cooked navy beans

1½ cups (265 g) cooked red beans

2 tablespoons liquid aminos (or tamari or soy sauce)

2 tablespoons maple syrup

2 tablespoons cocoa powder

1 tablespoon tomato paste

2 teaspoons ancho chile powder

2 teaspoons cumin

2 teaspoons smoked paprika

1 teaspoon dried parsley

1 teaspoon dried thyme

¼ teaspoon cayenne pepper, optional

2 teaspoons liquid smoke

Salt and black pepper to taste

1 batch Frites (page 80)

Tofu Sour Cream (page 33)

Additional toppings, such as chopped tomatoes, bell pepper, avocado, or green onions

IMPOSSIBLE CHEESEBURGER PIE

SERVES 6 TO 8

Cheeseburger. In pie form. No, it's not impossible—it's *impossibly easy*. This classic, hearty casserole was the first dish I ever cooked on my own, and when I went vegan, it was one of the first things I had to veganize. In this plant-based version, lentils take the place of ground beef and are combined with a mixture of Barbecue Sauce (page 31), ketchup, and mustard, poured into a biscuit crust, and topped with vegan cheddar cheese. It's as if your favorite cheeseburger got deconstructed and baked as a casserole, and it's *impossible* for it not to become one of your new favorite meals.

1. Preheat the oven to 450°F (230°C). Spray a 10-inch springform cake pan, 9 x 13-inch baking dish, or 10-inch pie dish with olive oil.

2. Heat the 2 teaspoons olive oil in a large shallow saucepan over medium heat. Add the onion and garlic and sauté until the onion is translucent. Add the lentils, broth, liquid aminos, Worcestershire sauce, liquid smoke, thyme, oregano, salt, and pepper. Simmer for 4 to 5 minutes, until the liquid has been absorbed. Remove from the heat.

3. Mix together the ketchup, Barbecue Sauce, and mustard; add to the lentil mixture.

4. Spread the biscuit dough on the bottom of the prepared baking dish. Spread the lentil mixture over the top of the dough. Bake for 15 minutes.

5. Sprinkle the grated cheese over the top of the lentil mixture. Top with the tomato slices. Return to the oven and bake for 5 minutes. Remove and top with the green onions. Serve warm.

PREP TIME: 30 minutes (*not including time to cook lentils*)
COOK TIME: 20 minutes

Olive oil spray

2 teaspoons extra virgin olive oil

½ medium yellow onion, finely chopped

2 garlic cloves, finely minced

2½ cups (400 g) cooked green lentils (see page 8)

¼ cup (60 ml) vegetable broth

2 tablespoons liquid aminos (or tamari or soy sauce)

2 teaspoons vegan Worcestershire sauce, optional

1 teaspoon liquid smoke

1 teaspoon dried thyme

½ teaspoon dried oregano

Salt and black pepper to taste

½ cup (125 ml) vegan ketchup

¼ cup (60 ml) Barbecue Sauce (page 31) or store-bought

¼ cup (60 ml) yellow or spicy brown mustard

1 batch Southern Biscuits dough (page 233), prepared through step 3

1 cup (120 g) Sunflower Cheddar (page 42), grated

2 tomatoes, sliced

2 green onions (white and green parts), finely sliced

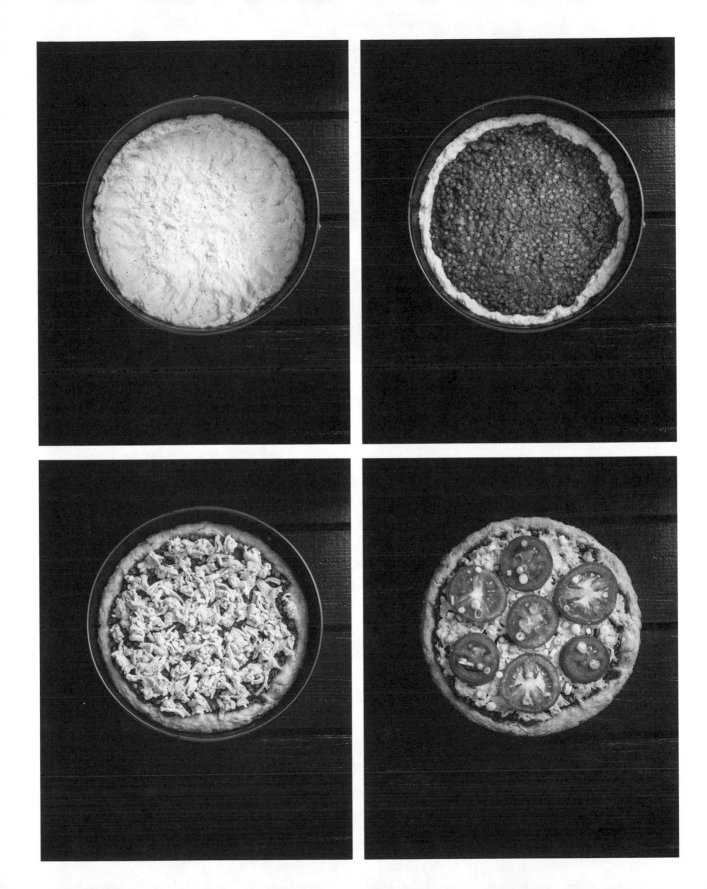

FIRE-ROASTED CHILE & SWEET POTATO ENCHILADAS

SERVES 6 TO 8

page 149

If you want to get your taste buds really excited, wait until you pull these enchiladas out of the oven. The aroma hits you first. The fire-roasted chile sauce is bubbling around the edges, and the cashew crema has slightly browned. Then there's the ten *agonizing* minutes you have to let the enchiladas "rest" before you can dig in. Once everything has settled and cooled down a bit, you can finally scoop out a section. The tortillas break open in some places, a chunk of cheesy sweet potato filling drops onto the table, though *you don't even care.* You're already cutting your first bite and pushing it through the extra sauce and crema on your plate.

PREP TIME: 60 minutes
COOK TIME: 30 minutes
DOWN TIME: 10 minutes

enchilada sauce

2 Anaheim or pasilla peppers

One 15-ounce (425 g) can unsalted diced fire-roasted tomatoes, with liquid

1½ cups (375 ml) vegetable broth

1 head roasted garlic (page 7)

Salt and black pepper to taste

sweet potato filling

2 teaspoons extra virgin olive oil

½ medium red onion, chopped

2 garlic cloves, minced

1 red bell pepper, chopped

4 cups (550 g) chopped (1-inch/2.5 cm cubes) sweet potatoes

2 teaspoons coconut sugar or vegan brown sugar

1½ teaspoons cumin

1 teaspoon smoked paprika

½ teaspoon ground cinnamon

½ teaspoon ancho chile powder

2 to 3 tablespoons nutritional yeast

1 tablespoon lemon juice

Salt and black pepper to taste

Olive oil spray

to make the enchilada sauce

1. Preheat the oven to 450°F (230°C). Line a baking sheet with parchment paper or a silicone baking mat.

2. If you have a gas stove, turn one of your stovetop burners to medium-high heat. Place the peppers on top of the burner. Use tongs to slowly turn them until all sides are black and charred (it's okay if they're not completely black). If you have an electric stove, turn on the broiler and raise one of the racks to the highest position. Place the peppers on the rack (or on a baking sheet on the rack) and cook, keeping a close eye on them. Turn them every couple minutes until each side is black and charred. When they're charred, remove them, and if you raised the oven temperature for the broiler, reduce it to 450°F (230°C).

3. Place the peppers on the prepared baking sheet and roast on a rack positioned in the center for 5 minutes, flipping halfway through to allow them to cook evenly. Remove from the oven and place the peppers in a plastic bag or airtight container to cool.

4. When the peppers have cooled, peel off the outer skin. Carefully trim off the tops and remove the seeds. Place the peppers in a blender. Add the tomatoes, broth, and roasted garlic and blend until smooth. Set aside.

5. Reduce the oven temperature to 350°F (175°C). Lightly spray a 9 x 13-inch baking pan with olive oil. Set aside.

to make the filling

1. Heat the oil in a large shallow saucepan over medium heat. Add the onion and garlic and sauté until the onion just starts to become translucent.

2. Add the bell pepper, sweet potatoes, coconut sugar, cumin, paprika, cinnamon, and chile powder. Sauté until the sweet potatoes are tender and can be easily pierced with a fork, 10 to 15 minutes. If the mixture begins to stick, add a few tablespoons of water or broth to deglaze the pan, and reduce the heat to medium-low.

3. Add the nutritional yeast, lemon juice, salt, and pepper; remove from the heat. Use a potato masher to mash the sweet potato slightly, leaving it a little chunky.

to make the cashew crema

Combine the cashew crema ingredients in a food processor and process until smooth. Set aside.

to assemble

1. Wrap the tortillas in a damp kitchen towel and microwave for 30 seconds. Remove from the microwave but keep them covered in the towel until ready to use.

2. Pour about ½ cup of the enchilada sauce into the bottom of the prepared baking dish, just enough to cover. Scoop ¼ to ⅓ cup of the filling down the middle of a tortilla. Roll it up and place it in the dish, seam side down. Repeat with the remaining tortillas.

3. Pour the remaining enchilada sauce over the tortillas, cover the dish with aluminum foil, and bake for about 20 minutes. Uncover, drizzle with the cashew crema, and return to the oven for 5 minutes. Remove from the oven and let rest 10 minutes before serving. Serve warm, topped with chopped green onions, cilantro, and/or avocado. Chill leftovers in an airtight container up to 1 week.

||||||||||||||||||||||||||||||||

VARIATION

▶ To save time or for a less spicy enchilada sauce, replace the Anaheim or pasilla peppers with 2 large roasted red bell peppers.

cashew crema

1 cup (160 g) raw cashews, soaked in water for at least 1 hour, *water reserved*

½ cup (125 ml) reserved soaking water

2 tablespoons lemon juice

1½ tablespoons nutritional yeast

1½ teaspoons white miso

1½ teaspoons white vinegar

½ teaspoon garlic powder

½ teaspoon onion powder

Salt to taste, optional

enchiladas

10 corn tortillas

Chopped green onions

Chopped fresh cilantro

Chopped avocado

TIPS

If you're short on time, the enchilada sauce and the cashew crema can be made in advance.

BBQ BACON BURGERS

MAKES 8 BURGERS

I think we can all agree there is a type of hunger that only a burger can satisfy. When that hunger arises, all you can think of is a meaty patty with all the fixin's. Nothing else will do. That's when this burger comes to the rescue. It's a hearty, BBQ-flavored patty made of beets, farro, and red lentils. Naturally, it's topped with Tempeh Bacon (page 25), homemade pickled red cabbage, and even more Barbecue Sauce (page 31). Plant-based cheese is a great addition, and I strongly recommend Cashew Blue Cheese (page 46). This is one succulently messy burger, so you may want to change out of your new white shirt.

to make the pickled red cabbage

1. Make the pickled red cabbage a day in advance. Chop the cabbage into quarters and cut out the core of each. Shred using a large box grater, or use a knife to make very thin slices. Place the shredded cabbage in a large colander and sprinkle salt over it. Toss to combine; leave the colander in the sink for 10 minutes to drain excess water.

2. After 10 minutes, quickly rinse off the salt and use a clean kitchen towel to pat the cabbage dry. In a large airtight container, mix the sherry vinegar, apple cider vinegar, coconut sugar, allspice, cloves, and bay leaves. Add the cabbage and stir to combine. Cover the container and chill 24 hours. Take out the allspice berries, cloves, and bay leaves before using. Leftovers can be kept chilled up to 1 month.

to make the burgers

1. Preheat the oven to 400°F (200°C). Line a baking sheet with parchment paper or a silicone baking mat.

2. Fit a steamer basket onto a small pot of water and bring to a boil. Place the beets in the steamer, cover, and steam until easily pierced with a fork, about 10 minutes. Remove from the steamer and cool for about 5 minutes.

{ RECIPE AND INGREDIENTS CONTINUE }

PREP TIME: 50 minutes (not including time to cook lentils and farro)
COOK TIME: 30 minutes
DOWN TIME: 24 hours (while red cabbage pickles)

pickled red cabbage

1 head red cabbage

Salt

1 cup (250 ml) sherry vinegar or red wine vinegar

½ cup (125 ml) apple cider vinegar

2 tablespoons coconut sugar or vegan brown sugar

3 to 4 allspice berries

3 to 4 whole cloves

2 bay leaves

burger patties

Water

1 cup (150 g) peeled, chopped beets

2½ cups (365 g) cooked farro (see page 10)

1½ cups (240 g) cooked red lentils (see page 8)

¼ cup (30 g) quinoa flour

2 garlic cloves

¼ cup (60 ml) Barbecue Sauce (page 31) or store-bought

3 tablespoons nutritional yeast

2 tablespoons liquid aminos (or tamari or soy sauce)

1 teaspoon cumin

1 teaspoon dried thyme

½ teaspoon ancho chile powder

½ teaspoon smoked paprika

1 teaspoon liquid smoke, optional

1 teaspoon vegan Worcestershire sauce, optional

Salt and black pepper to taste

3. While the beets are steaming, combine the farro, lentils, and quinoa flour in a large bowl. Use your hands to mash them together until they start holding together in clumps when squeezed. Set aside.

4. Combine the beets, garlic, barbecue sauce, nutritional yeast, liquid aminos, cumin, thyme, chile powder, paprika, liquid smoke (if using), Worcestershire sauce (if using), salt, and pepper in a food processor and process until mostly smooth (tiny pieces of beet are okay). Pour into the bowl with the farro mixture. Stir until fully combined.

5. Divide the mixture into 8 equal parts, shape into patties, and place on the baking sheet. Bake for 20 to 30 minutes, until firm, flipping once halfway through to ensure even cooking.

6. Before turning off the oven, place the burger buns on the oven rack for 2 minutes to heat them up. Remove and spread a layer of Barbecue Sauce on both halves of each bun. Place a few pieces of lettuce on the bottom bun and add the burger patty. Top with 2 to 3 bacon strips, some cashew blue cheese crumbles, and some pickled red cabbage. Top with the other half of the bun. Serve warm. Leftover patties can be chilled in an airtight container 4 to 5 days or frozen 1 month.

|||||||||||||||||||||||||||||

VARIATIONS

▶ Try using a different cheese, like Sunflower Cheddar (page 42), Tofu Chèvre (page 36), or a store-bought vegan cheese.

▶ To make gluten-free burgers, replace the farro with brown rice and use gluten-free buns.

sandwiches

8 vegan burger buns

Barbecue Sauce (page 31)

½ batch Tempeh Bacon (page 25)

½ batch Cashew Blue Cheese (page 46) or other vegan cheese of choice, optional

Mixed greens or lettuce

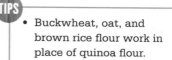

TIPS

- Buckwheat, oat, and brown rice flour work in place of quinoa flour.

- For perfectly round burgers, spray a biscuit cutter with olive oil and use it to shape your patty on the baking sheet.

- If you want to brown the outside of the burgers, spray a frying pan with olive oil and cook the baked patties over medium heat for a few minutes on each side.

- To make the burger prep much quicker, plan on cooking the farro and lentils and steaming the beets earlier that day or up to 3 days in advance.

NOT SOUP AGAIN!

Made-Over Classics and Brand-New Soups That Are Anything But Boring

For some reason I don't quite understand, many people think soup needs to be jazzed up with a sprinkle of cheese or bacon bits. For these plant-based soups, that is most definitely not the case. Whether you like a creamy bisque, a thick chowder, or a chunky stew, in this chapter you are sure to find a vegan soup that bursts with flavor, keeps you warm on a chilly night, and gives your bread something to sop up.

CREOLE CORN CHOWDER

SERVES 4 TO 6

PREP TIME: 10 minutes
COOK TIME: 30 minutes
DOWN TIME: 60 minutes *(while cashews soak)*

We all know that the best way to eat corn is straight off the cob, preferably grilled and drenched in vegan butter. The next best way is in corn chowder, preferably the spicy, Creole variety. We don't need loads of heavy cream to make it happen. A combo of cashews, coconut yogurt, non-dairy milk, and potatoes makes the creamiest corn chowder any side of the Mississippi. Top it with a couple handfuls of oyster crackers, just as I imagine they do down in the bayou (okay, okay, I just like *saying* "down in the bayou"—don't you?).

1. Combine the cashews and broth in a blender and blend until smooth. Set aside.
2. Heat the oil in a large pot over medium heat. Add the onion and garlic and sauté for about 3 minutes. Add the potatoes, bell peppers, and Anaheim pepper. Sauté for 3 to 4 minutes, stirring occasionally to prevent sticking.
3. Add the cashew mixture, water, paprika, oregano, thyme, mustard powder, and cayenne; bring to a boil. Reduce the heat and cover the pot, leaving the lid open a crack. Simmer for 20 minutes, stirring every few minutes to prevent sticking.
4. Add 2 cups (280 g) of the corn and the non-dairy milk, yogurt, lime juice, and liquid smoke. Use an immersion blender to blend the soup until mostly smooth but still a little chunky. Add the remaining 2 cups of corn, salt, and pepper, and remove from the heat. Serve hot, topped with the green onions, a drizzle of hot sauce, and oyster crackers (if using). Leftovers can be chilled in an airtight container 3 to 4 days.

¾ cup (120 g) raw cashews, soaked in water for at least 1 hour, *water discarded*

3 cups (750 ml) vegetable broth

1 teaspoon extra virgin olive oil

½ large red onion, diced

2 garlic cloves, minced

4 Yukon gold potatoes, chopped

1 red bell pepper, diced

½ green bell pepper, diced

1 tablespoon diced Anaheim pepper

1 cup (250 ml) water

2 teaspoons smoked paprika

1 teaspoon dried oregano

1 teaspoon dried thyme

½ teaspoon mustard powder

½ teaspoon cayenne pepper

4 cups (560 g) corn kernels (fresh or defrosted if frozen), divided

1 cup (250 ml) unsweetened non-dairy milk

¾ cup (170 g) plain coconut yogurt

1 tablespoon lime juice

½ teaspoon liquid smoke

1 teaspoon salt

Black pepper to taste

garnishes

Chopped green onions or chives

Hot sauce

Oyster crackers (omit for gluten-free)

BROCCOLI CHEDDAR SOUP

SERVES 4 TO 6

Years ago, when I worked in a French restaurant, it was my duty to make the cheese-based soup of the day. Of course, I had to use the chef's recipe, and to be perfectly honest, I never liked any of the soups, especially the broccoli cheddar; it tasted more like grease than cheesiness (much less broccoli). I'm sure that the head chef would not approve of this plant-based version with chickpeas and nutritional yeast, but if you love a rich, creamy, cheddary broccoli soup, I'm sure you'll enjoy my take! If you can find it, vegan pretzel bread makes the best accompaniment.

PREP TIME: 15 minutes
COOK TIME: 30 minutes

1 large head broccoli, including stems (about 1 pound/500 g)

Olive oil spray

Salt and black pepper to taste

1½ cups (255 g) cooked chickpeas (see page 8) or one 15-ounce (425 g) can, rinsed and drained

½ cup (35 g) nutritional yeast

2 tablespoons lemon juice

1 tablespoon tomato paste

1 teaspoon white miso

½ to 1 teaspoon liquid smoke, to taste

1 teaspoon garlic powder

½ teaspoon smoked paprika

¼ teaspoon turmeric

2 cups (500 ml) vegetable broth

2 cups (500 ml) water

1. Preheat the oven to 400°F (200°C). Line a baking sheet with parchment paper or a silicone baking mat.

2. Chop the broccoli head into florets and slice the stem into thin coins. Spread on the prepared baking sheet. Lightly spray with olive oil and add salt and pepper. Toss to coat. Roast for 20 minutes, flipping once halfway through to ensure even cooking.

3. In a blender, combine the chickpeas, nutritional yeast, lemon juice, tomato paste, miso, liquid smoke, garlic powder, paprika, turmeric, and broth. Blend until smooth. Add the cooked broccoli and pulse until mostly smooth (small chunks of broccoli are good).

4. Pour the mixture and the water into a large pot. Cook, stirring, over medium heat for about 2 minutes. Cover and cook, stirring occasionally, until heated through, about 8 minutes. Remove from the heat and serve hot. Leftovers can be chilled in an airtight container 3 to 4 days.

CAULIFLOWER BISQUE

SERVES 4 TO 6

I once ate a subtle, yet intensely herbal cauliflower bisque that was ultra-white and creamy beyond belief. It was as if all the most beautiful white things in life—the first snow, ruffly white sheets, hydrangeas, sand dollars, and the buildings of Santorini—all got together and manifested as a gorgeous soup. I tried for years to replicate it, but my results were never white—always light brown or orange. Then, I figured it out: Don't brown the shallots or cauliflower. Use water instead of broth. Let the flavor come from herbs in a bouquet garni that can be removed before blending. Add coconut milk. And voilà! The transcendent beauty of a velvety white soup is all yours!

PREP TIME: 10 minutes
COOK TIME: 25 minutes

3 to 4 fresh thyme sprigs

2 to 3 bay leaves

1 fresh rosemary sprig

2 teaspoons toasted sesame oil or extra virgin olive oil

¼ cup (30 g) chopped shallots

2 garlic cloves, minced

1 large head cauliflower, roughly chopped into small florets

3 cups (750 ml) water

1 cup (250 ml) canned lite coconut milk

1 tablespoon fresh lemon juice

Salt to taste

Truffle oil or toasted sesame oil for drizzling

1. Use a piece of kitchen twine to tie the thyme, bay leaves, and rosemary into a little bundle (bouquet). Set aside.

2. Heat the oil in a large shallow saucepan over medium heat. Add the shallots and garlic and cook, stirring occasionally, for about 2 minutes. Add the cauliflower and cook for 3 to 4 minutes.

3. Add the water and herb bouquet, bring to a boil, then reduce the heat and cover, leaving the lid open a crack. Simmer for 15 to 20 minutes, until the cauliflower is very tender.

4. Remove the bouquet and carefully transfer the mixture to a blender (in batches, if necessary). You can use an immersion blender instead, but the regular blender will likely yield a smoother soup. Add the coconut milk and lemon juice and blend until smooth. Add salt.

5. Serve with a drizzle of truffle oil. Leftovers can be chilled in an airtight container 3 to 4 days.

VARIATION

▶ For some extra flavor, if you don't care how white the bisque is, stir in ¼ cup (20 g) of nutritional yeast before serving, or use vegetable broth in place of the water.

WHITE BEAN & PORTOBELLO STEW

SERVES 6 TO 8

Cold, rainy weather. Fire in the fireplace. Fuzzy slippers covering your toes. Blanket wrapped around your shoulders. This thick, hearty stew. Crusty French baguette. Enough said.

1. Heat the oil in a large pot over medium heat. Add the leeks and garlic and sauté for 2 to 3 minutes, until fragrant. Add the carrot and celery and sauté for another 2 to 3 minutes. Add the mushrooms, liquid aminos, rosemary, thyme, sage, and fennel seeds. Sauté for 3 to 4 minutes.

2. Add the beans, broth, water, and miso. Bring to a boil, then reduce the heat and cover, leaving the lid open a crack. Simmer for 25 to 30 minutes.

3. When some of the liquid has reduced and the vegetables are tender, add the liquid smoke, salt, and black pepper. Fold in the kale and cook just until the kale begins to wilt, then remove from the heat.

4. Serve warm, with bread, if desired. Leftovers can be chilled in an airtight container up to 5 days.

TIP

You can purchase vegan broths that are chicken or beef flavored. They do not contain animal products, but they are seasoned to taste like their non-vegan counterparts.

PREP TIME: 15 minutes
COOK TIME: 40 minutes

2 teaspoons extra virgin olive oil

2 leeks (white part only), halved lengthwise and thinly sliced

2 garlic cloves, minced

1 carrot, chopped

1 celery rib, chopped

4 portobello mushrooms, sliced into ½-inch (1 cm) wide strips

1 tablespoon liquid aminos

1 tablespoon chopped fresh rosemary

1 tablespoon chopped fresh thyme

1 tablespoon chopped fresh sage

1 teaspoon fennel seeds

3 cups (525 g) cooked great Northern beans (see page 8) or two 15-ounce (425 g) cans, rinsed and drained

4 cups (1,000 ml) vegetable broth (chicken-flavored vegetable broth is best here; see tip)

1 cup (250 ml) water

1 teaspoon white miso

1 teaspoon liquid smoke

Salt and black pepper to taste

3 cups (40 g) roughly chopped kale

Crusty French bread or Southern Biscuits (page 233), optional

POTATO SAUERKRAUT SOUP WITH SAUSAGE CRUMBLES

SERVES 6 TO 8

Sure, we can all agree that a creamy potato soup is good. But what if it were blended with the tanginess of sauerkraut and tofu sour cream? And topped with sunflower sausage crumbles? Served with some crusty French bread? Now we're talking! But can you have all that and be vegan, too? Yes! One bite of this luscious soup will prove it.

1. Heat the oil in a large pot over medium heat. Add the onion and garlic and sauté until the onion is translucent. Add the potatoes and carrot and sauté for 2 to 3 minutes. Add the parsley, thyme, paprika, broth, and water; bring to a boil. Reduce the heat and cover, leaving the lid open a crack. Simmer for about 20 minutes.

2. Add the sauerkraut and use an immersion blender to blend the soup until mostly smooth (some chunks are good). Alternatively, blend the soup in batches in a regular blender. Stir in 1 cup of the sour cream. If you want a more sour-creamy taste, add the remaining ½ cup. Cook on medium-low heat until heated through, about 5 minutes. Add salt and pepper and remove from the heat.

3. Pour the soup into bowls. Top with a dollop of sour cream, a spoonful of sauerkraut, ¼ to ⅓ cup of sunflower sausage crumbles, and a pinch of fresh parsley (if using). Serve immediately. Leftovers can be chilled in an airtight container for 3 to 4 days.

PREP TIME: 10 minutes *(not including time to prepare Sunflower Sausage)*
COOK TIME: 30 minutes

1 teaspoon extra virgin olive oil

½ medium yellow onion, chopped

2 garlic cloves, minced

5 cups (625 g) chopped Yukon Gold potatoes

½ cup (80 g) chopped carrot

1 teaspoon dried parsley

1 teaspoon dried thyme

1 teaspoon smoked paprika

3 cups (750 ml) vegetable broth

2 cups (500 ml) water

1½ cups (385 g) sauerkraut, plus extra for garnish

1 to 1½ cups (225 to 340 g) Tofu Sour Cream (page 33), plus additional for garnish

Salt and black pepper to taste

½ batch Sunflower Sausage, crumbled (page 26)

Fresh parsley, optional

SPINACH ARTICHOKE SOUP

SERVES 6

W e've all been there. You're at a party by the snack table, shoveling spinach artichoke dip into your face. You can't stop, because *oh my god, it's spinach artichoke dip!* Soon, all the sourdough bread is gone so you nonchalantly scan the table for other things you can dip. You grab a tortilla chip, but it's not nearly as good. You wish you could eat it with a spoon and retain your dignity. My friend, there is a way! By disguising the dip as a soup, you can grab a grown-up spoon and finish off an entire bowl without any loss to your self-respect. Go on now. Fulfill your dreams.

PREP TIME: 5 minutes
COOK TIME: 30 minutes

cream

- 1½ cups (265 g) cooked great Northern beans (see page 8) or one 15-ounce (425 g) can, rinsed and drained
- 1 cup (250 ml) unsweetened non-dairy milk
- ¼ cup (20 g) nutritional yeast
- 3 tablespoons fresh lemon juice
- 1 tablespoon ume plum vinegar
- 2 teaspoons white miso
- 1 teaspoon Dijon mustard

soup

- 1 teaspoon extra virgin olive oil
- 2 shallots, chopped
- 1 to 2 garlic cloves, minced
- 2 cups (360 g) canned or frozen and thawed artichoke hearts
- 2 teaspoons dried basil
- 1 teaspoon dried oregano
- 3 cups (750 ml) vegetable broth
- 1 cup (250 ml) water
- 6 cups (180 g) packed spinach leaves or one 10-ounce (285 g) package frozen spinach, defrosted
- Salt and black pepper to taste
- Mini sourdough bread rounds, hollowed out for serving, optional

1. In a high-speed blender or food processor, combine the ingredients for the cream and blend until smooth. Set aside until ready to use.

2. In a large pot, heat the oil over medium heat for 1 minute. Add the shallots and garlic and sauté until fragrant and the shallots become slightly translucent. Add the artichoke hearts, basil, and oregano; sauté for 2 to 3 minutes. Add the broth and water and mix well. Cover and bring to a boil, then crack the lid and reduce the heat. Simmer for about 10 minutes.

3. When heated through and slightly thickened, remove the soup from the heat. Add the spinach and stir until incorporated and slightly wilted. Use an immersion blender to pulse the soup until it has a chunky (not smooth) consistency. Pour in the cream and mix until combined. Add salt and pepper.

4. Return to a simmer for 5 to 10 minutes, until heated through. Remove from the heat and serve inside the prepared bread bowls (if using).

TIPS

- Serving the soup with sourdough bread for dipping is a close runner-up to serving it in bread bowls.
- To fancy it up a bit, heat 1 teaspoon olive oil and 1 minced garlic clove in a frying pan until fragrant. Add 1½ cups halved artichoke hearts (canned or defrosted if frozen) and cook for 4 to 5 minutes on each side, until slightly browned. Top the soup with the pan-fried artichokes.

I'D MISS PIZZA.

Pizza-Party-Ready Vegan Pies

As the great Isa Chandra Moskowitz says, "Cake is a luxury. Pizza is a right." Don't think that going vegan means your days of stealing the last slice, folding it in half to keep the toppings from slipping off, and shoving it in your mouth are gone. You will still get to lick the marinara sauce off your fingers and eat the doughy crusts your crazy friend would just as soon throw away. These are your rights as a human! Take advantage of them!

PIZZA DOUGH, THREE WAYS

The scariest part about making pizza at home is the dough: "It takes too long," "Will the yeast activate?," "Will the dough rise?," "I'm afraid of rolling pins!," and the list goes on. There are a lot of excuses for not making your own pizza dough, but the truth is that once you get the hang of it, it's a piece of pie (pun intended).

Here are a few pointers to keep in mind:

- The water must always be precisely 110°F (45°C). Use a candy thermometer to make sure. Any more and the yeast will die; any less and the yeast can't activate. Microwaving the water for 1 minute usually does the trick, but if it gets too hot, stick the cup in the refrigerator for a couple minutes and check again.

- You can use a stand mixer fitted with a dough hook to mix your dough, but it isn't necessary.

- Add flour until you have a soft ball of dough. Sometimes you won't use the full amount listed in the ingredients, and sometimes you'll use more.

- A well-floured surface is paramount to peaceful dough rolling (i.e., no "it's-sticking-to-everything!!!" panic attacks).

- The best surface to cook your pizza on is a preheated pizza stone. You will, however, need a good pizza peel to transfer your pizza to the stone. If you don't have a pizza stone, don't sweat it. A round metal pizza pan or even a baking sheet will also work.

BASIC PIZZA DOUGH

MAKES TWO 10-INCH PIZZA CRUSTS

This dough is perfect for a softer, chewier crust, the kind that allows you to fold your slice in half.

1. Combine the water and sugar in a large bowl or in the bowl of a stand mixer fitted with a dough hook. Add the yeast and set aside. Let it sit and activate for 10 minutes, or until a thick foamy layer forms on the top.

2. After the yeast has activated, mix in the oil and salt. Add the flour ½ cup at a time and stir (or mix) after each addition until combined. If you are not using a stand mixer, use your hands to knead the dough when it gets too difficult to stir. Continue to add flour, ½ cup at a time, until you have a soft ball of dough (you may not need all 3 cups). If it is too dry and crumbly, add olive oil by the teaspoon until it is no longer dry. If it is too sticky, add more flour by the tablespoon until you can touch the ball without it sticking to your finger.

3. Lightly spray the inside of a large bowl with olive oil. Place the ball of dough in the bowl, cover with a damp kitchen towel, and store in a warm, not-too-drafty place. Let it rise for 1 hour, or until doubled in size.

4. Gently punch down the doubled ball of dough a couple of times. Turn it out onto a floured surface and knead for about 1 minute.

5. Split the dough in half and use as directed in your pizza recipe of choice. Leftover dough can be placed in a resealable plastic bag and refrigerated 3 to 4 days or frozen 1 month.

PREP TIME: 30 minutes
DOWN TIME: 60 minutes

1 cup (250 ml) warm water, heated to 110°F (45°C)

1 teaspoon vegan sugar

2¼ teaspoons active dry yeast

2 tablespoons extra virgin olive oil

1 teaspoon salt

2½ to 3 cups (325 to 390 g) bread flour, divided, plus more for kneading

Olive oil spray

SPICED OR HERBED PIZZA DOUGH

MAKES TWO 10-INCH PIZZA CRUSTS

SF NF PA

This recipe also yields a soft crust, but it is studded with herbs or spices, taking the flavor of your pizza to the next level.

PREP TIME: 30 minutes
DOWN TIME: 60 minutes

1 cup (250 ml) warm water, heated to 110°F (45°C)

1 teaspoon vegan sugar

2¼ teaspoons active dry yeast

3 cups (390 g) bread flour, divided, plus more for kneading

Herbs or spices of choice (see variations)

2 tablespoons extra virgin olive oil

1 teaspoon salt

Olive oil spray

1. Combine the water and sugar in a large bowl or in the bowl of a stand mixer fitted with a dough hook. Add the yeast and set aside. Let it sit and activate for 10 minutes, or until a thick foamy layer forms on the top.

2. In a separate large bowl, whisk together the flour with the herbs or spices.

3. After the yeast has activated, mix in the oil and salt. Add the flour mixture ½ cup at a time and stir (or mix) after each addition until combined. If you are not using a stand mixer, use your hands to knead the dough when it gets too difficult to stir. Continue to add flour until you have a soft ball of dough (you may not need all 3 cups). If it is too dry and crumbly, add olive oil by the teaspoon until it is no longer dry. If it is too sticky, add more flour by the tablespoon until you can touch the ball without it sticking to your finger.

4. Lightly spray the inside of a large bowl with olive oil. Place the dough in the bowl, cover with a damp kitchen towel, and store in a warm, not-too-drafty place. Let it rise for 1 hour, or until doubled in size.

5. Gently punch down the doubled ball of dough a couple of times. Turn it out onto a floured surface and knead for about 1 minute. Split the dough in half and use as directed in your pizza recipe of choice. Leftover dough can be placed in a resealable plastic bag and refrigerated 3 to 4 days or frozen 1 month.

VARIATIONS

▶ For Caraway Seed Crust, add 2 tablespoons caraway seeds to the flour.

▶ For Fennel & Sage Crust, add 1½ tablespoons fennel seeds and 1½ teaspoons dried sage to the flour.

▶ For Mixed Herb Crust, add 1½ teaspoons dried rosemary, 1½ teaspoons dried thyme, and 1½ teaspoons dried parsley to the flour.

▶ For Italian Herb Crust, add 1½ teaspoons dried basil, 1½ teaspoons dried oregano, and 1½ teaspoons dried marjoram to the flour.

▶ For Curry-Spiced Crust, add 2 teaspoons curry powder and 1 teaspoon garam masala to the flour.

▶ For Onion & Garlic Crust, add 1½ teaspoons onion powder and 1½ teaspoons garlic powder to the flour.

▶ For Hot & Spicy Crust, add 2 teaspoons crushed red pepper, 1 teaspoon cumin, and 1 teaspoon ancho chile powder to the flour.

CORNMEAL PIZZA DOUGH

MAKES TWO 10-INCH PIZZA CRUSTS

The cornmeal in this dough will give you a crispier, crunchier crust. No toppings will be sliding off these pizza slices!

1. Combine the water and sugar in a large bowl or in the bowl of a stand mixer fitted with a dough hook. Add the yeast and set aside. Let it sit and activate for 10 minutes, or until a thick foamy layer forms on the top.

2. In a large bowl, whisk together 2 cups of the flour and the cornmeal. Set aside.

3. After the yeast has activated, mix in the oil and salt. Add the flour mixture ½ cup at a time and stir (or mix) after each addition until combined. If you are not using a stand mixer, use your hands to knead the dough when it gets too difficult to stir. Continue to add the flour mixture until you have a soft ball of dough (you may not need all 2½ cups). If it is too dry and crumbly, add olive oil by the teaspoon until it is no longer dry. If it is too sticky, add the remaining bread flour by the tablespoon until you can touch the ball without it sticking to your finger.

4. Lightly spray the inside of a large bowl with olive oil. Place the dough in the bowl, cover with a damp kitchen towel, and store in a warm, not-too-drafty place. Let it rise for 1 hour, or until doubled in size.

5. Gently punch down the doubled ball of dough a couple of times. Turn it out onto a floured surface and knead for about 1 minute. Split the dough in half and use as directed in your pizza recipe of choice. Leftover dough can be placed in a resealable plastic bag and refrigerated 3 to 4 days or frozen 1 month.

PREP TIME: 30 minutes
DOWN TIME: 60 minutes

1½ cups (375 ml) warm water, heated to 110°F (45°C)

1 teaspoon vegan sugar

2¼ teaspoons active dry yeast

2 cups (260 g) + ½ cup (65 g) bread flour (if needed), divided, plus more for kneading

1½ cups (210 g) fine-ground cornmeal

2 tablespoons extra virgin olive oil

1 teaspoon salt

Olive oil spray

ROASTED GARLIC WHITE PIZZA WITH MACADAMIA RICOTTA

MAKES 1 PIZZA

It's pretty rare that you go out of your way to make a pizza from scratch just for yourself, right? This is one of my favorite pizzas to share because people can't get over how creamy the white sauce is or how tasty the Macadamia Ricotta (page 41) is when it gets slightly toasted. I've made it for non-vegan friends who've gone home and made it again for themselves. You know those friends who don't believe that pizza can be good without loads of greasy cheese? This is the pizza you should share with them.

1. If you're using a pizza stone, put it in the oven. If not, lightly dust a pizza pan or baking sheet with cornmeal; set aside. Preheat the oven to 475°F (250°C).

2. Mix the non-dairy milk with the vinegar in a cup and set aside for at least 5 minutes.

3. Meanwhile, fill a pot with about 2 inches of water. Bring to a boil. Place the cauliflower florets in a steamer basket, fit it in the pot, cover, and steam for about 10 minutes, until the florets are easily pierced with a fork. Remove and let cool for a few minutes.

4. Gently squeeze each clove of garlic from its skin into a food processor. Add the steamed cauliflower, milk mixture, cashews, lemon juice, miso, nutritional yeast, salt, and pepper. Process until smooth.

5. Heat a large frying pan over medium heat. Add the spinach and the water. Sauté until the spinach has just begun to wilt. Remove from the heat.

6. Roll out the pizza dough on a floured surface to desired size, making sure the dough is at least ¼ inch (.5 cm) thick. Spread the spinach on top, leaving a ½-inch (1 cm) crust around the perimeter. Spoon the white sauce on top of the spinach. Crumble the Macadamia Ricotta on top of the sauce.

7. Transfer the pizza to the pizza stone or place on the prepared pan. Bake for 10 to 12 minutes, until the crust has risen and is lightly golden. Slice and serve hot.

PREP TIME: 45 minutes *(not including time to prepare pizza dough or Macadamia Ricotta)*
COOK TIME: 15 minutes
DOWN TIME: 1 hour *(while cashews soak)*

roasted garlic white sauce
½ cup (125 ml) non-dairy milk
1 teaspoon apple cider vinegar
Water
½ small head cauliflower, cut into florets
1 head roasted garlic (page 7)
¼ cup (40 g) cashews, soaked in water at least 1 hour, *water discarded*
1 tablespoon lemon juice
1½ teaspoons white miso
1 teaspoon nutritional yeast
Salt and black pepper to taste

pizza
1 bunch spinach, stems removed, leaves roughly chopped
1 tablespoon water
½ batch Basic Pizza Dough (page 179)
Flour for rolling
Macadamia Ricotta (page 41)

> **TIP**
> The roasted garlic white sauce makes enough for 2 pizzas, so you will have some left over. It makes a wonderful pasta sauce or sandwich spread.

ROASTED VEGGIE DEEP-DISH PIZZA

MAKES 1 PIZZA

Pizza is always a mood elevator, but deep dish is something special. Years ago, during a very tumultuous time in my life, I hopped on a plane to visit a dear childhood friend. She picked me up from the airport and made one stop on the way home—to pick up a deep-dish pizza from her favorite pizzeria. We cracked open a bottle of wine, ate pizza, and talked for hours. After that evening, my life (or at least my outlook) really turned around. When you eat deep-dish pizza, layers of gooey sauce and melty cheese seep out, and devouring a thick, heavenly piece is so satisfying. But I also can't help but feel that the depth of this—vegan!—pizza also deepens its ability to improve your mood.

1. In a medium bowl, whisk together the pizza sauce ingredients. Chill until ready to use.

2. Preheat the oven to 400°F (200°C). Line a baking sheet with parchment paper or a silicone baking mat. Spread the mushrooms, zucchini, bell pepper, and red onion on the prepared pan. Spray with olive oil and sprinkle on the basil, oregano, salt, and pepper. Toss to fully coat each piece. Roast for 15 minutes, tossing once halfway through to ensure even cooking. Remove from the oven. Add the cherry tomatoes and gently toss together.

3. Increase the oven temperature to 475°F (250°C). Lightly spray a 10-inch springform pan (preferably) or cake pan with olive oil. Place the dough into the prepared pan and press it into the bottom and up the sides. If using a springform pan, do not leave any dough hanging over the edge of the pan (it will crack and tear when you release the sides).

4. Slice the Macarella discs into ¼-inch (.5 cm) thick medallions. Spread ¼ cup (60 ml) pizza sauce on the pizza dough in the bottom of the pan. Add a layer of medallions (it's okay if there are gaps between them). Top with half the vegetables. Spoon about ½ cup (120 ml) of pizza sauce over the vegeta-

PREP TIME: 30 minutes *(not including time to prepare pizza dough or Macarella)*
COOK TIME: 30 minutes

pizza sauce

One 15-ounce (445 ml) can unsalted tomato sauce

One 6-ounce (170 g) can tomato paste

1 tablespoon extra virgin olive oil

1 teaspoon dried basil

1 teaspoon dried oregano

¼ teaspoon garlic powder

Salt and black pepper to taste

roasted veggies

8 ounces (225 g) sliced button or cremini mushrooms

2 zucchini, sliced

½ yellow or orange bell pepper, thinly sliced

½ medium red onion, thinly sliced

Olive oil spray

1 tablespoon dried basil

2 teaspoons dried oregano

Salt and black pepper to taste

2 cups (360 g) halved cherry tomatoes

pizza

1 batch Cornmeal Pizza Dough (page 181), *not divided in half*

Flour for rolling

4 Macarella discs (page 49)

bles, and top with the remaining vegetables. Add one more layer of medallions over the vegetables, and spread the remaining pizza sauce over the top.

5. Bake for 30 minutes, or until the crust is firm and golden. Remove from the oven and let it rest in the pan for 10 minutes. If you used a springform pan, remove the outer ring (first you may need to run a knife along the rim to loosen the crust from the pan), slice, and serve. If you used a regular cake pan, slice it in the pan and remove it slice by slice.

KABOCHA, CARAMELIZED ONION & PORCINI MUSHROOM PIZZA

MAKES 1 PIZZA

The idea of a cheeseless pizza is a little scary for some. If there's no cheese, where does the flavor come from? Fact: It comes from the toppings and the pizza crust itself. On cheese pizzas, the toppings' flavors are partially masked by the heavy, greasy cheese. When you take that away, you can play with an endless variety of flavor profiles—and guess what? Your pizzas will taste much more interesting! Here, roasted, pureed kabocha squash is spread on a cornmeal crust, then topped with sweet caramelized onions and earthy porcini mushrooms. Robust, sweet, smoky, earthy, and herbal. Trust me, the cheese will not be missed.

1. Place the mushrooms in a bowl and cover with hot water. Soak for 10 minutes, or until tender; drain off the water.

2. If you're using a pizza stone, put it in the oven. If not, lightly dust a pizza pan or baking sheet with cornmeal; set aside. Preheat the oven to 425°F (220°C).

3. Line a baking sheet with parchment paper or a silicone baking mat.

4. Place the squash cubes on the prepared baking sheet and generously spray with olive oil. Sprinkle with the cinnamon, cumin, nutmeg, paprika, salt, and pepper; toss to coat. Roast for 30 minutes, tossing once halfway through to ensure even cooking. When the pieces are easily pierced with a fork, remove and cool for about 5 minutes.

5. Meanwhile, heat 1 teaspoon of the oil in a large frying pan over medium heat until it begins to simmer. Add the onions, toss until fully coated, and cook until translucent. Reduce the heat to medium-low and mix in the coconut sugar. Continue to cook, stirring every 3 to 4 minutes, for 25 to 30 minutes. If the onions begin to stick too much, deglaze the pan with a little water and reduce the heat just a bit more. When the onions are dark and very soft, add salt and remove from the heat. Transfer to a bowl and set aside.

6. Heat the remaining 1 teaspoon oil over medium heat in the same frying pan. Add the rehydrated mushrooms, thyme,

PREP TIME: 60 minutes (not including time to prepare the pizza dough)
COOK TIME: 10 minutes

2 cups (90 g) dried porcini mushrooms

Hot water

1 small kabocha squash, halved, seeded, peeled, and cubed (see tips)

Olive oil spray

1 teaspoon cinnamon

1 teaspoon cumin

½ teaspoon nutmeg

½ teaspoon smoked paprika

Salt and black pepper to taste

2 teaspoons extra virgin olive oil, divided

1 large red onion, halved and very thinly sliced (use a mandoline, if possible)

Pinch of coconut sugar or vegan brown sugar

2 teaspoons chopped fresh thyme

½ teaspoon garlic powder

½ teaspoon onion powder

2 to 3 tablespoons nutritional yeast, to taste

1 tablespoon fresh lemon juice

2 teaspoons maple syrup

½ batch Cornmeal Pizza Dough (page 181)

Flour for rolling

garlic powder, and onion powder and cook, stirring every couple minutes to prevent sticking, for 5 minutes, or until heated through and beginning to brown. Add salt and pepper and remove from the heat.

7. After the squash is out of oven, increase the oven temperature to 425°F (220°C).

8. Place the squash pieces, nutritional yeast, lemon juice, and maple syrup in a food processor. Process until smooth, pausing to scrape the sides as necessary. Set aside.

9. Roll out the pizza dough on a floured surface to desired size, making sure the dough is at least ¼ inch (.5 cm) thick. Spread the kabocha puree on top, leaving a ½-inch (1 cm) crust around the perimeter. Top with the caramelized onions and mushrooms (you may not be able to fit it all). Transfer the pizza to the pizza stone or prepared pan. Bake for 10 to 12 minutes, until the crust has risen and is lightly golden. Slice and serve while hot.

TIPS

• Use a sharp knife to prepare the kabocha. Halve, then flip one half cut side down and slice off the top inch (by the stem) and bottom inch. Set on the flat bottom end and peel the skin off by *very* carefully running the knife from the top to the bottom. Chop the flesh into small chunks; repeat with the other half.

• This pizza can be doubled without cooking extra ingredients. Simply use both halves of the Cornmeal Pizza Dough and split the squash, onion, and mushrooms between the two. I like to save the ingredients and make the same pizza again the next night.

POTATO-LEEK PIZZA WITH CORNMEAL CRUST

MAKES 1 PIZZA

Clean. Simple. Elegant. These are not words one would typically associate with a pizza, but this, my friend, is not your ordinary pizza. A crisp cornmeal crust provides a platform for a light-yet-luscious leek spread, layers of gorgeous potato slices, and rosemary. These simple flavors will envelop you like a warm blanket. Don't pair this pizza with a beer and a loud sporting event on TV. It's the kind you want while sipping a dry white wine and listening to the Beatles (I recommend *The White Album*, if only to color coordinate). If you absolutely must have cheese, crumble some Tofu Chèvre (page 36) over the top.

PREP TIME: 15 minutes
COOK TIME: 12 minutes
DOWN TIME: 1 hour

3 medium red potatoes

½ teaspoon salt, plus more to taste

1 teaspoon + 1 tablespoon extra virgin olive oil, divided

1 leek (white part only), halved lengthwise and sliced (see tip)

1 teaspoon dried rosemary

½ teaspoon fresh lemon juice

½ batch Cornmeal Pizza Dough (page 181)

Flour for rolling

1 tablespoon chopped fresh rosemary

Olive oil spray

Black pepper to taste

1. Using a mandoline or incredible knife skills, slice the potatoes very, very super thin. Did I mention they should be thin?

2. Place the potato slices in a large shallow bowl. Toss with the salt, cover with water, and soak for 1 hour. Drain off the water and lay the slices on a towel. Gently pat them dry.

3. If you're using a pizza stone, put it in the oven. If not, lightly dust a pizza pan or baking sheet with cornmeal; set aside. Preheat the oven to 475°F (250°C).

4. Heat 1 teaspoon of the oil in a large frying pan over medium heat. Set aside 2 tablespoons of the sliced leeks and add the rest to the pan. Sauté for 3 minutes, or until they become just soft and fragrant. Transfer to a food processor; add the remaining 1 tablespoon oil, dried rosemary, and lemon juice. Process until almost smooth (a small leek chunk here or there won't hurt); add salt to taste.

5. Roll out the pizza dough on a floured surface to desired size, making sure the dough is at least ¼ inch (.5 cm) thick. Spread the leek mixture on top (it will be a thin layer, perhaps spotty in some places), leaving a ½-inch (1 cm) crust around the perimeter. Layer the potato slices in a pretty pattern or scatter them randomly on top of the leeks. Lightly spray with olive oil and sprinkle the remaining 2 tablespoons of leeks and the fresh rosemary over the potatoes. Sprinkle on salt and pepper.

6. Transfer the pizza to the pizza stone or prepared pan. Bake for 10 to 12 minutes, until the crust has risen and is lightly golden. Slice and serve hot.

||||||||||||||||||||||||||||

VARIATION

▶ If you love leeks and can't get enough of them, double the leek spread ingredients and make a thicker layer on the pizza. A few testers and I preferred it this way.

TIP

When shopping for leeks, look for long thin stalks rather than short, fat ones, which tend to be woodier and more fibrous. To clean, trim and discard the top green part and the bottom root end; slice the remainder in half lengthwise. Clean under running water by slowly flipping the layers like you would a deck of cards.

SEITAN REUBEN PIZZA WITH CARAWAY SEED CRUST

MAKES 1 PIZZA

I love combining two of my favorite foods or dishes to create one superdish (some people refer to this process as *fusion*). It's a guaranteed win 98 percent of the time (notice this book is lacking a recipe for French Onion Cupcakes?). This recipe marries a vegan Reuben with one of the top three best food groups, pizza, for an experience you will not soon forget. Thinly sliced seitan is "corned" in a tart and tangy marinade, then paired with Swiss cheese sauce, sauerkraut, and a creamy Russian dressing. Then it's all piled on a pizza crust studded with caraway seeds. I have a feeling you're about to become a huge fan of the superdish, too.

PREP TIME: 50 minutes (*not including time to prepare seitan or pizza dough*)

COOK TIME: 15 minutes

DOWN TIME: 3 to 4 hours (*while cashews soak and seitan marinates*)

corned seitan

½ batch Homemade Seitan (page 28) or store bought

½ cup (125 ml) beet juice (see tip)

¼ cup (125 ml) brown rice vinegar

¼ cup (60 ml) water

2 tablespoons liquid aminos (or tamari or soy sauce)

1 tablespoon juice from a jar of capers, optional

1 tablespoon Dijon mustard

½ teaspoon smoked salt or regular salt

½ teaspoon ground allspice

½ teaspoon ground cloves

½ teaspoon ground ginger

½ teaspoon smoked paprika

¼ teaspoon cayenne pepper

Several dashes of black pepper

Swiss cheese sauce

½ cup (75 g) raw almonds, soaked in water for 3 to 4 hours, *water reserved*

1 tablespoon tahini

2 teaspoons nutritional yeast

1 teaspoon white miso

½ teaspoon garlic powder

½ teaspoon onion powder

Salt to taste

Russian dressing

¼ cup (55 g) vegan mayonnaise

1½ tablespoons vegan ketchup

1½ teaspoons red wine vinegar

1. Using a mandoline (or a sharp knife, carefully), slice the seitan into very, very, very thin strips. In a shallow bowl or baking dish, combine the beet juice, vinegar, water, liquid aminos, caper juice (if using), mustard, salt, allspice, cloves, ginger, paprika, cayenne, and pepper. Add the seitan strips and toss until completely coated. Place in the refrigerator and marinate for at least 1 hour (or up to 24 hours), tossing every so often to recoat each strip.

2. Combine the Swiss cheese sauce ingredients, including 9 tablespoons of the reserved soaking water, in a food processor; process until mostly smooth (it's okay if it's a little gritty). If it is not getting smooth, add 1 more tablespoon of reserved water. Chill until ready to use. This can be made up to 2 days in advance.

3. In a small bowl, mix the Russian dressing ingredients and set aside. This can be made up to 2 days in advance and chilled in an airtight container.

4. If you're using a pizza stone, put it in the oven. If not, lightly dust a pizza pan or baking sheet with cornmeal; set aside. Preheat the oven to 475°F (250°C).

5. Roll out the pizza dough on a floured surface to desired size, making sure the dough is at least ¼ inch (.5 cm) thick. Spread the Swiss cheese sauce on top, leaving a ½-inch (1 cm) crust around the perimeter. Top with the seitan. Transfer to

the pizza stone or prepared pizza pan. Bake for 10 to 12 minutes, until the seitan is warm and the crust has risen and is lightly golden. Remove from the oven, top with the sauerkraut, and drizzle with the Russian dressing. Slice and serve immediately.

||||||||||||||||||||||||||||

VARIATION

▶ Forget the pizza and layer the seitan, sauerkraut, Swiss cheese sauce, and Russian dressing between two pieces of toasted pumpernickel bread for the greatest deli sandwich ever!

1 teaspoon tomato paste

½ teaspoon dried dill

½ teaspoon smoked paprika

2 tablespoons sweet pickle relish

pizza

½ batch Caraway Seed Crust dough (page 180, see variation)

Flour for rolling

½ cup (130 g) sauerkraut

TIP

Beet juice can usually be found in the juice section of your grocery or natural food store. If you can't find it, puree some steamed beets and use ½ cup of the puree.

BUFFALO CAULIFLOWER CALZONES WITH CASHEW BLUE CHEESE

MAKES 2 LARGE CALZONES OR 4 MINI CALZONES (SERVES 2 TO 4)

page 176

Buffalo cauliflower is the key to changing the mind of those who refuse to believe vegan food could possibly taste good. A Buffalo cauliflower calzone with Cashew Blue Cheese is the key to *blowing their minds*! With that super-spicy "Buffalo" flavor, no one cares whether it's chicken or cauliflower—especially when it's coated in a nutty chickpea flour crust and stuffed in a soft, doughy pizza pocket along with a healthy amount of tangy Cashew Blue Cheese. Need to impress an omnivore? Make this.

1. If using a pizza stone, put it in the oven. If not, lightly dust a pizza pan or baking sheet with cornmeal; set aside. Lightly spray a 9 x 13-inch baking dish with olive oil. Preheat the oven to 450°F (230°C).

2. In a small bowl, mix the hot sauce, tomato paste, and agave syrup. Mix in the arrowroot powder, salt, and pepper. Set aside.

3. In a large bowl, mix the non-dairy milk, chickpea flour, garlic powder, and paprika. Dredge one cauliflower floret at a time in the mixture and place in the prepared baking dish. Bake for 20 minutes (if you're preheating a pizza stone, place the baking sheet on top of it).

4. Remove from the oven and use a spatula to loosen any florets sticking to the dish. Pour the hot sauce mixture over the cauliflower, toss to coat, and bake 5 minutes. Remove from the oven and set aside.

5. Increase the oven temperature to 475°F (250°C).

6. Split the pizza dough into 2 or 4 pieces. Roll each piece out on a floured surface into a rough circle (about 10 inches/25 cm across for 2 large calzones, or 5 inches/13 cm for 4 mini calzones).

7. On half of each dough circle, place a pile of Buffalo cauliflower (about 1½ cups for large calzones, ¾ cup for mini calzones), leaving a 1-inch (2.5 cm) perimeter between the pile and the edge of the dough. Over the cauliflower, crumble

PREP TIME: 45 minutes (*not including time to prepare pizza dough or Cashew Blue Cheese*)

COOK TIME: 12 minutes

buffalo cauliflower

Olive oil spray

1 cup (250 ml) hot sauce

2 tablespoons tomato paste

1 tablespoon agave syrup

1½ tablespoons arrowroot powder or cornstarch

½ teaspoon salt

Black pepper to taste

1 cup (250 ml) non-dairy milk

1 cup (110 g) chickpea flour

½ teaspoon garlic powder

½ teaspoon smoked paprika

1 large head cauliflower, chopped into florets

calzones

½ batch Basic Pizza Dough (page 179)

Flour for rolling

½ batch Cashew Blue Cheese (page 46)

Water

Olive oil spray

about ¼ cup of the Cashew Blue Cheese for large calzones, 2 tablespoons for mini calzones. Brush a little water on the edge of the dough on the side closest to the fillings. Fold the empty half over the cauliflower so the edges meet, creating a half-circle. Fold the edges over to seal and prevent any filling from leaking out. Use a fork to crimp the edges. Lightly spray the tops with olive oil.

8. Gently transfer the calzones to the pizza stone or prepared baking sheet. Bake for 10 to 12 minutes, until the dough has risen and is firm and golden. Remove from the oven and serve immediately. Leftover Buffalo cauliflower can be chilled in an airtight container for 3 to 4 days or eaten while you're waiting for the pizza to come out of the oven.

||||||||||||||||||||||||||||||

VARIATIONS

▶ If you would like to make a regular pizza rather than calzones, reserve ¼ cup of the sauce when preparing the cauliflower. Roll out the pizza dough on a floured surface to your desired size, making sure the dough is at least ¼ inch (.5 cm) thick. Spread the reserved hot sauce on the dough, leaving a ½-inch (1 cm) crust around the perimeter. Crumble the Cashew Blue Cheese on top of the sauce and top the cheese with as much cauliflower as you can fit. Transfer to the pizza stone or a prepared pizza pan. Bake for 10 to 12 minutes, until the crust has risen and is lightly golden. Slice and serve hot.

▶ If Buffalo sauce is not your thing, try replacing the hot sauce or a portion of it with Barbecue Sauce (page 31).

MINI PIZZA-STUFFED MUSHROOMS

MAKES 12 MINI PIZZA MUSHROOMS

page 177

PREP TIME: 10 minutes *(not including time to prepare Macarella)*
COOK TIME: 15 minutes

W̲e̲ all have those moments when we want a homemade meal that is really good but doesn't require a ton of legwork. Pizza isn't what usually comes to mind (unless you use a premade crust), but what if, instead of buying a premade crust, you used mushrooms as your pizza base? Oddly, when paired with pizza sauce, cheese, and your favorite toppings, the mushroom itself will remind you of soft, chewy pizza dough. Best of all, they're healthy and take less than 30 minutes to get on the table. How's that for a no-fuss meal?

12 large cremini mushrooms or very small portobellos (each roughly 2 to 3 inches/5 to 8 cm in diameter)

Olive oil spray

3 tablespoons diced green bell pepper

3 tablespoons diced red onion

3 tablespoons sliced black olives

1 cup (250 ml) Pizza Sauce (page 184)

2 Macarella discs, sliced into thin medallions (page 49)

1. Preheat the oven to 400°F (200°C). Line a baking sheet with parchment paper or a silicone baking mat.

2. Remove the stems from the mushrooms. (They're great sautéed, roasted, or mixed into a stew or chili for added texture.) Use a teaspoon to gently scrape out the insides of each mushroom cap, creating a clean bowl. Lightly spray the top of each cap with olive oil and place them cap side down ("bowl" side up) on the prepared baking sheet.

3. In a bowl, mix the bell pepper, red onion, olives, and pizza sauce. Scoop the mixture into each mushroom, filling to the brim.

4. Bake for 8 to 10 minutes, until the mushrooms have softened slightly.

5. Top each mushroom with a Macarella medallion and return to the oven for 4 minutes. Broil for 1 minute, then remove. Serve hot.

VARIATIONS

▶ To use fresh, unfirm Macarella (page 49), prepare it through step 2 while the mushrooms are in the oven. Instead of molding the cheese in containers, top each mushroom with a spoonful of the warm cheese. For the remainder of the cheese, follow steps 3 and 4 in the Macarella recipe. Bake the mushrooms for 2 to 3 minutes, then broil for 1 minute.

▶ You could also try a different cheese. Tofu Chèvre (page 36) would be awfully nice!

▶ Mix up the "toppings" you mix with the pizza sauce. Try artichoke hearts, pepperoncini, jalapeños, Sunflower Sausage (page 26), or Tempeh Bacon (page 25).

▶ Try switching up the size of the mushrooms. You could do 4 large portobellos for more of a "personal" pizza or about 20 smaller creminis for delicious two-bite appetizers.

▶ If you're in a pinch, use store-bought vegan mozzarella shreds, such as Follow Your Heart Vegan Gourmet Shreds.

CAN'T I BE PESCATARIAN INSTEAD?

Seafood-Inspired Dishes That Will Reel You In

Being pescatarian is the step many people take when they want to be vegetarian or vegan but aren't down with giving up all animal flesh. It may seem like a less-harmful middle ground, but the seafood industry is destroying our oceans, and I hate to be a Debbie Downer, but it's pretty much why the seahorse is almost extinct. I urge you to research further—and while you're at it, try some of the replacements in this chapter. Chances are you won't miss seafood at all!

JACKFRUIT "TUNA" SALAD SANDWICH

~~~~~~

SERVES 4

If tuna salad sandwiches are totally your jam, then get ready for this new addition to your sandwich lineup. Jackfruit's shredded meat texture and super-absorbent nature make it a fantastic meat substitute (as you know if you've tried BBQ Jackfruit Fajitas, page 104, or Jackfruit Nacho Supreme, page 150). It also makes a great substitute for canned tuna! Mashed white beans, vegan mayonnaise, mustard, pickled relish, and "fishy"-tasting kelp granules help give this salad that taste you know and love.

1. Place the jackfruit in a colander and thoroughly rinse it. Use two forks or your fingers to tear it into shreds. Set aside.
2. In a large bowl, mash the beans with a fork or potato masher. Add the rest of the salad ingredients and mix well. Fold in the shredded jackfruit.
3. Generously spread some of the salad onto 1 slice of bread. Add your preferred sandwich fixings and top with another slice of bread. Repeat with remaining ingredients. Chill leftover salad in an airtight container up to 1 week.

||||||||||||||||||||||||||||

VARIATION

▶ To make a Jackfruit "Tuna" Melt, top the salad with some Sunflower Cheddar (page 42) or Macarella (page 49) and cook the sandwich in a greased frying pan, 3 to 4 minutes on each side, until golden and heated through.

PREP TIME: 15 minutes

salad

One 20-ounce (565 g) can jackfruit (packed in water or brine, not syrup), rinsed and drained

1½ cups (265 g) cooked great Northern white beans (see page 8) or one 15-ounce (425 g) can, rinsed and drained

1 teaspoon kelp granules

½ teaspoon dried tarragon

¼ cup (55 g) vegan mayonnaise

2 tablespoons pickled relish

1½ tablespoons Dijon mustard

Juice of 1 lemon

8 slices of bread (gluten-free if necessary)

Sandwich fixings (lettuce, tomato, avocado, etc.)

WILD MUSHROOM SUSHI

MAKES 3 ROLLS

Sushi is usually associated with fish and lots of it, but in actuality, sushi can be made with any number of ingredients as long as it includes cooked, vinegared rice. Lucky for us, rice is already vegan, so all we have to do is make our sushi with plants and we're golden! For this version, we get to stuff our nori rolls with assorted mushrooms sautéed in a miso-tamari sauce and slices of fresh avocado. I've replaced half of the rice with quinoa for some added protein, but using all rice would work just as well.

1. Heat the oil in a large frying pan over medium heat. In a small cup, mix the tamari and miso with a fork. Add all the mushrooms to the pan and toss to coat with the oil. Add the tamari mixture and stir to coat. Cook until the mushrooms have softened and reduced in size, about 8 minutes. Add salt and pepper. Remove from the heat and set aside to cool.

2. In a large bowl, mix the rice, quinoa, vinegar, mirin, and salt.

3. Wrap a bamboo sushi rolling mat (available at most cooking supply stores) in a large sheet of plastic wrap and lay out flat. Lay 1 sheet of nori, smooth side up, on top of the mat. The nori should be lying lengthwise from left to right (the longer dimension from left to right).

4. Fill a little bowl with water. Dip your fingers in the water and use them to spread about one third of the rice mixture onto the nori, leaving about ½ inch (1 cm) clear at the end of the nori farthest from you. (Keeping your fingers wet will help keep the rice from sticking to them.) It's okay if there are small bare patches.

5. About 2 inches (5 cm) from the edge closest to you, going from left to right, lay out a strip of avocado on the rice. Spread one third of the mushrooms in a strip on top of the avocado.

PREP TIME: 30 minutes (*not including time to cook rice and quinoa*)
COOK TIME: 10 minutes

1 teaspoon extra virgin olive oil

1 tablespoon tamari or soy sauce

½ teaspoon white miso

1½ cups (90 g) sliced shiitake mushrooms

1½ cups (90 g) sliced oyster mushrooms

1½ cups (85 g) bunapi mushrooms

Salt and black pepper to taste

1 cup (160 g) cooked brown rice (see page 9)

1 cup (160 g) cooked quinoa or additional cooked brown rice

1 tablespoon brown rice vinegar

1 teaspoon mirin

¼ teaspoon salt

3 rectangular nori sheets

Water

½ avocado, peeled, pitted, and sliced into thin strips

6. Wet the empty ½-inch of the nori farthest from you with a bit of water so that when you roll it over, the nori will stick. Using the rolling mat, roll the sushi tightly over the strip of ingredients, using your fingers to keep it packed in as much as possible. Use the mat to hold the roll firmly for a few seconds before unrolling the mat and transferring the roll to a cutting board.

7. Using a sharp knife (a dull knife will destroy the roll, trust me), slice the roll in half. Then slice each half into four pieces, making a total of eight pieces. Repeat with the remaining ingredients. Serve immediately.

TIP

Be patient. If you've never rolled sushi, your first few (or ten) rolls may not be the prettiest. It's okay. You'll get the hang of it.

ORANGE-MISO MUSHROOM SCALLOPS WITH ORANGES, FENNEL & FORBIDDEN RICE

SERVES 2

King oyster mushrooms have a very thick, dense, and spongelike stem. When you slice those stems into 1-inch pieces, they resemble scallops and, amazingly, cook very similarly and have the same kind of texture. Here, the mushroom "scallops" are braised in an orange-miso sauce and served with oranges and fennel over black forbidden rice for a truly elegant meal.

PREP TIME: 10 minutes (*not including time to cook the rice*)
COOK TIME: 10 minutes

4 large, thick-stemmed king oyster mushrooms, stems only (see tip)

2 tablespoons vegan butter, divided

Salt and black pepper to taste

3 tablespoons white wine

3 tablespoons orange juice

1 tablespoon agave syrup or Happy Bee Honey (page 34)

1½ teaspoons white miso

½ teaspoon dried rosemary, crushed between your fingers

1 navel orange, peeled and sliced into round cross-sections

1 blood orange, peeled and sliced into round cross-sections

1 small fennel bulb, halved and thinly sliced

2 cups (320 g) cooked forbidden rice (see page 9)

1. Trim the root ends from the mushroom stems and slice into ¾- to 1-inch-round (2.5 cm) "scallops." Rinse and pat dry.

2. Melt 1 tablespoon of the vegan butter in a large frying pan over medium heat. Add salt and pepper to the scallops and place them, cut side down, in the pan. Cook for about 1 minute, until slightly crisp and golden on the bottom, then flip them. Cook for 1 minute on the other side, then transfer to a plate.

3. Melt the remaining 1 tablespoon of butter in the same pan over medium heat. Add the wine, orange juice, agave syrup, miso, and rosemary; stir until combined. Add the oranges (reserving a few slices for garnish, if desired) and fennel and cook (gently moving the oranges only a couple times to prevent sticking) until the sauce has thickened, 3 to 4 minutes. Add the scallops and sauté until heated through, about 1 minute. Remove from the heat. Add more salt and pepper, if desired.

4. Divide the rice between two plates. Use a slotted spoon to scoop the oranges first, then fennel, then scallops onto the rice. Generously spoon the sauce over the scallops (using a nonslotted spoon). If you reserved a few orange slices, use them to garnish the dish. Serve immediately.

TIP

King oyster mushrooms are also known as king trumpet mushrooms. Only the stems are used in this recipe; the leftover caps can be mixed into other recipes that call for mushrooms, such as Wild Mushroom Sushi (page 198) or Beluga Lentil & Couscous Salad (page 114).

ARTICHOKE CRAB CAKES WITH SRIRACHA TARTAR SAUCE

SERVES 3 TO 4

Flaky, soft, briny. No, I'm not talking about crab; I'm talking about artichoke hearts, silly! Those three traits were the main reason I decided to use artichoke hearts as the base for recreating vegan crab cakes. Old Bay Seasoning brings that classic Chesapeake Bay flavor (always a great ingredient for seafood-inspired dishes), and vegan mayonnaise works as a binder so you don't need eggs. They're quickly pan-fried and served with a hot and tangy sriracha tartar sauce for a quick, unforgettable meal that will make you happy to leave the crabs under the sea.

1. In a small bowl, whisk together the Sriracha Tartar Sauce ingredients. Chill until ready to use.

2. Place the oyster crackers in a food processor and process into the consistency of coarse flour with small chunks. Set aside in a small bowl.

3. Place the artichoke hearts in a food processor and pulse 6 to 7 times, until broken up but still chunky. Transfer to a large bowl. Add the scallions, red bell pepper, corn kernels, Old Bay, kelp granules, garlic powder, dried parsley, mayonnaise, and salt and pepper. Stir in the oyster cracker "flour."

4. Use a ¼-cup (60 ml) measuring cup to scoop out the artichoke mixture. Using your hands, shape patties and place on a plate.

5. Set a large frying pan, preferably cast iron, over medium heat. Pour in enough oil to coat the bottom and heat for 2 to 3 minutes. Line a plate with paper towels.

6. Place 3 to 4 patties in the pan and cook for 3 to 4 minutes on each side, until crisp and browned all over. Place on the plate with more paper towels on top to absorb the excess oil. Repeat with the remaining patties, adding more oil as necessary, until all are cooked. Serve topped with the Sriracha Tartar Sauce and remaining scallions.

PREP TIME: 10 minutes
COOK TIME: 20 minutes

sriracha tartar sauce
½ cup (110 g) vegan mayonnaise

1 to 2 tablespoons sriracha

1 tablespoon juice from a jar of capers

1 tablespoon lemon juice

artichoke crab cakes
1 cup (53 g) oyster crackers or crushed saltine crackers

Two 15-ounce (425 g) cans artichoke hearts, rinsed and drained well

3 to 4 scallions, finely chopped, plus more for garnish

¼ cup (35 g) finely diced red bell pepper

¼ cup (35 g) corn kernels (fresh or defrosted if frozen)

2 teaspoons Old Bay Seasoning

½ teaspoon kelp granules, optional

½ teaspoon garlic powder

½ teaspoon dried parsley

¼ cup (55 g) vegan mayonnaise

Salt and black pepper to taste

Canola oil for frying

VARIATION

▶ If you do not wish to fry the fritters, preheat the oven to 400°F (200°C), line a baking sheet with parchment paper or a silicone baking mat, and lightly spray with olive oil. Spread the patties on the prepared sheet and lightly spray with olive oil. Bake for 20 to 25 minutes, until firm and golden, flipping once halfway through to ensure even cooking.

BAJA DELISH TACOS WITH MANGO SALSA

SERVES 2 TO 3

It's time to turn your kitchen into a little seaside taco shack—the kind where surfers can run up from the ocean, grab a taco, then get back to riding the waves. You'll practically feel the cool breeze blowing through your sun-bleached locks as you top these breaded chickpea fillets with fresh mango salsa. Plop yourself down to enjoy your light yet filling taco, and you'll find yourself transported to the sandy beach with hot volleyball players knocking the ball back and forth. Just as you swallow your last bite, you'll be ready to grab your board. Surf's up!

1. In a large bowl, mix the Mango Salsa ingredients. Chill until ready to use.

2. Line a 9 x 5-inch loaf pan with parchment paper. Set aside.

3. In a small bowl, whisk together the chickpea flour, kelp granules, Old Bay, onion powder, garlic powder, paprika, salt, dill, and pepper.

4. Bring the water to a boil, then whisk in the chickpea flour mixture and reduce the heat to medium-high. Continue to whisk for 3 to 4 minutes, until the mixture has the texture of a very thick, lumpy pudding. Whisk in the oil and remove from the heat. Pour into the prepared loaf pan and use a rubber spatula to spread it evenly. Refrigerate at least 2 to 3 hours or overnight.

5. When the mixture has chilled and hardened, remove from the refrigerator. Use the parchment paper to lift the block out of the pan. Slice the block widthwise into 6 strips (fillets).

6. Pour the non-dairy milk into one shallow bowl, the arrowroot powder into another, and the bread crumbs into another. Using one hand for the wet ingredients and one hand for the dry, dredge one chickpea fillet in the milk and then in the arrowroot powder. Tap off the excess arrowroot powder, then dredge the fillet in the milk again, and finally in the bread crumbs. When fully coated, set on a plate and repeat with the remaining fillets.

PREP TIME: 30 minutes
COOK TIME: 20 minutes
DOWN TIME: 2 to 3 hours

mango salsa

2 mangos, pitted, peeled, and diced small

1 red bell pepper, diced

½ cup (135 g) diced red onion

⅓ cup (15 g) chopped cilantro

2 tablespoons diced jalapeño

Juice of 1 lime

Salt to taste

chickpea fillets

1 cup (110 g) chickpea flour

½ teaspoon kelp granules

½ teaspoon Old Bay Seasoning

½ teaspoon onion powder

½ teaspoon garlic powder

½ teaspoon smoked paprika

½ teaspoon salt

¼ teaspoon dried dill

Several dashes of black pepper

2 cups (500 ml) water

2 teaspoons extra virgin olive oil

1 cup (250 ml) non-dairy milk

¾ cup (105 g) arrowroot powder

1 cup (180 g) gluten-free brown rice bread crumbs (see tip)

Olive oil spray

tacos

6 corn tortillas

1 cup (50 g) shredded cabbage

2 to 3 radishes, thinly sliced, optional

Sriracha Tartar Sauce (page 202), optional

7. Line a plate with paper towels. Heat a large frying pan, preferably cast iron, over medium heat for 3 to 4 minutes. Liberally spray the bottom of the pan with olive oil (or pour in just enough olive oil to very thinly coat the bottom and heat for 2 to 3 minutes). Place the fillets in the pan and cook for 3 to 4 minutes on each side, until crisp and golden brown all over. Transfer the fillets to the paper towels.

8. Respray the pan with olive oil, add 1 tortilla, and cook for 30 seconds on each side, until heated but still soft and pliable. Remove from the pan, place on a plate, and cover with a clean kitchen towel. Repeat with the remaining tortillas.

9. To assemble the tacos, sprinkle a couple pinches of shredded cabbage and radish slices (if using) into the middle of a heated tortilla. Top with a chickpea fillet and the Mango Salsa. Serve with Sriracha Tartar Sauce, if using.

IIIIIIIIIIIIIIIIIIIIIIIIIIII

VARIATION

▶ Switch out the chickpea fillets for Faux Fish (page 207).

TIP

Gluten-free brown rice bread crumbs make a perfect crust for these fillets. They can usually be found in the gluten-free section of your grocery store. Regular bread crumbs should work as well, but look for a variety with a finer crumb.

BEER-BATTERED FAUX FISH & CHIPS

SERVES 4

Me, before trying this recipe: "I don't *love* battered and fried foods so I'm not totally sure how much I'll like this dish." Me, after trying this recipe: "I wanna dip everything in this batter and fry it! And eat it! *Everything*!" It doesn't matter if you like or dislike fried fish, or even fried food in general: you are totally going to be a fan of this fried faux fish. Old Bay Seasoning and kelp granules give it a seafoody taste, and when you squeeze lemon juice over the final product and dip it into a bit of malt vinegar, you'll feel like you're hanging out at a seaside British pub. Pass me a pint!

PREP TIME: 15 minutes
COOK TIME: 30 minutes
DOWNTIME: 60 minutes

faux fish

1 cup (130 g) unbleached all-purpose flour

½ cup (65 g) corn flour

½ cup (70 g) cornmeal (fine to medium grind)

2 teaspoons baking powder

3 teaspoons Old Bay Seasoning, divided

1 teaspoon salt, divided

½ teaspoon onion powder

½ teaspoon garlic powder

2 cups (500 ml) pale amber vegan beer, plus additional if needed

Two 14-ounce (490 g) blocks extra-firm tofu, pressed for 30 minutes

¼ cup (60 ml) lemon juice

1 teaspoon dried dill

1 teaspoon kelp granules

Canola oil, for frying

1 cup (140 g) cornstarch or arrowroot powder

chips

3 to 4 large red potatoes, cut into 8 wedges each

Olive oil spray

Salt and black pepper to taste

Lemon wedges

Malt vinegar, optional

Sriracha Tartar Sauce (page 202), optional

1. In a large bowl, whisk together the flour, corn flour, cornmeal, baking powder, 1 teaspoon of the Old Bay, ½ teaspoon of the salt, and the onion and garlic powder. Slowly mix in the beer until the consistency is slightly thinner than pancake batter. If needed, add beer by the tablespoon to thin it. Refrigerate for 1 hour.

2. Turn one block of tofu on its side and slice it in half, creating 2 sheets half as thick as the original block but equal in length and width. Slice those 2 sheets in half lengthwise, creating 4 long strips. Repeat with the other block of tofu.

3. In a 9 x 13-inch glass baking dish, mix the lemon juice, dill, kelp granules, the remaining 2 teaspoons Old Bay, and the remaining ½ teaspoon salt. Place the tofu strips in the baking dish to soak up some of the marinade, then flip them over so the other side can soak. Refrigerate for 30 to 60 minutes, until the beer batter is ready.

4. Meanwhile, to make the chips, preheat the oven to 400°F (200°C) and raise one oven rack to the highest position. Line a baking sheet with parchment paper or a silicone baking mat. Spread the potato wedges on the sheet and generously spray with olive oil. Add salt and pepper and toss to coat. Bake for 30 minutes, flipping once halfway through to ensure even cooking. Remove and turn off the oven heat. If the chips finish before the faux fish, cover with a kitchen towel and return them to the oven, heat off.

{ RECIPE CONTINUES }

5. Line a plate with paper towels. Set a large shallow saucepan over medium heat. Fill the bottom of the pan with about 3 inches (7.5 cm) of oil and heat until it begins to shimmer.

6. While the oil is heating, pour the cornstarch into a shallow bowl. Using one hand, dredge 2 strips of tofu through the cornstarch and use your fingers to rub off any excess powder. Drop the strips in the beer batter and, with your other hand, turn until completely covered. Use tongs to gently transfer the strips, one at a time, to the frying pan. Cook both strips for about 1 minute on each side, until perfectly crisp and golden. Use the tongs to transfer them to the paper towels to soak up excess oil. Repeat with the remaining tofu.

7. Serve the faux fish warm with the baked chips, lemon wedges (to squeeze over the faux fish), vinegar (if using), and Sriracha Tartar Sauce (if using).

MY FRIENDS WON'T WANT TO COME OVER FOR DINNER.

Fancy Dinner Party Recipes Sure to Impress

A big fear when becoming vegan is of losing one's social life. Choosing to live a compassionate lifestyle may upset some of your friends because they feel insecure, had a not-so-appetizing experience with vegan food in the past, or don't understand the diet. The key is to show them that you and your taste buds are still the same—and the best way is by cooking for them, fancy dinner-party style. Here are some dishes guaranteed to amaze even your foodiest of pals.

CARROT CASHEW PÂTÉ

MAKES 1½ CUPS

An appetizer can set the tone for an entire dinner party. If it's terrible, your guests will look forward to the rest of the meal with dread. They'll pick at their food and mutter, "That explains it" when you tell them it's vegan. But serve an appetizer that is a guaranteed hit, like this pâté, and your guests will excitedly ask for the recipe. When you tell them it's vegan you'll get the coveted response, "Whaaaaaaaaat? This is *vegan*? No way!" They'll be pumped for dinner, and over dessert they'll say they might give veganism a try . . . if you promise to teach them how to cook.

PREP TIME: 10 minutes

DOWN TIME: 2 hours (partially while cashews soak)

1 cup (160 g) raw cashews, soaked in water for at least 1 hour, *water discarded*

1 cup (110 g) grated carrot

2 tablespoons liquid aminos

1 teaspoon lemon juice

½ teaspoon white miso

½ teaspoon thyme

½ teaspoon paprika

Salt and black pepper to taste

Bread, pita, crackers, or veggies for dipping

1. In a food processor, combine the cashews and carrot and process for about 1 minute. Add the liquid aminos, lemon juice, miso, thyme, paprika, salt, and pepper; process until smooth, pausing to scrape the sides as necessary.

2. Chill 1 hour prior to serving to allow the flavors to fully marry. Serve with your preferred dippers.

GREEK BRUSCHETTA WITH HEART OF PALM TAPENADE & TOFU FETA

It's a warm summer evening and a few of your friends have come over with a bottle of crisp white wine to dine al fresco. You scan your refrigerator, notice you have some leftover Tofu Feta (page 44), and know exactly what you're going to serve. Your friends talk and laugh with you in the kitchen while you whip up a fragrant and delectable heart of palm tapenade and slice some bread. Your friends will love the feta paired with the tapenade, and you'll just smile, sip your wine, and give yourself a little mental pat on the back.

PREP TIME: **10 minutes** (not including preparing Tofu Feta)

About 20 black olives, pitted and rinsed

About 20 green olives, pitted and rinsed

4 to 5 heart of palm spears

3 tablespoons capers

3 tablespoons lemon juice

3 to 4 tablespoons chopped fresh parsley

Salt to taste

⅓ batch Tofu Feta (page 44)

1 sourdough baguette, thinly sliced

1. Combine the black olives, green olives, hearts of palm, capers, lemon juice, parsley, and salt in a food processor and pulse until all are fairly uniform in size and no piece is larger than a lentil. Chill in an airtight container until ready to use. It will keep for 4 to 5 days.

2. Scoop 1 to 2 tablespoons of tapenade onto each slice of bread and sprinkle Tofu Feta on top. Serve immediately.

||||||||||||||||||||||||

VARIATION

▶ To make this dish gluten-free, serve with gluten-free bread or crackers.

TOFU & AVOCADO TARTARE

SERVES 4

The term *tartare* is generally reserved for finely chopped raw meat or fish, often served with tartar sauce. In my pre-vegetarian days I refused to try it, so it wasn't until I tasted a few variations of vegan tartares that I began to see what all the fuss was about. This recipe is inspired by a tofu and avocado tartare my husband and I had in a restaurant in Barcelona. It's perfect to serve to your guests in place of an ordinary salad, and I'll bet that after they taste a vegan tartare, there'll be no going back to the original.

1. Combine the lemon juice, beet juice, rice vinegar, miso, and nutritional yeast in a shallow baking dish.

2. Place the tofu in a food processor and pulse just a few times, until all the pieces are about the size of the tip of your pinkie finger (but not pureed). Transfer the tofu to the baking dish with the marinade. Toss to combine. Cover and chill at least 2 to 3 hours; overnight is even better.

3. About 30 minutes before you assemble the tartare, combine the avocados and lime juice in a medium bowl and gently mash together. You want it to be like a very chunky guacamole. Add salt, cover, and chill about 30 minutes.

4. Lightly spray the inside of a 3- to 3½-inch biscuit cutter with olive oil.

5. Remove the tofu from the refrigerator and taste. Add salt if desired. Transfer to a fine-mesh sieve and use the back of a large spoon to press on the tofu, draining as much liquid as possible. When you can't get any more liquid to release, set the sieve over a bowl.

6. Arrange the cucumber slices in an overlapping circle on the center of each serving plate. Make the circle large enough so the inside of the ring can be tucked underneath the tartare but the slices will remain mostly visible and uncovered. Place the biscuit cutter in the center of the ring. Scoop one-quarter of the avocado mixture into the bottom of the form; use your fingers to press into an even layer. Fill the remainder of the

PREP TIME: 30 minutes
DOWN TIME: 2 to 3 hours or overnight

¼ cup (60 ml) fresh lemon juice

3 tablespoons beet juice

2 tablespoons rice vinegar

1 tablespoon white miso

2 teaspoons nutritional yeast

One 14-ounce (395 g) block extra-firm tofu

2 avocados, pitted and peeled

2 tablespoons fresh lime juice

Salt to taste

Olive oil spray

1 cucumber, very thinly sliced (use a mandoline if possible)

Balsamic vinegar, for drizzling

Black sesame seeds or regular sesame seeds

Microgreens

biscuit cutter with the tofu and use your fingers to gently pack it in and make a flat top. Very gently lift the biscuit cutter straight up to reveal a little "tower" of tartare. Wipe down the biscuit cutter, respray with olive oil, and repeat with the remaining avocado and tofu.

7. To finish, drizzle the balsamic vinegar on the plate around the perimeter of the cucumbers. Sprinkle sesame seeds over the top and place a couple pieces of microgreens on the tartare. Serve immediately.

PORTOBELLO CARPACCIO

SERVES 4

Some words just sound fancier than others. When you say them, no matter what they mean, people think you're classy. Words like *canapé*, *plethora*, and *Sacha Baron Cohen*. *Carpaccio* is also one of these words, even though all it means is to marinate and very thinly slice something and lay it on a plate. In the past, carpaccio was strictly reserved for steak, but times have changed. Many fruits or vegetables could take the place of steak in this recipe, but portobello mushrooms are my favorite. It's extremely easy to prepare and looks absolutely stunning when plated.

PREP TIME: 30 minutes
COOK TIME: 8 minutes

- 3 tablespoons fresh lemon juice, divided
- 3 tablespoons extra virgin olive oil, divided
- ½ tablespoon red wine vinegar
- ½ tablespoon liquid aminos (or tamari or soy sauce)
- ½ teaspoon dried oregano
- ½ teaspoon dried basil
- ½ teaspoon liquid smoke
- 4 medium/large portobello mushrooms, destemmed and gills removed
- 3 tablespoons diced roasted red pepper
- 1 tablespoon capers
- 1½ cups (40 g) microgreens
- Crusty olive loaf or other bread, for serving

1. Preheat the oven to 400°F (200°C). Line a baking sheet with parchment paper or a silicone baking mat.
2. Mix 1 tablespoon of the lemon juice, 1 tablespoon of the oil, and the vinegar, liquid aminos, oregano, basil, and liquid smoke in a small bowl.
3. Use a pastry brush to brush both sides of each mushroom with the sauce. Place them on the baking sheet, underside up, to rest for 10 minutes. Reserve the extra sauce.
4. After 10 minutes, place the baking sheet in the oven and roast for 4 minutes. Flip the mushrooms, brush the tops with the remaining sauce, and roast for 4 minutes. Remove and allow to cool for about 10 minutes.
5. When the mushrooms have cooled, use a serrated knife to very thinly slice them on a bias (diagonally). If not serving right away, chill in an airtight container until ready to serve.
6. Arrange the slices in an overlapping pattern on a platter or individual serving plates. Sprinkle the roasted red pepper and capers over the mushrooms and top with the microgreens. Drizzle with the remaining 2 tablespoons lemon juice and 2 tablespoons oil; add salt. Serve immediately with the bread.

GNOCCHI ALLA VODKA

SERVES 4 TO 6

page 209

PREP TIME: 30 minutes
COOK TIME: 30 minutes
DOWN TIME: 60 minutes (*while cashews soak and potatoes bake*)

You've been planning this little dinner party for weeks. You want to prepare something that screams "casual elegance." Something that lets you tell your friends, "I made it from scratch," and they'll tell everyone you're "like, basically the vegan Giada De Laurentiis—and just as gorgeous." So you decide to make this gnocchi from scratch (which is much easier than it sounds) and serve it with a sauce so simple you have time to throw together a nice salad, make some garlic bread, and perhaps even brush your hair. Now get your beautiful self in the kitchen!

gnocchi

4 russet potatoes or other potatoes

Water

Salt to taste

1 to 3 cups (130 to 390 g) whole wheat flour (or bread flour, if not using russet potatoes)

vodka sauce

¾ cup (120 g) raw cashews, soaked in water for at least 1 hour, *water reserved*

1 tablespoon vegan butter

2 shallots, diced

½ to ¾ cup (125 to 205 ml) vodka, to taste (see variations)

One 15-ounce (445 ml) can unsalted tomato sauce

½ cup (120 g) tomato paste

1 teaspoon red pepper flakes, plus more for seasoning

Salt and black pepper to taste

to make the gnocchi

1. Preheat the oven to 400°F (200°C). Place the potatoes on a baking sheet and bake for 1 hour, or until easily pierced with a fork. Remove from the oven and slice in half lengthwise.

2. Fill an 8-quart (or larger) pot almost to the top with water and bring to a boil. Add a bit of salt to the water.

3. When the potatoes are cool enough to touch (but not completely cool—you want them to be as warm as possible), peel the skins and place the insides in a large bowl.

4. Ideally, run the potatoes through a ricer. Alternatively, mash them (until you think your arm will fall off and the potatoes are very smooth) or puree in a food processor. Add salt.

5. Add the flour to the potatoes ¼ cup at a time, using your hands to work the flour in with each addition. You want to use as little flour as possible to achieve a perfect ball of dough. When you think you have the right consistency, tear off a tiny piece, roll it into a ball, and drop it into the boiling water. If it rises to the top without falling apart, that's good, but if it tastes gummy, add flour to the dough by the tablespoon until it is firmer. If the ball falls apart when you drop it in, add water to the dough by the teaspoon.

6. Turn the burner heat to low while you form the gnocchi; it will take a little while.

7. Turn the dough out onto a floured surface. Tear off a piece and roll into a long rope about ¾ inch (2 cm) in diameter.

Cut the rope in half, then, with the two shorter ropes next to each other, slice them into ½-inch (1 cm) "pillows." Continue with the rest of the dough.

8. Use a fork to shape the gnocchi. Use your thumb to roll each gnocchi "pillow" down to the end. You will get ridges on one side and a "dimple" on the other side that holds whatever sauce you cook it in. Repeat until the entire ball of dough has been rolled into gnocchi.

9. Turn the water back up to a boil. Line two baking sheets with parchment paper.

10. In batches of 10 to 15, drop the gnocchi into the boiling water. They will dance around for a while; when they rise to the top and stay there for a couple of seconds, they are done. Don't leave them at the top of the water for more than a few seconds. Use a slotted spoon to transfer them to the lined baking sheets, making sure none are touching. You may use them right away or freeze for later use (see tips).

to make the vodka sauce

1. In a food processor or blender, combine the cashews and ¾ cup (205 ml) reserved soaking water; process until completely smooth. Set aside.

2. Melt the vegan butter in a large frying pan over medium heat. Add the shallots and sauté until they become slightly translucent. Add the vodka, tomato sauce, and tomato paste. Bring to a boil, then reduce the heat and simmer for 15 to 20 minutes, until the sauce has reduced by one-quarter.

3. Add the cashew mixture and simmer for 3 to 4 minutes, until heated through. Add the red pepper flakes, salt, and pepper. Add the fresh or defrosted (see tips) gnocchi and simmer until the gnocchi is heated through. Serve immediately. Perhaps you could even try topping it with some Pecan Parmesan (page 38)!

TIPS

- To freeze, let the gnocchi cool, then place the baking sheet(s) in the freezer. When frozen, transfer them to an airtight container and freeze until ready to use. They will keep in the freezer for 1 to 2 months. Defrost in the refrigerator 8 hours prior to using.

- If you are in a time crunch, feel free to use store-bought gnocchi. No judging here. Just be sure to read the ingredients because many brands contain egg.

|||||||||||||||||||||||||||||||||

VARIATIONS

▶ Add a little protein by adding 1½ cups cooked chickpeas or white beans (see page 8) or one 15-ounce (425 g) can, rinsed and drained, to the sauce along with the gnocchi.

▶ Is vodka not your thing? Replace it with a vegan white wine, nix it altogether, or try the Pan-Fried Gnocchi & Acorn Squash with Hazelnut-Sage Pesto (page 249).

SALISBURY SEITAN PHYLLO POUCHES WITH ROSEMARY MASHED POTATOES

Do you have friends who are more the meat and potatoes type? I know I do. In fact, before going vegetarian and later vegan, my husband loved a meal of steak and potatoes. When I served him this meal, his first words were, "This is the coolest thing I've ever seen food do!" He may have temporarily forgot that the food didn't make itself into this fabulous dinner, and that, in fact, there was a human working in the kitchen. The point, though, is that this is *the* recipe to serve to your meat and potatoes friends to show them that being vegan isn't a sacrifice.

1. Whisk together 1 cup of the broth with the arrowroot powder, then mix with the remaining 2 cups of broth. Set aside.

2. To make the gravy, heat the oil in a large shallow saucepan over medium heat. Add the onion and garlic and sauté until the onion is translucent. Add the sage, thyme, paprika, pepper, liquid aminos, mustard, and broth mixture. Bring to a boil, then reduce the heat and simmer for about 15 minutes. Add the nutritional yeast, lemon juice, and salt.

3. Pour half the gravy into a bowl, cover to keep warm, and set aside. Add the sliced seitan to the pan and simmer for 5 to 10 minutes, until the seitan is heated through. Remove from the heat and cover the pan to keep it warm.

4. Preheat the oven to 350°F (175°C). Line a baking sheet with parchment paper or a silicone baking mat.

5. Roll out the phyllo dough sheets. Slice them in half widthwise to make two 6½ x 9-inch rectangular stacks. Combine the two stacks and place a damp towel over the stack so they do not dry out. Lay out 1 sheet of phyllo dough and spray with olive oil. Lay out another sheet on top of that sheet and spray with olive oil. Repeat until you have a stack of 4 oiled sheets. Scoop about ⅔ cup (120 to 130 g) of the seitan mixture into the middle of the stack. Gather the corners and open edges of the phyllo dough and twist into a closed pouch. If you like, tie

{ RECIPE CONTINUES }

PREP TIME: 30 minutes (*not including time to prepare Homemade Seitan*)
COOK TIME: 30 minutes

gravy

- **3 cups (750 ml) vegetable broth, divided, plus extra if needed**
- **3 tablespoons arrowroot powder or cornstarch**
- **2 tablespoons extra virgin olive oil**
- **1 small yellow onion, diced**
- **2 garlic cloves, minced**
- **½ teaspoon dried sage**
- **½ teaspoon dried thyme**
- **¼ teaspoon paprika**
- **⅛ teaspoon black pepper**
- **2 tablespoons liquid aminos**
- **½ teaspoon Dijon mustard**
- **2 tablespoons nutritional yeast**
- **1 tablespoon lemon juice**
- **Salt to taste**

pouches

- **1 batch Homemade Seitan (page 28) or store-bought, very thinly sliced**
- **Twelve 13 x 18-inch sheets vegan phyllo dough (e.g., Fillo Factory brand)**
- **Olive oil spray**

mashed potatoes

- **4 Yukon gold potatoes (peeled or unpeeled—your preference), cut in half, steamed, and kept warm in a covered pot**
- **¼ cup (60 ml) non-dairy milk, plus additional to taste**
- **1 tablespoon extra virgin olive oil**
- **1 teaspoon dried rosemary**
- **Salt to taste**

the pouch with a little piece of kitchen twine. Repeat with the remaining phyllo sheets and seitan mixture until you have 6 pouches.

6. Place the pouches on the prepared baking sheet and spray with olive oil. Bake for 30 minutes, or until the pouches are golden.

7. While the pouches are in the oven, place the steamed potatoes in a large bowl and use a potato masher to mash them until smooth. Add the oil and non-dairy milk; stir until combined. Add milk by the tablespoon if it's not creamy enough for your taste. Add the rosemary and salt. Cover and keep warm until ready to use.

8. While the pouches are in the oven, pour the remaining gravy into the original pan and cook over medium-low heat until heated through. If it thickens too much, add water or broth by the tablespoon until it thins out to your liking. Keep warm.

9. When the pouches are done, remove from the oven. If you used kitchen twine to tie the pouches, remove it. Spread about ¼ cup of the remaining gravy on each plate. Top with ½ cup of mashed potatoes, then a seitan pouch. Serve immediately.

TIP

If you want to prepare part of the meal ahead of time, the gravy and the seitan mixture can be made a day in advance and chilled in an airtight container. Lightly reheat the seitan mixture before making the pouches. It's best to prepare the pouches right before serving to prevent sogginess.

NO WAY. I'M ITALIAN! (OR SOUTHERN/ GERMAN/MEXICAN/ FRENCH!)

Dishes Inspired by Not-So-Vegan Cuisines

One excuse I hear a lot is heritage or geographical location. Are you telling me that you don't eat plants in Louisiana? Or that because you're from Spain, you must eat meat? Peer pressure, especially from your family, can make eating a certain way feel mandatory, but if you examine your culture's diet, you're sure to find plant-based options or recipes that are easily veganized. Try the recipes in this chapter and get creative with your own cuisine. Regardless of where you come from, you can go vegan.

ROASTED CORN, GREEN CHILE & TOFU CHÈVRE QUESADILLAS WITH AVOCADO CREMA

SERVES 2

Beans, rice, tortillas, salsa, guacamole—the list of vegan Mexican food options goes on and on! It is very easy to avoid meat in Mexican dishes; many times all you have to do is ask for no *queso* (though it's also good to make sure the beans and rice were not cooked in lard or animal broth). This recipe takes one of my favorite Mexican food staples (the quesadilla), fills it with Tofu Chèvre (page 36), roasted corn, and green chiles, and tops it with a quick and easy avocado-cashew crema. It's sure to satisfy your Mexican food cravings!

1. Preheat the oven to 400°F (200°C).
2. Combine the avocado crema ingredients in a food processor and process until smooth. Chill until ready to use.
3. Line a baking sheet with parchment paper and spread the corn on it. Lightly spray with olive oil, sprinkle with the paprika, salt, and pepper, and toss to fully coat. Roast for 10 minutes, flipping once halfway through. Remove from the oven.
4. Lay out 1 tortilla and spread half the tofu chèvre on one half. Top with half the roasted corn and half the green chiles. Fold the bare half of the tortilla over the fillings and lightly press down to seal. Repeat with the remaining ingredients.
5. Heat a large frying pan over medium heat. Lightly spray the pan with olive oil. Place the quesadillas in the pan and lightly spray the tops with olive oil. Cook for 2 to 3 minutes on each side, until golden and heated through. Slice each quesadilla into four quarters and serve immediately, topped with the Avocado Crema.

PREP TIME: 20 minutes (*not including time to prepare Tofu Chèvre*)
COOK TIME: 5 minutes
DOWN TIME: 60 minutes (*while cashews soak*)

avocado crema

½ cup (80 g) raw cashews, soaked in water for at least 1 hour, *water reserved*

¼ cup (60 ml) reserved soaking water

1 small avocado, pitted and peeled

1 garlic clove

2 tablespoons lime juice

1 teaspoon nutritional yeast

½ teaspoon smoked paprika

Dash of cayenne pepper

Salt and black pepper to taste

quesadillas

1 cup (140 g) corn kernels (fresh or defrosted if frozen)

Olive oil spray

A few dashes of smoked paprika

Salt and black pepper to taste

2 large flour tortillas (gluten-free if necessary)

½ batch Tofu Chèvre (page 36)

2 to 3 tablespoons diced canned green chiles

CAULIFLOWER PICCATA

SERVES 2 TO 4

PREP TIME: 5 minutes
COOK TIME: 35 minutes

Italian cuisine is one of the easiest to veganize. It's already rich in vegetables, fruits, beans, grains, pasta, and bread. Butter is not readily used in Italy, because olive oil is the preferred cooking fat. You'll find that the only things you need to do are remove the cheese and replace the meat. Classic steak or chicken piccata can be made more compassionate by switching out the meat for cauliflower steaks. Roasting cross sections from a head of cauliflower gives you a chewy, meaty alternative that readily absorbs the lemony piccata sauce. Served over orzo or rice, it's *molto bene!*

2 large heads of cauliflower, leaves removed

Olive oil spray

Salt and black pepper to taste

1 tablespoon vegan butter

3 large shallots, finely diced

⅓ cup (80 ml) vegetable broth

2 teaspoons arrowroot powder

⅓ cup (80 ml) white wine

¼ cup (60 ml) lemon juice

¼ cup (50 g) capers

1 teaspoon agave syrup

6 to 8 lemon slices with rind, optional

1. Preheat the oven to 400°F (200°C). Line a baking sheet with parchment paper or a silicone baking mat.
2. Slice the cauliflower heads in half vertically. From each of those halves, slice parallel to the original cut to form two ¾- to 1-inch-thick (2 cm) steaks. If the cauliflowers are small, make just 1 steak from each half and reserve the remaining florets.
3. Lay the cauliflower steaks and remaining florets on the prepared baking sheet. Spray with olive oil on both sides. Sprinkle with salt and pepper. Roast for 20 to 25 minutes, flipping once halfway through to ensure even cooking. Remove from the oven and set aside.
4. Melt the vegan butter in a large frying pan over medium heat. Add the shallots and cook until they start to become translucent. In a cup, use a fork to whisk together the broth and arrowroot powder. Add that mixture and the wine to the pan. Reduce the heat to medium-low and simmer for about 5 minutes. Mix in the lemon juice, capers, and agave syrup.
5. Add the cauliflower steaks and spoon the sauce over them. Cook for 2 to 3 minutes, until heated through. Serve garnished with lemon slices, if using.

PRETZEL DUMPLINGS WITH MUSHROOM-SAUERKRAUT GRAVY

SERVES 4 TO 5 (MAKES 10 TO 12 DUMPLINGS)

On a flight aboard a German airline, my husband and I were accidentally served non-vegan pretzel dumplings in a creamy mushroom gravy. We were tantalized by the dish until a stewardess took it away. For months and months, I dreamed of re-creating that dish we were teased with. This vegan version is even *more* appetizing than the original, made with two of everyone's favorite German vegan foods: sauerkraut and soft pretzels. Soft pretzels are almost always vegan (though some may use butter or an egg wash to keep the salt on or be sweetened with honey, so it's good to check). They make for a hearty, flavorful dumpling, while sauerkraut makes this mushroom gravy very robust.

1. Place the pretzel pieces in a large bowl. Add the warm non-dairy milk to the bowl and stir until all the pieces are submerged. Cover and let sit for 30 minutes.

2. After 30 minutes, use a potato masher to mash the pretzel pieces for a couple minutes, until a little mushier, with chunks still remaining. Add the shallots, bread crumbs, flour, garlic powder, parsley, salt, and pepper.

3. While the pretzel pieces are soaking, start the gravy. In a medium bowl or large measuring cup, whisk together 2 cups of the broth with the arrowroot powder. Set aside.

4. Heat the oil in a large pot or saucepan over medium heat. Add the onion and garlic and sauté until the onion is just starting to become translucent. Add the mushrooms and cook until tender, stirring occasionally. Add the broth mixture and the remaining 2 cups of broth. Stir in the sauerkraut, sage, thyme, and pepper.

5. Bring to a boil, then quickly reduce the heat and simmer for 10 minutes, stirring occasionally, until slightly thickened and reduced. Add the nutritional yeast, taste, and add salt if necessary.

PREP TIME: 20 minutes
COOK TIME: 35 minutes
DOWN TIME: 30 minutes

dumplings

4 medium soft pretzels, chopped into ½-inch (1 cm) chunks (see tips)

1¾ cups (430 ml) warm non-dairy milk (see tips)

¼ cup (30 g) chopped shallots

6 tablespoons (60 g) bread crumbs

5 tablespoons (55 g) whole wheat flour

¼ teaspoon garlic powder

¼ cup (10 g) chopped fresh parsley

Salt and black pepper to taste

gravy

4 cups (1,000 ml) vegetable broth, divided

3 tablespoons arrowroot powder

1 teaspoon extra virgin olive oil

½ medium yellow onion, diced

1 garlic clove, minced

8 ounces (225 g) sliced button or cremini mushrooms

½ cup to ¾ cup (130 to 195 g) sauerkraut (depending on preference), optional

1 teaspoon dried sage

1 teaspoon dried thyme

⅛ teaspoon black pepper

2 tablespoons nutritional yeast

Salt to taste

6. Measure out a scoop of the mixture (using a ⅓-cup/80 ml scoop for smaller dumplings or a ½-cup/120 ml scoop for larger dumplings). Gently shape into a ball and place into the gravy. Repeat with the remaining dumpling mixture. It is okay if the dumplings are close or barely touching, but try to space them evenly. Simmer (not boil!) for 15 minutes. Gently flip over the dumplings and simmer for 5 more minutes. Use a slotted spoon to scoop out the dumplings; serve them topped with the gravy. Leftovers can be chilled in an airtight container 1 to 2 days.

TIPS

- I use Kim & Scott's Gourmet Pretzels in Traditional Bavarian, a vegan brand of frozen soft pretzels available at a variety of stores (see www.kimandscotts.com for details). Bake them and let them sit out to cool a few hours before making the dumplings.

- If you purchase pretzels from a bakery, do so a day or two prior to making the dumplings so they can get a little stale, and opt for unsalted if possible. Otherwise, brush most of the salt off before tearing them into pieces.

- To warm the non-dairy milk, microwave for about 1 minute or warm on the stovetop over medium heat for a couple minutes. It should be warm but not too warm to comfortably touch.

ASPARAGUS QUICHE

SERVES 6 TO 8

page 223

Meat, cheese, butter, and eggs all play a large role in French dishes, but that doesn't mean they're impossible to veganize! Take this quiche, for example. The classic French quiche is easily made vegan: use store-bought puff pastry (e.g., Pepperidge Farm, which is vegan and available in the freezer section of most grocery stores) for the crust and create an egglike filling using a combination of tofu and chickpea flour. It's a perfect meal for any time of the day. Serve with a small salad and follow with a tiny cup of *café*, and you'll feel like you're in Paris in the springtime.

PREP TIME: 20 minutes
COOK TIME: 25 minutes

Olive oil spray

1 sheet vegan puff pastry, defrosted according to box directions

½ bundle asparagus (8 to 12 spears), bottoms trimmed

1 teaspoon extra virgin olive oil

1 leek (white part only), halved lengthwise and sliced

2 teaspoons chopped fresh thyme

½ cup (50 g) sliced sun-dried tomatoes (if hard, rehydrated in water until softened)

Half of a 14-ounce block (about 200 g) extra-firm tofu

1 cup (250 ml) non-dairy milk

¾ cup (85 g) chickpea flour

¼ cup (20 g) nutritional yeast

1 tablespoon fresh lemon juice

1 teaspoon black salt (kala namak) or regular salt

1 teaspoon garlic powder

¾ teaspoon mustard powder

½ teaspoon onion powder

¼ teaspoon turmeric

¼ teaspoon black pepper

1. Preheat the oven to 400°F (200°C). Lightly spray a 10-inch tart pan (with a removable base) with olive oil.

2. If the puff pastry sheet is too small to fill the tart pan, roll it out on a floured surface. Press it into the pan. Let ½ inch (1 cm) hang over the edge; trim the rest.

3. Chop the asparagus in half and set aside the top halves (with the tips). Chop the bottom halves into 1-inch (2.5 cm) segments.

4. Heat the oil in a large frying pan over medium heat. Add the leek and cook for about 2 minutes. Add the asparagus and thyme and cook until softened, about 5 minutes. Add the sun-dried tomatoes and remove from the heat. Transfer to a large bowl.

5. Gently squeeze the tofu to release extra water. In a food processor, combine the tofu, non-dairy milk, chickpea flour, nutritional yeast, lemon juice, salt, garlic powder, mustard powder, onion powder, turmeric, and pepper. Process until smooth. Pour into the bowl with the cooked vegetables and mix until fully combined. Transfer to the prepared puff pastry crust. Use a rubber spatula to spread it. Arrange the top halves of the asparagus on top of the quiche. Use the rubber spatula to gently press them in so they are still visible but not resting on top of the quiche.

6. Bake for 25 to 30 minutes, until the quiche is set and golden on the top and a toothpick inserted into the center comes out mostly clean. Remove from the oven and cool in the pan for 10 minutes. Remove the tart from the pan and slice, or slice and serve straight from the pan. Leftovers can be covered with plastic wrap and chilled 2 to 3 days.

||||||||||||||||||||||||||||

VARIATION

▶ Asparagus not in season? Don't like that vegetable? Use whatever fresh veggies you have on hand. Sliced mushrooms, diced broccoli and bell peppers, and greens like spinach or chard are great in quiches.

SOUTHERN BISCUITS WITH SAUSAGE & GRAVY

SERVES 4

My family has roots in Ohio and Virginia, and my grandpa is a country boy through and through. Whenever we'd go out for breakfast to his favorite diner, he would always order a plate of biscuits 'n' gravy—the epitome of country food. I would watch him devour his fluffy biscuits overflowing with creamy white gravy and bits of sausage scattered here and there. This vegan version reminds me of him every time I make it. Puffy, buttery biscuits loaded with vegan Sunflower Sausage (page 26) and tons of rich, velvety white gravy. I think this dish would do my ol' country grandpa proud.

PREP TIME: 35 minutes *(not including time to prepare Sunflower Sausage)*
COOK TIME: 25 minutes

biscuits

- ¾ cup (180 ml) non-dairy milk
- ¼ cup (60 ml) non-dairy creamer (or increase the non-dairy milk to 1 cup/250 ml)
- 1 tablespoon apple cider vinegar
- 2 cups (260 g) unbleached all-purpose flour
- 1 tablespoon baking powder
- 1 teaspoon baking soda
- 1 teaspoon salt
- ⅓ cup (70 g) vegan butter, kept very cold (see tip)

gravy

- 2 tablespoons extra virgin olive oil
- ½ cup (135 g) diced yellow onion
- 2 garlic cloves, minced
- ¼ cup (30 g) unbleached all-purpose flour
- 3 cups (750 ml) non-dairy milk, plus additional if needed
- ½ teaspoon dried sage
- ½ teaspoon dried thyme
- ⅛ teaspoon black pepper
- A few dashes of nutmeg
- 1 tablespoon nutritional yeast, optional
- Salt to taste

- 1 tablespoon non-dairy milk
- 1 tablespoon vegan butter, melted
- 1 batch Sunflower Sausage crumbles (page 26), cooked

1. Preheat the oven to 450°F (230°C). Line a baking sheet with parchment paper or a silicone baking mat. Whisk together the non-dairy milk, creamer, and vinegar in a small bowl; place in the refrigerator.

2. In a large bowl, whisk together the flour, baking powder, baking soda, and salt. Add the very cold vegan butter and use a pastry cutter or butter knife to very quickly cut the butter into the flour until it is the consistency of bread crumbs.

3. Add the milk mixture and mix with a spoon until just combined. Turn it out onto a floured surface and knead for a couple minutes into a pliable dough. Use your hands to flatten the dough into a 1-inch (2.5 cm) thick rectangle. Fold it in half widthwise, then again to make a square. Repeat two to three more times. Flatten and stretch the dough into a ¾-inch (2 cm) thick round.

4. Use a biscuit cutter or the rim of a glass to cut out biscuits; place them on the baking sheet. When you can't cut any more, roll up the dough, flatten it out, and cut out more biscuits. Repeat until there is no dough left. Set the pan aside in a cool area.

5. To make the gravy, heat the oil in a large shallow saucepan over medium heat. Add the onion and garlic and sauté until the onion just starts to become translucent. Add the flour and cook, stirring constantly, for about 2 minutes, until the flour turns golden.

{ RECIPE CONTINUES }

6. Slowly whisk in the 3 cups non-dairy milk and bring to a boil. Reduce the heat to low and add the sage, thyme, pepper, and nutmeg. Simmer, whisking frequently, for 15 minutes, or until the milk has reduced by about one-third and has thickened. Add the nutritional yeast, taste, and add salt. Turn the heat down to low to keep warm until ready to serve. If the gravy thickens too much, stir in a couple tablespoons of milk.

7. To finish the biscuits, use your thumb to make a tiny well on the top of each. In a small bowl, mix the 1 tablespoon non-dairy milk and the melted vegan butter. Use a pastry brush to brush on top of each biscuit. Bake for 12 to 15 minutes, until the tops are golden.

8. Serve hot, topped with the sunflower sausage and gravy.

||||||||||||||||||||||||||||

VARIATION

▶ Place ⅓ cup (80 ml) extra virgin olive oil in the freezer. When it is mostly frozen, remove and use in place of the butter for a slightly stronger, more savory flavor.

TIP

Place the ⅓ cup vegan butter in the freezer about 10 minutes before you use it. Super-cold butter is the key to biscuit success.

BUT I HATE [INSERT VEGETABLE HERE].

Recipes to Convert Veggie-Haters into Lovers

Most of us have at least one vegetable that we still push around our plates, try to hide under other foods, or feed to the dog when no one's looking. If you've ever said, "But Mom, I haaaate peas" or "Cauliflower makes me gag," you may think you aren't vegan material. The truth of the matter is that—no offense—Mom hasn't prepared those vegetables the right way yet. Hand her this book and no vegetable will stand in the way of your compassion again!

EGGPLANT MEATBALL SUBS WITH SPICY MARINARA SAUCE

SERVES 2 TO 4

Who doesn't love a sloppy ol' meatball sub? Anyone? The "meat" in these meatballs is actually roasted eggplant mixed with amaranth, an ancient Mexican grain that gets very sticky when cooked (making it a very good binder). Roasting the eggplant takes away the typical mushy sliminess that tends to drive people away. The meatballs are very boldly flavored but are even better when combined with the incredibly easy Spicy Marinara Sauce. They're so good even the biggest of eggplant-haters won't detect the eggplant.

PREP TIME: 25 minutes
COOK TIME: 30 minutes

subs

3 cups (300 g) diced eggplant

Olive oil spray

2 tablespoons liquid aminos (or tamari or soy sauce)

Salt and black pepper to taste

¼ cup (190 g) amaranth

¾ cup (180 ml) vegetable broth

1 teaspoon extra virgin olive oil

½ medium yellow onion, diced

1 garlic clove, minced

1 tablespoon nutritional yeast

2 teaspoons dried basil

1 teaspoon dried oregano

1 teaspoon liquid smoke

¼ cup (28 g) chickpea flour

2 mini sandwich baguettes or 1 long baguette, sliced into 2 to 4 sections

spicy marinara sauce

One 15-ounce (425 g) can unsalted, diced fire-roasted tomatoes, with liquid

¼ cup (60 ml) vegetable broth

1 tablespoon tomato paste

1 teaspoon sriracha

1 teaspoon dried basil

Salt and black pepper to taste

1. Preheat the oven to 400°F (200°C). Line a baking sheet with parchment paper or a silicone baking mat. Spread the eggplant chunks on the baking sheet. Lightly spray with olive oil and drizzle the liquid aminos over them. Sprinkle with salt and pepper, then toss to fully coat. Roast for 20 minutes, tossing once halfway through to ensure even cooking. When they are tender and caramelized, remove from the oven and let cool for about 5 minutes.

2. Meanwhile, combine the amaranth and broth in a small pot and cover. Bring to a boil, then reduce the heat and crack the lid just a hair. Simmer until the liquid has cooked away, 10 to 15 minutes. Fluff with a fork and set aside.

3. Also while the eggplant is in the oven, heat the oil in a small frying pan over medium heat for about 1 minute. Add the onion and garlic and sauté until the onion is translucent. Remove from the heat.

4. Combine the eggplant, onion and garlic, nutritional yeast, basil, oregano, and liquid smoke in a food processor. Pulse just a few times until it is broken up and mushy, but still a tad chunky.

5. Add the eggplant mixture and chickpea flour to the cooked amaranth and mix. Use a tablespoon or ice cream scoop to scoop about 2 tablespoons of the mixture into your hand. Shape into a ball and place on the same parchment-covered baking sheet you used for the eggplant chunks. Repeat until all the mixture is used.

6. Bake for 25 to 30 minutes, until the meatballs feel solid and are slightly browned on the outside.

7. While the meatballs are baking, make the marinara sauce: Combine the tomatoes, broth, tomato paste, sriracha, and basil in a medium pot. Bring to a boil, reduce the heat, and simmer for 10 to 15 minutes. Use an immersion blender to pulse the sauce a few times to break up the tomato chunks into smaller pieces. Alternatively, carefully transfer the sauce to a blender and blend just until you have a thick, chunky sauce. Taste and add salt and pepper.

8. Carefully slice the baguette lengthwise, leaving the top and bottom connected. Spread a couple spoonfuls of marinara sauce on the bottom half of the sandwich. Add 3 to 4 meatballs and spoon a few spoonfuls of sauce over them. Messy is good. Serve immediately.

||||||||||||||||||||||||||||

VARIATION

▶ Take this sandwich up a notch by melting some Macarella (page 49) on top of the meatballs. After you've assembled the sandwich and covered the meatballs in sauce, place 2 to 3 slices of cheese on top of the meatballs and place the sandwich, open faced, on a baking sheet. Use a sheet of aluminum foil to make a tent over the sandwiches. Broil for a couple minutes, just until the cheese starts to get melty. Serve immediately.

RED VELVET BEET SMOOTHIE WITH CASHEW CREAM ICING

MAKES 1 LARGE OR 2 SMALL SMOOTHIES

GF **SF**

I was tricked into liking beets at a young age. I was told they were really, really good but my mom was going to eat them all if I didn't do something about it, so naturally, like any five-year-old would, I grabbed my fork and tried to eat them all. However, I know not all of us are competitive enough to have acquired a taste for the brightly hued roots at age five. For haters, beets are best enjoyed when disguised as something sweet. I love to use cooked beets in red velvet cupcakes and raw beets in red velvet smoothies. No, I'm not trying to trick you into eating beets. It's just that I'm going to drink this entire smoothie if you don't have some. . . .

cashew cream "icing"

¼ cup (40 g) raw cashews, soaked in water for at least 1 hour, *water reserved*

1 teaspoon vegan sugar or sugar substitute (see tips)

smoothie

¾ cup (115 g) chopped or grated raw red beets (see tips)

4 to 6 strawberries

1 frozen banana, peeled

1 cup (250 ml) cold non-dairy milk

2 Medjool dates, pitted

3 tablespoons cocoa powder or cacao powder

1 tablespoon flaxseed meal

1 tablespoon agave syrup

1. In a food processor, combine the cashews, ¼ cup (60 ml) of the reserved soaking water, and the sugar. Process until smooth. Chill until ready to use.

2. In a blender, combine the smoothie ingredients and process until smooth, pausing to scrape the sides as necessary. Serve immediately, topped with the "icing."

||||||||||||||||||||||||||||

VARIATION

▶ If you have some Coconut Whipped Cream (page 276) on hand, try a dollop of that instead of the Cashew Cream Icing.

TIPS

- Stevia is a plant-based, zero-calorie sugar substitute with no noticeable aftertaste (unlike some brands of artificial sweeteners). It's also great in coffee or tea.

- If your blender is not that powerful, steam the beets for about 5 minutes (not until they are completely soft) and let them cool prior to using them. Taste before serving—you may need to mix in more agave syrup to make up for the decrease in sweetness

CHIPS & PEASAMOLE

SERVES 4

Guacamole is the queen of all dips (hummus is king). Even though the fat from avocados is good for you, I can understand why you may sometimes want to lighten up that absolutely perfect dip. That's where peas come in. Mashing peas into guacamole, or Peasamole, is the best way to get this high-protein little legume into a pea-hater's life. Peasamole is so ridiculously addictive that I wouldn't be surprised if people started calling it the grand duchess of dips.

1. Preheat the oven to 350°F (175°C). Line two baking sheets with parchment paper or silicone baking mats.

2. Generously spray both sides of 1 tortilla with olive oil. Place it on a cutting board. Repeat with another tortilla and place on top of the first tortilla. Repeat with the remaining tortillas until you have a stack. Slice into 6 triangles for a total of 36 chips. Spread the chips over the sheets (no overlapping) and lightly sprinkle with salt. Bake for 8 to 10 minutes, until the edges are crisp and curled up. Remove from the oven. Let them cool (and continue to get crispier) completely on the sheets.

3. In a food processor, combine the peas, avocado, lime juice, cilantro, cumin, garlic powder, onion powder, paprika, and cayenne. Pulse into a thick chunky sauce, similar to guacamole. Add salt and pepper and garnish with the remaining peas.

4. Serve the dip with the chips.

PREP TIME: 10 minutes
COOK TIME: 10 minutes

chips
6 corn tortillas
Olive oil spray
Salt to taste

peasamole
1½ cups (210 g) frozen peas, defrosted, plus more for garnish
½ cup (100 g) mashed avocado (from about 1 small avocado)
2 tablespoons lime juice
2 tablespoons chopped fresh cilantro
½ teaspoon cumin
½ teaspoon garlic powder
½ teaspoon onion powder
¼ teaspoon paprika
⅛ teaspoon cayenne pepper, or to taste
Salt and black pepper to taste

SWEET & SOUR CAULIFLOWER

SERVES 3 TO 4

Cauliflower, in my opinion, is the *It* vegetable. There is nothing it can't do. However, some don't realize that when you roast cauliflower, it takes on a whole new, stronger, nuttier taste and a chewier texture. It also becomes a perfect sponge for whatever sauce you cook it in. In case you weren't yet swayed by Barbecue Sauce (page 31), Buffalo Sauce (page 192), or Piccata Sauce (page 227), now sweet & sour joins the ranks of Sauces That Make Cauliflower Awesome. After roasting the cauliflower, throwing in big chunks of pineapple (a must for sweet & sour anything, right?), and smothering it in this thick and tangy sauce, you too will be convinced.

PREP TIME: 10 minutes
COOK TIME: 20 minutes

cauliflower

1 large head of cauliflower, broken into florets

Olive oil spray

Several dashes of garlic powder

Several dashes of cumin

Several dashes of smoked paprika

Salt and black pepper to taste

sweet & sour sauce

Juice of 1 lemon

½ cup (80 g) finely diced pineapple + 1 cup (160 g) diced, divided

½ cup (125 ml) water

⅓ cup (80 ml) rice vinegar

¼ cup (40 g) coconut sugar

3 tablespoons sliced sun-dried tomatoes (if hard, rehydrated in water until softened)

1 tablespoon tamari or soy sauce

½ tablespoon sriracha

½ teaspoon ground ginger

1 tablespoon cornstarch mixed with ¼ cup (60 ml) water until fully dissolved

½ red bell pepper, diced

Salt to taste

Cooked rice, quinoa, or other grain (see page 9)

Sesame seeds, optional

1. Preheat the oven to 450°F (230°C). Line a baking sheet with parchment paper. Spread the cauliflower on the parchment. Lightly spray with olive oil and sprinkle with the garlic powder, cumin, paprika, salt, and pepper. Toss to fully coat.

2. Roast for 20 minutes, tossing halfway through to ensure even cooking. Remove from the heat.

3. While the cauliflower bakes, combine the lemon juice, ½ cup of the pineapple, water, vinegar, coconut sugar, sun-dried tomatoes, tamari, sriracha, and ginger. Process until smooth.

4. Transfer the mixture to a large shallow saucepan, bring to a boil, and immediately reduce to low heat. Stir in the cornstarch mixture and stir until fully combined. Add the remaining 1 cup of pineapple, bell pepper, and salt; continue to cook for about 5 minutes, stirring occasionally to prevent sticking. Add the roasted cauliflower and stir to fully coat each piece. Serve immediately with rice and top with sesame seeds, if desired.

ROASTED GARLIC HUMMUS & BROCCOLI BOWL

SERVES 2 TO 3

Broccoli has always been the hardest vegetable for me to warm up to. After all my years avoiding it, I tried to give it a second chance when I became vegan. I tried many ways of preparing it, and all my experimenting led to three conclusions: 1) broccoli is best when roasted, 2) it is great when cloaked in a thick sauce as a disguise, and 3) grains make good company for it. This recipe embodies all three: roasted broccoli served atop a bowl of quinoa and covered with a heavenly roasted garlic hummus. If even *I* like broccoli this way, you should have no problems digging in.

1. Preheat the oven to 425°F (220°C). Line a baking sheet with parchment paper or a silicone baking mat.

2. In a food processor, combine the roasted garlic flesh, chickpeas, tahini, and lemon juice. Process until smooth. Drizzle in the broth until the sauce is thick but drips slowly off a spoon. Add salt and pepper. Set aside.

3. Spread the broccoli and shallots on the prepared sheet. Generously spray with olive oil. Sprinkle with the rosemary, thyme, parsley, salt, and pepper; toss to coat. Roast for 20 minutes or until the broccoli is tender and caramelized, flipping once halfway through to ensure even cooking.

4. Divide the quinoa among two or three bowls. Top with the roasted vegetables and pour the hummus over them. Serve immediately.

PREP TIME: 20 minutes (*not including time to roast garlic*)
COOK TIME: 20 minutes

roasted garlic hummus

1 head roasted garlic (page 7), flesh squeezed from each clove

1½ cups (255 g) cooked chickpeas (see page 8) or one 15-ounce (425 g) can, rinsed and drained

2 tablespoons tahini

2 tablespoons lemon juice

½ cup vegetable broth (you may not use all of it)

Salt and black pepper to taste

the bowl

1 large bunch broccoli, chopped into florets, stems sliced

4 large shallot bulbs, quartered

Olive oil spray

1 teaspoon dried rosemary

1 teaspoon dried thyme

1 teaspoon dried parsley

Salt and black pepper to taste

3 cups (480 g) cooked red or white quinoa (see page 9)

BALSAMIC MAPLE BRUSSELS SPROUTS & SWEET POTATO

page 235

SERVES 4 TO 6

There's no bigger hater of brussels sprouts than my husband. That said, he goes for seconds and thirds of this recipe. Roasting brussels sprouts is the key to converting nonbelievers, and coating them in a sweet, tart, and savory balsamic sauce is the key to bringing them back for more.

PREP TIME: 20 minutes
COOK TIME: 40 minutes

Olive oil spray

5 tablespoons + ¼ cup (60 ml) balsamic vinegar, divided

3 tablespoons maple syrup

2 tablespoons extra virgin olive oil

1 tablespoon liquid aminos

¼ cup (20 g) nutritional yeast

18 to 20 brussels sprouts

2 large sweet potatoes, peeled and chopped into 1-inch (2.5 cm) pieces

⅓ cup (45 g) dried cranberries

⅓ cup (130 g) chopped pistachios, optional

1. Preheat the oven to 400°F (200°C). Lightly spray a 9 x 13-inch baking dish with olive oil and set aside. Mix 5 tablespoons of the vinegar with the maple syrup, oil, liquid aminos, and nutritional yeast in a large bowl. Set aside.

2. Trim the brussels sprouts of any dirty, yellow, or wilted outer leaves and rinse. Trim the stems off and cut the sprouts in half lengthwise. Add the brussels sprouts and sweet potatoes to the large bowl. Toss to coat every piece with the sauce.

3. Pour the contents of the bowl into the prepared baking dish. Cover with aluminum foil. Bake for 20 minutes. Remove the foil, toss to recoat in the sauce, and bake, uncovered, for 20 more minutes.

4. Meanwhile, to make the glaze, bring the remaining ¼ cup vinegar to a boil over medium (not high) heat in a small pot. When it begins to boil, reduce the heat and simmer for 3 to 4 minutes. Remove from the heat and let cool.

5. When the vegetables are tender and caramelized, add the cranberries, pistachios (if using), and glaze; toss to combine. Serve immediately..

I DON'T WANT TO BE LEFT OUT AT POTLUCKS AND FAMILY GET-TOGETHERS.

Vegan Recipes That Will WOW the Crowds

Being the only vegan at a potluck or family get-together causes panic in even the strongest of herbivores. Will I have enough to eat? Will they eat what I bring? Will Uncle Ed wave a turkey leg in my face as a "joke"? You need to turn your worry into determination to show your friends and family how great vegan food is. Be positive, happy, and the bearer of delicious foods. And who knows? Maybe next time you won't be the only vegan!

PAN-FRIED GNOCCHI & ACORN SQUASH WITH HAZELNUT-SAGE PESTO

Winter squashes scream fall, and every October I want them all: butternut, acorn, kabocha, delicata, red kuri, pumpkin, and more. And I want them in everything. This recipe features my favorite combination: roasted acorn squash with pan-fried gnocchi and an autumnal pesto made with hazelnuts and fresh sage leaves. It doesn't take terribly long to prepare and would be perfect for a potluck after an afternoon spent picking apples with friends or for a dinner party to celebrate the changing leaves.

PREP TIME: 10 minutes *(not including time to prepare gnocchi, if making from scratch)*

COOK TIME: 20 minutes

pesto
⅓ cup (55 g) hazelnuts

2 to 3 garlic cloves

2 tablespoons nutritional yeast

1 tablespoon lemon juice

2 cups (60 g) packed fresh basil

½ cup (15 g) fresh sage

2 tablespoons extra virgin olive oil

2 tablespoons vegetable broth

Salt and black pepper to taste

gnocchi & squash
4 cups (500 g) chopped acorn squash

Olive oil spray

1 teaspoon dried thyme

½ teaspoon ground cinnamon

¼ teaspoon ground nutmeg

Salt and black pepper to taste

2 tablespoons extra virgin olive oil

1 batch gnocchi (page 218) or one 16-ounce (455 g) package store-bought (see tip)

Pecan Parmesan (page 38), for topping

1. Combine the hazelnuts and garlic in a food processor and pulse until broken up. Add the nutritional yeast, lemon juice, basil, and sage; process until a paste forms. Add the oil and broth and process until smooth. Add salt and pepper and chill until ready to use.

2. Preheat the oven to 400°F (200°C). Line a baking sheet with parchment paper or a silicone baking mat. Spread the acorn squash on the sheet, spray with olive oil, and sprinkle with the thyme, cinnamon, nutmeg, salt, and pepper. Bake for 20 minutes, flipping once to ensure even cooking. When tender, remove from the oven.

3. Heat the 2 tablespoons of oil in a large, shallow saucepan over medium heat. Add the gnocchi and cook, stirring occasionally, until heated through and lightly browned. Remove from the heat. Add the cooked acorn squash and pesto and gently fold together until combined (you don't want to mash the gnocchi or squash). Serve warm, topped with Pecan Parmesan.

TIP

If you are purchasing gnocchi, be sure to check the ingredients. Some contain egg or even dairy. If using homemade gnocchi, boil before adding to the sauce; they are only warmed, not cooked, in step 3.

MAPLE-BAKED BEANS & CORNBREAD CASSEROLE

SERVES 12 TO 14

I'm just going to come right out and say it: I love casseroles. I was raised in a casserole-lovin' family and in my pre-vegan days, a rectangular dish filled with something cooked in a can of condensed soup and topped with potato chips or corn flakes or bread crumbs was the epitome of comfort. If you're like me, never fear—since going vegan, the casseroles have only gotten better. Take this casserole of smoky, barbecue-y, maple-y beans baked with a layer of cornbread on top. Now imagine digging into a bowlful while sitting at a table with your loved ones, the sound of familiar voices and laughter dancing in your ears. This casserole has "cozy" written all over it.

PREP TIME: 30 minutes
COOK TIME: 25 minutes

maple-baked beans

1 teaspoon extra virgin olive oil

1 small sweet onion, diced

2 garlic cloves, minced

Two 15-ounce (425 g) cans navy beans, rinsed and drained

One 15-ounce (425 g) can unsalted diced tomatoes, with liquid

⅔ cup (160 ml) Barbecue Sauce (page 31) or store-bought

⅓ cup (80 ml) maple syrup

2 tablespoons tomato paste

1½ tablespoons apple cider vinegar

1½ tablespoons Dijon mustard

1 tablespoon liquid aminos (or tamari or soy sauce)

1 teaspoon sriracha

½ teaspoon liquid smoke

½ teaspoon cumin

½ teaspoon ground cinnamon

A few dashes of nutmeg

1½ tablespoons nutritional yeast, optional

Salt and black pepper to taste

cornbread

1½ cups (375 ml) non-dairy milk

1 tablespoon apple cider vinegar

1 tablespoon flaxseed meal

2 tablespoons warm water

2 cups (280 g) cornmeal (fine or coarse grind)

1 cup (130 g) whole wheat pastry flour

1. Preheat the oven to 400°F (200°C). Lightly spray a 9 x 13-inch baking dish with olive oil.

2. Heat the oil in a large pot over medium heat. Add the onion and garlic and sauté until the onion starts to become translucent. Add the beans, tomatoes, Barbecue Sauce, maple syrup, tomato paste, 1½ tablespoons vinegar, mustard, liquid aminos, sriracha, liquid smoke, cumin, cinnamon, and nutmeg. Bring to a boil, then reduce the heat and simmer, stirring occasionally, for 15 minutes. Stir in the nutritional yeast (if using), salt, and pepper. Remove from the heat.

3. While the beans are simmering, make the cornbread batter. In a measuring cup, combine the non-dairy milk and 1 tablespoon vinegar. In a small bowl, combine the flaxseed meal and warm water. Let both mixtures sit for at least 5 minutes.

4. In a large bowl, whisk together the cornmeal, flour, baking powder, baking soda, salt, paprika, nutmeg, and cayenne. Add the milk mixture, flaxseed meal mixture, melted vegan butter, and maple syrup. Mix until just combined.

5. Pour the beans into the prepared baking dish. Using a rubber spatula, spread the cornbread batter on top. Bake for 25 minutes, or until a toothpick inserted into the center of the cornbread comes out clean. Remove from the oven and serve warm. Leftovers can be covered and chilled 3 to 4 days.

1 tablespoon baking powder

½ teaspoon baking soda

½ teaspoon salt

¼ teaspoon smoked paprika

¼ teaspoon ground nutmeg

¼ teaspoon cayenne powder, optional

⅓ cup (70 g) melted vegan butter

2 tablespoons maple syrup

SEITAN-MUSHROOM ROAST WITH WILD RICE STUFFING

SERVES 8 TO 10

page 247

As a vegan it's common to worry about being unable to participate in family holiday traditions, but being with loved ones is what's important. Plus, there was a first time your aunt made *that* pie or your grandmother made *that* gravy. You can create a new tradition too by bringing this succulent roast as a replacement for the turkey (or at least a second option). The stuffing can also be served alone as a side dish. Your family members may raise their eyebrows (or even tease you a bit), but remember, they have emotions tied up in the same traditions you do, and they'll soon realize it's not about what's on the table but about who's sitting around it.

to make the stuffing

1. Add the water and wild rice to a medium pot and bring to a boil. Reduce the heat, cover, and simmer for about 45 minutes.

2. Melt the vegan butter in a large shallow saucepan over medium heat. Add the onion and garlic and sauté until the onion just begins to become translucent. Add the butternut squash, carrot, celery, rosemary, thyme, and sage; sauté for 8 to 10 minutes, until the squash and carrots are easily pierced with a fork but not mushy. Remove from the heat.

3. Drain the cooked rice and add to the vegetables. Mix in the nutritional yeast, then fold in the cranberries and pecans. Cover until ready to use.

to make the seitan

1. Preheat the oven to 350°F (175°C). Set out a baking sheet. Lay out 2 pieces of aluminum foil, each about 16 to 18 inches long, so that one overlaps the other, horizontally, by about 5 to 6 inches. Lightly spray the foil with olive oil.

2. In a large bowl, whisk together the vital wheat gluten, chickpea flour, nutritional yeast, onion powder, thyme, sage, cumin, salt, and pepper.

PREP TIME: 90 minutes
COOK TIME: 60 minutes

stuffing

3 cups (750 ml) water

1 cup (185 g) wild rice, rinsed

1 tablespoon vegan butter

1 medium yellow onion, diced

1 to 2 garlic cloves, minced

2 cups (250 g) chopped butternut squash (in ½-inch/1 cm pieces)

1 cup (160 g) chopped carrot (in ½-inch/1 cm pieces)

½ cup (60 g) chopped celery (in ½-inch/1 cm pieces)

1 tablespoon chopped fresh rosemary

1 tablespoon fresh thyme leaves

1 tablespoon chopped fresh sage

3 tablespoons nutritional yeast, optional

¾ cup (105 g) dried cranberries

⅔ cup (85 g) chopped pecans

seitan

Olive oil spray

2¼ cups (315 g) vital wheat gluten

⅔ cup (40 g) chickpea flour

½ cup (35 g) nutritional yeast

2 teaspoons onion powder

1 teaspoon dried thyme

1 teaspoon dried sage

1 teaspoon cumin

½ teaspoon salt

¼ teaspoon black pepper

2 garlic cloves, minced

2 cups (140 g) sliced cremini mushrooms

3. In the bowl of a food processor, pulse the garlic cloves a few times, then add the mushrooms. Pulse until the mushroom pieces are no larger than ¼ inch (.5 cm). Pour the mushrooms and garlic into a small bowl and add the broth, soy sauce, oil, and liquid smoke. Mix to combine.

4. Pour the broth mixture into the gluten mixture and use a wooden spoon to mix them as much as possible. When you can no longer use your spoon, use your hands to knead the dough until it comes together into a ball.

5. Turn the seitan ball onto the prepared foil and use your hand to flatten and stretch it into a roughly 9 x 13-inch rectangle. Place 2 cups of stuffing in a strip lengthwise down the middle of the rectangle. Take the side of the seitan closest to you and fold it over the stuffing, using your fingers to tuck in the stuffing tightly. Continue to roll it over and press firmly to create a tight seam along the length of the log. Press the ends closed. Use a pastry brush to brush the log with additional broth.

6. Fold each side of the foil over the top of the log until it is tightly wrapped and sealed. Transfer to the baking sheet and bake for 60 to 70 minutes, turning the log over three to four times to ensure it cooks evenly. Peel back the foil and use a fork to test the roast; when it feels pretty firm, it is done.

7. Remove from the oven and let rest in the foil for about 10 minutes before unwrapping, slicing into ½- to 1-inch rounds, and serving. Alternatively, place the roast on a platter and let the guest slice it and serve themselves. Chill leftovers in an airtight container for up to 5 days or freeze for up to a month.

1⅔ cups (410 ml) vegetable broth, plus extra for basting

3 tablespoons soy sauce (or tamari or liquid aminos)

1 tablespoon extra virgin olive oil

1 teaspoon liquid smoke

FINGERLING POTATOES, GREEN BEANS & CARAMELIZED SHALLOTS WITH DIJON-THYME VINAIGRETTE

SERVES 4 TO 8

Vegetarians and vegans always get stuck bringing the vegetable side dish to gatherings. It's your duty to show your family how fabulous vegetables can be by creating something that's elegant and delectable with a lot of "wow" factor. This is one of those dishes. Green beans may seem kind of boring, but when you pair them with potatoes, you start to get people's interest. Serving anything with the word *caramelized* in it will earn you plenty of fans, but you'll really have everyone's attention when you drizzle on the Dijon-thyme dressing. Be prepared to bring home an empty serving plate!

1. Bring a large pot of water to a boil.
2. Preheat the oven to 400°F (200°C). Line a baking sheet with parchment paper or a silicone baking mat. Spread the potatoes on the sheet. Lightly spray with olive oil and sprinkle with salt and pepper. Roast for 20 to 25 minutes, flipping once halfway through, until easily pierced with a fork.
3. Prepare an ice bath (a bowl full of water and ice). Place the green beans in the boiling water and cook for about 2 minutes. Immediately transfer to the ice bath. Let them sit for 1 minute, then drain and set aside.
4. Melt 1½ teaspoons of the vegan butter in a large shallow saucepan over medium heat. Add the shallots and cook, stirring occasionally, for about 15 minutes, until light brown. Add the remaining 1½ teaspoons of vegan butter and melt. Add the green beans and sauté until tender. Add the lemon juice and season with salt and pepper. Mix in the roasted potatoes.
5. To make the vinaigrette, combine all the ingredients in a cup and stir with a fork until fully incorporated.
6. To serve, transfer the green beans, potatoes, and shallots to a serving dish and top with the vinaigrette.

PREP TIME: 10 minutes
COOK TIME: 25 minutes

Water

1 pound (455 g) fingerling potatoes, halved lengthwise

Olive oil spray

Salt and black pepper to taste

Ice

½ pound (223 g) fresh green beans, ends trimmed

1 tablespoon vegan butter, divided

5 to 6 shallots, thinly sliced

Juice of ½ lemon

Dijon-thyme vinaigrette

3 tablespoons sherry vinegar

2 tablespoons Dijon mustard

1½ tablespoons agave syrup

1 tablespoon chopped fresh thyme

Pinch of salt

CREAMY CURRIED TEMPEH SALAD WITH DRIED CHERRIES & ALMONDS

SERVES 4 (DOUBLE OR TRIPLE FOR LARGER CROWDS)

PREP TIME: 10 minutes
COOK TIME: 20 minutes

Water

One 8-ounce (225 g) package tempeh

1 tablespoon liquid aminos (or tamari or soy sauce)

⅓ cup (80 g) vegan mayonnaise

⅓ cup (75 g) plain coconut yogurt

2 teaspoons tahini

2 tablespoons curry powder

½ teaspoon smoked paprika

½ teaspoon ground cinnamon

1 celery rib, diced

2 tablespoons chopped scallions

2 tablespoons chopped fresh cilantro

⅓ cup (50 g) roughly chopped dried cherries

⅓ cup (50 g) roughly chopped almonds

Salt and black pepper to taste

optional
Leaves from 2 heads of endive

Microgreens or other mixed greens

Sandwich bread

Heading to a Fourth of July cookout and need a salad that can stand the heat? Going to a work potluck with the endless table of bowls of food and need something that will stand out? Or perhaps you're hosting a party and want a satisfying appetizer? This salad works for all that and more. Its rich and creamy sauce, chunks of tender tempeh, bursts of flavorful cherries, and crunchy almonds are sure to please everyone no matter how you serve it—by itself, as part of a larger salad, scooped into little endive "boats" for hors d'oeuvres, or stuffed into sandwiches.

1. Fill the bottom of a medium pot with 1 to 2 inches of water and bring to a boil. Place a steamer basket in the pot and add the tempeh, crumbled into roughly ½- to 1-inch (1 to 2.5 cm) chunks, making sure not to crumble it too small. Cover the steamer basket and let the tempeh steam for 20 minutes, stirring once halfway through. When it is tender, remove from the heat.

2. Drain the water and transfer the tempeh into the pot. Heat over medium-low heat and stir in the liquid aminos. Cook, stirring, until about 2 minutes after the liquid has been absorbed. Remove from the heat and let cool.

3. In a large bowl, mix the mayonnaise, yogurt, and tahini. Stir in the curry powder, paprika, and cinnamon. Mix in the celery, scallions, cilantro, cherries, and almonds. Mix in the cooked tempeh. Taste and add salt and pepper. Chill at least 1 hour to let the flavors marry.

4. Serve by itself, scooped into endive leaves, with microgreens or mixed greens, or in a sandwich. Leftovers can be chilled in an airtight container 3 to 4 days.

VARIATIONS

▶ Mix it up—try replacing the dried cherries with raisins, currants, or even fresh fruit like apple or mango. The almonds can be replaced with walnuts, pecans, cashews, pistachios, or even peanuts. Pumpkin seeds are a good nut-free option.

CHEESY VEGGIE STROMBOLI

SERVES 12 TO 14

page 247

You know those party pinwheel sandwiches with the rubbery slices of yellow cheese and processed cold cuts all wrapped up in a soggy tortilla? This stromboli is like those puny sandwiches on super-delicious vegan steroids. There's loads of veggies and melty Macarella all wrapped up in a doughy pizza crust with a crisp outer shell. It's so amazing, I screamed the first time I cut into it, a scare-the-dog-to-death sort of scream. If you want to make people scream (or at least oooh and ahhh) at your next party, make this stromboli. It can feed a small army and is perfect served hot or cold.

PREP TIME: 20 minutes (*not including time to prepare Macarella*)
COOK TIME: 30 minutes

1 teaspoon extra virgin olive oil

½ medium red onion, diced

3 garlic cloves, minced

8 ounces (225 g) sliced cremini mushrooms

2 cups (240 g) sliced zucchini

One 15-ounce (425 g) can unsalted diced tomatoes, with liquid

2 teaspoons dried basil

1½ teaspoons dried oregano

½ teaspoon smoked paprika

Salt and black pepper to taste

½ bunch chard, destemmed and chopped

1 batch Basic Pizza Dough (page 179, prepared through step 4)

3 to 4 Macarella discs (page 49)

2 cups (280 g) chopped roasted red bell pepper

1 cup (180 g) sliced black olives

Olive oil spray

1. Preheat the oven to 450°F (230°C). Line a large (roughly 13 x 17½-inch) baking sheet with parchment paper or a silicone baking mat.

2. Heat the oil in a large shallow saucepan over medium heat. Add the onion and garlic and sauté for 2 to 3 minutes. Add the mushrooms, zucchini, tomatoes, basil, oregano, and paprika. Cook for 10 to 15 minutes, stirring occasionally, until the zucchini is tender. Add the salt and pepper. Add the chard and cook just until it begins to wilt. Remove from the heat and drain off excess liquid.

3. Lightly flour the prepared baking sheet. Place the ball of pizza dough in the middle and stretch and roll it out to fill the baking sheet.

4. Thinly slice the Macarella discs into very thin medallions (with a mandoline, if possible). Spread the medallions over the pizza dough, leaving a 1-inch (2.5 cm) perimeter around the edge of the dough. Sprinkle the roasted bell pepper and olives over the medallions; top with the vegetable mixture. Fold the short ends of the rectangle over the filling. Starting with the long side closest to you, roll the dough over the filling and continue rolling into a log. Gently roll the log to fit diagonally across the baking sheet, seam side down (as much as possible), and lightly spray with olive oil. Bake for 30 minutes, until the dough is firm and golden. Remove from the oven and let rest for at least 10 minutes before slicing and serving warm or cool. Leftovers can be chilled in an airtight container 3 to 4 days.

||||||||||||||||||||||||||||

VARIATION

▶ Try replacing the Macarella with Tofu Chèvre (page 36) and the vegetables with Roasted Ratatouille (page 88).

YOU CAN'T BAKE WITHOUT BUTTER OR EGGS!

Vegan Desserts That Aren't Missing a Thing

There's always that moment when someone considering going vegan thinks, "Sure, I could give up milk and eggs," then realizes everything those animal products go into. "I don't know if I could never have another cookie, though" is usually the follow-up. The truth is that plants offer a large variety of ways to mimic the actions of eggs, butter, and milk. The recipes in this chapter explore some of those methods and satisfy your sweet tooth in the process.

SALTED CARAMEL PEANUT BUTTER BARS

MAKES 16 BARS

Though eggs are very prominent in baking, they're not difficult to replace. There are several ways to mimic the binding action of egg. In this recipe, mashed banana steps up to the plate. As a bonus, the banana pairs beautifully with the maple syrup and peanut butter (which also adds some binding action). A date-based salted caramel sauce is swirled into the top to complete an unforgettable treat.

PREP TIME: 15 minutes
COOK TIME: 25 minutes

salted caramel swirl

7 Medjool dates, pitted

3 tablespoons almond milk or other non-dairy milk

1 teaspoon arrowroot powder

¼ teaspoon salt

peanut butter bars

1 cup (130 g) whole wheat pastry flour

1 teaspoon baking powder

½ teaspoon salt

1 large ripe banana, mashed

½ cup (130 g) smooth peanut butter

½ cup (125 ml) maple syrup

1 tablespoon canola oil

1 teaspoon almond extract or vanilla extract

1. Preheat the oven to 350°F (175°C). Line an 8 x 8-inch baking dish with parchment paper with some overhanging the sides (making it easier to remove the bars later).

2. In a blender, combine the dates and almond milk. Blend into a smooth, velvety paste, stopping to scrape the sides every minute or so. (This may take several minutes.) When smooth, transfer to a small bowl; mix in the arrowroot powder and salt. Set aside.

3. In a large bowl, whisk together the flour, baking powder, and salt. In a medium bowl, mix the banana, peanut butter, maple syrup, oil, and almond extract. Add the banana mixture to the flour mixture and mix until combined. Spread this very thick batter in the prepared baking dish. Use a rubber spatula to smooth the top as much as possible.

4. Drizzle or drop small spoonfuls of the caramel over the top, making sure *not* to spread it out. To create a marbled effect, run a butter knife through the caramel and batter a few times in one direction and then a few times in the opposite direction, making sure *not* to cut all the way through the batter to the dish.

5. Bake for 20 to 25 minutes, until a toothpick inserted into the center comes out clean. Let cool in the dish for a few minutes before using the parchment paper to lift out the bars and place on a cooling rack. Cool completely, then slice. Store leftovers in an airtight container.

||||||||||||||||||||||||||

VARIATION

▶ Make it gluten-free by substituting gluten-free all-purpose flour for the whole wheat flour.

SPICED CARROT CAKE CUPCAKES WITH CREAM CHEESE FROSTING

MAKES 12 CUPCAKES

"**N**ever trust a person who doesn't like carrot cake" is what I always say. Actually, I've never said that until just now, but it's still true. In fact, I dare you to make these sweet and spicy vegan carrot cake cupcakes topped with puffy clouds of cream cheese frosting and find anyone who doesn't like them. If you do come across such a person, you have my permission to snatch that cupcake back (so it can be finished by someone who appreciates it), but I would do so with one raised eyebrow.

PREP TIME: 35 minutes
COOK TIME: 20 minutes

¾ cup (185 ml) non-dairy milk

1 teaspoon apple cider vinegar

1¾ cups (225 g) whole wheat pastry flour

2 teaspoons ground cinnamon

1½ teaspoons baking powder

1 teaspoon ground ginger

½ teaspoon ground cloves

½ teaspoon ground nutmeg

½ teaspoon salt

¼ teaspoon ground cardamom

½ cup (125 ml) Happy Bee Honey (page 34) or agave syrup

⅓ cup (70 g) vegan butter, melted

1 tablespoon flaxseed meal

1 teaspoon vanilla extract

1½ cups (165 g) grated carrots

½ cup (60 g) packed raisins, optional

cream cheese frosting

1½ cups (380 g) vegan cream cheese

5 tablespoons vegan powdered sugar or powdered xylitol

2 tablespoons agave syrup

2 teaspoons fresh lemon juice

1 teaspoon vanilla extract

1. Preheat the oven to 350°F (175°C). Line a 12-cup muffin tin with cupcake liners.
2. In a cup, mix the non-dairy milk and vinegar. Let sit for at least 10 minutes.
3. In a large bowl, whisk together the flour, cinnamon, baking powder, ginger, cloves, nutmeg, salt, and cardamom.
4. In a medium bowl, mix the Happy Bee Honey, vegan butter, flaxseed meal, and vanilla. Stir in the milk mixture. Mix in the grated carrots. Add the carrot mixture to the flour mixture and stir until just combined. Fold in the raisins, if using.
5. Divide the batter among the 12 cupcake liners, making sure not to fill them more than two-thirds. Bake for 20 minutes, or until a toothpick inserted into the center comes out clean. Let cool in the muffin tin for about 5 minutes before transferring the cupcakes to a cooling rack to cool completely.
6. While the cupcakes cool, make the frosting. In a bowl, use a fork to stir together the cream cheese, powdered sugar, agave syrup, lemon juice, and vanilla. If desired, transfer to a pastry bag or a resealable plastic bag with the tip of one corner cut out.
7. Using the pastry bag or a rubber spatula, top the cooled cupcakes with the frosting and serve. If not serving immediately, chill in an airtight container 1 to 2 days. If you'd like to freeze the cupcakes, wait to frost them until they have defrosted.

ROSEMARY-LEMON POUND CAKE WITH LEMON GLAZE

Originally, the recipe for pound cake included 1 pound each of butter, eggs, sugar, and flour. I don't know about you, but to me that sounds like one heavy cake! For vegan pound cakes, you can recreate that moist denseness using coconut oil instead of butter, silken tofu in place of eggs, and coconut sugar and agave syrup to bring the sweetness. This version has a lemony twist with a touch of fresh rosemary. The result is a bright, sweet, citrusy, yet subtly herbaceous cake perfect for serving with afternoon tea (or whenever cake is appropriate). And—bonus—you don't have to be a weightlifter to get it out of the oven!

1. Preheat the oven to 350°F (175°C). Line a loaf pan with parchment paper, leaving some overhang on the sides, and set aside.

2. In a small cup, mix the non-dairy milk and vinegar. Let sit for at least 10 minutes.

3. In a medium bowl, combine the flour, 1 tablespoon of rosemary, baking powder, and salt.

4. In a mixer fitted with a whisk attachment (or in a large bowl, using a hand mixer), blend the coconut oil and sugar together. With the mixer running at low speed, add the agave syrup, pureed tofu, lemon juice, milk mixture, vanilla, and the 1 teaspoon lemon zest.

5. Add the flour mixture to the wet ingredients in three batches, mixing after each addition just until smooth.

6. Pour into the prepared pan and bake for 50 to 60 minutes, until raised in the center and a toothpick inserted into the center comes out dry and almost clean (a few crumbs are okay).

7. Cool the cake in the pan for 15 minutes. Set a wire rack on a sheet pan with sides (to catch the glaze). Use the parchment paper to lift the still-warm cake out of the pan and transfer to the rack to cool completely.

PREP TIME: 20 minutes
COOK TIME: 50 minutes
DOWN TIME: 30 minutes

¼ cup (60 ml) non-dairy milk

1 teaspoon apple cider vinegar

1½ cups (195 g) whole wheat pastry flour

1 tablespoon chopped fresh rosemary, plus extra for garnish

1½ teaspoons baking powder

½ teaspoon salt

½ cup (105 g) coconut oil, melted

½ cup (75 g) coconut sugar

⅓ cup (80 ml) agave syrup or Happy Bee Honey (page 34)

Half of a 12-ounce package (about 170 g) extra-firm silken tofu (the vacuum-packed kind), pureed

¼ cup (60 ml) fresh lemon juice

1 teaspoon vanilla extract

1 teaspoon lemon zest, plus extra for garnish

glaze

½ cup (60 g) vegan powdered sugar or powdered xylitol

1 to 2 tablespoons fresh lemon juice

8. While the cake cools, make the glaze. In a small bowl, whisk together the powdered sugar and 1 tablespoon of the lemon juice. If it is too thick, whisk in the remaining tablespoon of juice. Spoon the glaze over the cooled cake and sprinkle the extra lemon zest and chopped rosemary over the top. When the glaze has set (gotten a little firm), slice the cake and serve.

BUTTERSCOTCH BREAD PUDDING

SERVES 6 TO 8

Fellow carboholics know that bread pudding is just the ultimate way to consume bread. Pieces of bread baked in a sweet, creamy sauce? Yeah, it's one of the best things ever. This bread pudding is baked with dried apricots, walnuts, and homemade butterscotch sauce. Then it's drizzled with even more butterscotch sauce. Carbolicious *and* compassionate.

1. Melt the vegan butter in a medium pot over medium heat. Add the coconut sugar, creamer, non-dairy milk, and agave syrup and bring to a boil. Quickly reduce the heat and simmer for 5 minutes, stirring occasionally. Stir in the vanilla and salt, then the arrowroot powder. Remove from the heat and let the sauce cool completely. The final product will lightly coat the back of a spoon and be thick, but not as thick as maple syrup. (This can be made up to 1 week in advance and chilled in an airtight container until ready to use. If it separates, stir and it will be fine.)

2. Preheat the oven to 350°F (175°C). Lightly spray an 8 x 8-inch baking dish, 8- to 10-inch cake pan or cast-iron pan, or six to eight 8-ounce ramekins with cooking spray.

3. In a large bowl, combine the bread, dried apricots, and walnuts (if using). In a medium bowl, mix the non-dairy milk, applesauce, coconut sugar, vanilla, cinnamon, cloves, nutmeg, salt, and ½ cup (125 ml) of the prepared butterscotch sauce. Add the milk mixture to the bread mixture and stir until thoroughly combined. Soak for about 5 minutes.

4. Transfer the mixture to the prepared baking dish, pan, or ramekins. Bake for 30 to 40 minutes (or 20 to 25 minutes for ramekins), until the top is set and beginning to turn golden brown. Remove and let cool in the pan for about 10 minutes. Serve each portion in a bowl (or in its own ramekin) with a drizzle of the remaining butterscotch sauce and the Coconut Whipped Cream (if using).

||||||||||||||||||||||||||||||||

VARIATIONS

▶ Try switching out the dried apricots for another dried fruit like figs, dates, or raisins. The walnuts are interchangeable, too; this would be great with pecans, almonds, cashews, or hazelnuts. Or go crazy and throw in some chocolate chips while you're at it!

PREP TIME: 15 minutes
COOK TIME: 40 minutes
DOWN TIME: 45 minutes

butterscotch sauce

½ cup (105 g) vegan butter

½ cup (75 g) coconut sugar or vegan brown sugar

½ cup (125 ml) soy or coconut creamer or canned coconut milk

½ cup (125 ml) non-dairy milk

¼ cup (60 ml) agave syrup

2 teaspoons vanilla extract

⅛ teaspoon salt

1 tablespoon arrowroot powder or cornstarch

bread pudding

Cooking spray

6 cups (360 g) cubed sourdough or French bread, preferably slightly stale

1 cup (165 g) chopped dried apricots

½ cup (50 g) chopped walnuts, optional

1¾ cups (435 ml) non-dairy milk

½ cup (120 g) unsweetened applesauce

¼ cup (40 g) coconut sugar or vegan brown sugar

1 teaspoon vanilla extract

1 teaspoon ground cinnamon

¼ teaspoon ground cloves

¼ teaspoon ground nutmeg

¼ teaspoon salt

Coconut Whipped Cream (page 276), optional

MINI NO-BAKE FRUIT CHEESECAKES

MAKES 12 MINI CHEESECAKES

In my pre-vegan days, I must've attempted to bake cheesecakes 157 times. They were all epic fails. When I went vegan and began making no-bake cheesecakes, they were all huge wins. Even if you aren't much of a cheesecake whisperer either, you'll find that the crust for these cheesecakes is über-simple and holds together like a dream. The fruity, nut-based cheesecake is richer and lusher than any non-vegan cheesecake I've ever tasted. Plus, they're mini, which automatically makes them cuter, not to mention more portable and easier to share with a crowd. It's fruity, no-fail, no-bake cheesecakes for the win!

1. Line a 12-cup muffin tin with muffin liners, or lightly grease with cooking spray. Combine the almonds, dates, oil, and salt in a food processor and process until the mixture is crumbly and holds together if pinched. Divide equally among the 12 wells of the muffin tin, about 1 tablespoon each, and use your fingers to press it flat into the bottoms. Place the pan in the freezer.

2. Combine all the filling ingredients in a food processor and process until smooth, pausing to scrape the sides as necessary. Remove the muffin tin from the freezer and scoop the filling onto each crust, filling the wells almost to the top. Use a spoon or rubber spatula to smooth the tops. Freeze for 30 minutes, then refrigerate for 1 hour before serving. Serve topped with the additional fruit.

PREP TIME: 40 minutes

DOWN TIME: 3 hours *(partially while cashews soak)*

crust

Cooking spray, optional

1 cup (150 g) raw almonds

7 to 8 Medjool dates, pitted

2 teaspoons coconut oil

Pinch of salt

filling

2 cups (320 g) raw cashews, soaked in water for 3 to 4 hours, *water discarded*

1 cup (about 130 g) chopped fruit(s) of choice (e.g., strawberries, raspberries, blueberries, blackberries, mango, pineapple), plus extra for topping

½ cup (105 g) coconut oil, melted

½ cup (125 ml) agave syrup

2 tablespoons fresh lemon juice

1 teaspoon vanilla extract

Pinch of salt

||||||||||||||||||||||||

VARIATION

▶ Make even *tinier* mini cheesecakes by using a 24-well mini muffin tin.

ICED OATMEAL COOKIES

MAKES 20 TO 24 COOKIES

page 259

Who hasn't overdosed on those crispy iced oatmeal cookies, inhaling them until Mom had to pry the pink and white plastic packaging from their grubby, crumb-covered little hands? These cookies are a healthy spin on that childhood favorite, only a bit chewier, like traditional oatmeal cookies. Applesauce and flaxseed meal replace the eggs, while non-dairy milk makes the most perfect icing. And now that we're grown-ups, the only thing keeping you from eating them all is if you choose to share (but that's what a double batch is for, right?).

PREP TIME: 15 minutes
COOK TIME: 10 minutes

¼ cup (60 ml) non-dairy milk

1 tablespoon apple cider vinegar

1¼ cups (160 g) unbleached all-purpose flour

¾ cup (75 g) rolled oats

1 teaspoon ground cinnamon

½ teaspoon baking powder

½ teaspoon baking soda

½ teaspoon ground ginger

½ teaspoon salt

¼ teaspoon ground cloves

¼ teaspoon ground nutmeg

⅓ cup (80 ml) melted coconut oil or canola oil

⅓ cup (50 g) coconut sugar or vegan brown sugar

¼ cup (60 g) unsweetened applesauce

2 tablespoons maple syrup

1½ teaspoons flaxseed meal

1 teaspoon almond extract or vanilla extract

Cooking spray

icing

1 cup (120 g) vegan powdered sugar or powdered xylitol

2 tablespoons non-dairy milk

1. Preheat the oven to 350°F (175°C). Line two baking sheets with parchment paper or silicone baking mats.

2. In a cup, mix the non-dairy milk and the vinegar. Let sit for at least 5 minutes.

3. In a large bowl, whisk together the flour, oats, cinnamon, baking powder, baking soda, ginger, salt, cloves, and nutmeg.

4. In a medium bowl, stir or use an electric hand mixer to combine the coconut oil, coconut sugar, applesauce, maple syrup, flaxseed meal, and almond extract. Mix in the milk mixture. Add the mixture to the flour mixture and stir until just combined.

5. Use a tablespoon or ice cream scoop to place heaping spoonfuls of dough onto the prepared baking sheets. Wet your fingers or spray them with cooking spray, then use them to flatten each cookie and gently shape into rounds. Bake for 8 to 10 minutes, until set and the bottoms are beginning to turn golden brown. Remove from the oven; cool the cookies on the sheet for 3 to 4 minutes before transferring them to a cooling rack to cool completely.

6. While the cookies cool, use a fork to mix the powdered sugar and non-dairy milk. When the cookies are cool, spoon all the icing over the cookies. Let sit until the icing has slightly hardened. Chill leftovers in an airtight container for 3 to 4 days.

VARIATION

▶ Leave the icing off and use the cookies to make Ice Cream Sandwiches (page 292)!

WAIT, IS CHOCOLATE VEGAN?

Desserts That Highlight Chocolate—Don't Worry, It's Vegan!

The day after I went vegan, I had a chocolate craving—and my heart filled with dread. "I'll never be able to have chocolate again! What have I done?" I quickly learned that there is tons of vegan chocolate out there, just waiting to be devoured. All you have to do is check the ingredients. Whew! Here are some recipes to help you use it all up.

CHOCOLATE CHIP BROWNIES

SERVES 16

Brownies are just the *ultimate* when it comes to chocolate, right? Aside from eating chocolate straight, these brownies have got to be the best way to satisfy chocolate cravings. There are four forms of chocolate in them: melted dark chocolate, cocoa powder, chocolate extract, and chocolate chips studded throughout each piece. All that chocolate creates the thickest, densest, fudgiest brownies you may ever sink your teeth into!

1. Preheat the oven to 350°F (175°C). Lightly spray an 8 x 8-inch baking dish with cooking spray. Line the dish with parchment paper, leaving some hanging over the edges so you'll be able to lift the brownies out of the pan easily.

2. In a small bowl or cup, whisk together the flaxseed meal and warm water. Set aside. In a medium bowl, mix the flour, cocoa, baking powder, baking soda, and salt.

3. In a double boiler or a glass dish on top of a pot of boiling water, melt the chocolate with the vegan butter, stirring until it's completely smooth. Remove from the heat. Add the agave syrup, coconut sugar, chocolate extract, and flaxseed meal mixture and mix thoroughly.

4. Add the flour mixture to the melted chocolate mixture and stir until just combined. Fold in the chocolate chips. The batter should be very thick, almost like cookie dough.

5. Spread the batter in the prepared baking dish. Bake for 20 minutes, or until a toothpick inserted into the center comes out mostly clean (a couple crumbs are okay). Remove from the oven and cool in the pan for about 5 minutes. Using the parchment paper, lift the brownies and transfer to a cooling rack to cool completely before slicing. Store leftovers in an airtight container at room temperature or in the refrigerator for 3 to 4 days.

PREP TIME: 20 minutes
COOK TIME: 20 minutes

Cooking spray

1½ tablespoons flaxseed meal

3 tablespoons warm water

1 cup (130 g) unbleached all-purpose flour

3 tablespoons cocoa powder (see tip)

1½ teaspoons baking powder

½ teaspoon baking soda

½ teaspoon salt

1 cup (180 g) chopped vegan dark chocolate (see tip)

6 tablespoons vegan butter

¼ cup (40 ml) agave syrup or Happy Bee Honey (page 34)

¼ cup (40 g) coconut sugar or vegan brown sugar

2 teaspoons chocolate extract

1 cup (180 g) vegan chocolate chips

VARIATION

▶ Replace half the chocolate chips with chopped nuts or, if it's wintertime, chopped candy canes.

TIP
Be sure to splurge on high-quality chocolate and cocoa; you won't regret it!

DOUBLE CHOCOLATE TRUFFLES

MAKES 20 TRUFFLES

I once read that when you bite into a non-vegan baked good or candy, the dairy in the item coats the inside of your mouth, thus making it hard for you to fully taste the other flavors. To me, this is tragic, especially when it comes to chocolate candy. I want to taste *all* of the chocolate. I want the chocolate flavor to knock me on my butt! When you take a bite of these little truffles, your mind goes blank for a moment. The chocolate flavor overwhelms your senses as you feel euphoria rush over you. Just as chocolate candy should.

PREP TIME: 35 minutes
DOWN TIME: 24 hours + 30 minutes

ganache filling

1 cup (180 g) vegan dark chocolate chips

½ cup (125 ml) full-fat canned coconut milk

½ tablespoon melted vegan butter

chocolate coating

¾ cup (135 g) chopped vegan dark chocolate

1 teaspoon coconut oil

toppings

Cacao nibs

Mini vegan chocolate chips

Chopped nuts

Melted vegan chocolate

1. To make the ganache, place the chocolate chips in a bowl and set aside. Pour the coconut milk into a small pot and bring to a boil. When it is boiling, pour it over the chocolate chips. Let it sit for about 2 minutes, then gently stir until it is completely combined and smooth. Add the melted vegan butter, stir again, and cool at room temperature. When it has completely cooled, cover and refrigerate overnight.

2. The next day, line a baking sheet with waxed paper. Scoop heaping ½-tablespoonfuls and use your hands to roll the scoops into balls. (Your hands will get messy but you'll be okay with it because they're covered in chocolate.) It's okay if the balls are misshapen.

3. Place the baking sheet in the refrigerator 10 to 15 minutes. Remove and reshape the ganache balls into (mostly) perfect spheres if necessary, then chill for another 10 to 15 minutes.

4. To make the coating, in a double boiler or a glass dish on top of a pot of boiling water, melt the chocolate with the coconut oil, stirring, until it's completely smooth. Remove from the heat.

5. Use a spoon to dip one ganache ball at a time into the coating, then carefully place the truffle on the lined baking sheet. Top each with your chosen topping(s), or let them cool completely, then drizzle more melted chocolate over them. Keep chilled until ready to serve.

VARIATIONS

If you like your truffles flavored, it is easy to infuse this recipe with other flavors without taking away from the chocolate rush. Try:

▶ Espresso—Soak ¼ cup (25 g) espresso beans in the coconut milk for at least 2 hours. Prior to boiling the coconut milk, run it through a fine-mesh strainer to remove the espresso beans. Garnish the top of each truffle with a new (unsoaked) espresso bean.

▶ Lavender—Soak 2 table-spoons dried lavender in the coconut milk for at least 2 hours. Prior to boiling the coconut milk, run it through a fine-mesh strainer to remove the lavender. Garnish the top of each truffle with a few sprigs of (unsoaked) dried lavender.

▶ Ginger—Stir 1 teaspoon ground ginger into the ganache when you add the melted butter. Garnish the top of each truffle with a couple tiny pieces of candied ginger.

▶ Sea Salt—Stir ¼ teaspoon ground sea salt into the ga-nache when you add the melted butter. Garnish the top of each truffle with a couple tiny chunks of Himalayan sea salt.

▶ Chile Pepper—Stir ¼ tea-spoon cayenne pepper into the ganache when you add the melted butter. Garnish the top of each truffle with a few crushed red pepper flakes.

MOLASSES-HAZELNUT CHOCOLATE MOUSSE TART WITH COCONUT WHIPPED CREAM

Silken tofu and raw cashews blended together create a perfect non-dairy base for a chocolate mousse that can only be described as legendary. If you wanted to stop and just eat the mousse, no one would blame you, but if you like to give your mousse a delicious little nest to rest in, then the molasses-hazelnut crust is absolutely necessary. Blackstrap molasses not only adds vitamins and minerals (hello, iron!) but also gives the hazelnut crust a gingerbread flavor. Topped with a cloud of fluffy Coconut Whipped Cream, you have a treat that is sure to please every chocoholic.

1. If you plan to make the whipped cream, place a large bowl and the beaters from an electric mixer in the refrigerator.

2. Combine the hazelnuts, dates, oat flour, molasses, and salt in the bowl of a food processor. Pulse until smooth and crumbly, scraping the sides as needed.

3. Line the bottom of a tart pan or springform pan with parchment paper. Press the crust mixture into the bottom of the pan and (if using a tart pan) up the sides. If there is excess oil (from overprocessing), use paper towels to blot away the oil. Place the pan in the freezer for 1 hour.

4. In a double boiler or a glass dish on top of a pot of boiling water, melt the chocolate, stirring, until it's completely smooth. Remove from the heat.

5. In a blender or food processor, combine the melted chocolate with the cashews, tofu, cocoa powder, and coconut sugar. Process until smooth, pausing to scrape the sides as needed. Pour the mixture on top of the frozen crust. Use a rubber spatula to smooth out. Refrigerate for at least 2 hours.

6. If you are making the whipped cream, just before you're ready to serve, remove the coconut milk from the refrigerator and use a can opener to open the can. All of the fat should have separated from the liquid and you should have a mound of hardened coconut milk fat at the top. Spoon it out into your refrigerated bowl, leaving the watery liquid in the can (reserve for smoothies or for drinking). Use a handheld mixer with the

PREP TIME: 30 minutes
DOWN TIME: 5 to 7 hours

crust

2½ cups (400 g) hazelnuts

14 Medjool dates, pitted

5 tablespoons oat flour (certified gluten-free if necessary)

1½ tablespoons blackstrap molasses or regular molasses

¼ teaspoon salt

mousse

1 cup (180 g) chopped vegan dark chocolate

1 cup (160 g) raw cashews, soaked in water for 3 to 4 hours, *water discarded*

One 12-ounce (340 g) package extra-firm silken tofu (the vacuum-packed kind)

1 tablespoon cocoa powder

¼ cup (40 g) coconut sugar or vegan brown sugar

coconut whipped cream (optional)

One 13.5-ounce (400 ml) can coconut milk, refrigerated overnight (see tips)

1 to 2 teaspoons vegan powdered sugar or powdered xylitol

optional toppings

Blackstrap molasses or regular molasses

Chocolate chips

Cacao nibs

Chopped hazelnuts

Sea salt

refrigerated beaters to whip the cream until light and fluffy. Mix in the powdered sugar and chill until ready to use.

7. When the tart has chilled for at least 2 hours, remove and slice. Serve each slice with a dollop of whipped cream, a drizzle of molasses, and a sprinkle of toppings of choice.

||||||||||||||||||||||||||

VARIATION

▶ Instead of a large tart pan or springform pan, make individual tarts by using six mini tart pans.

TIPS

- Certain brands of canned coconut milk are better than others for making whipped cream. I have good results with Thai Kitchen and Native Forest. Trader Joe's Coconut Cream works well, too, and yields more solid cream than regular coconut milk does.

- If you refrigerate the can upside down, when you open it, all you will have to do is drain off the water and scoop out the fat. If you forget to turn it upside down, don't worry—just proceed with the instructions as they are.

FLOURLESS CHOCOLATE DECADENCE CAKE

SERVES 8

PREP TIME: 15 minutes
COOK TIME: 85 minutes
DOWN TIME: 2 to 3 hours or overnight

Cooking spray

1½ cups (255 g) cooked chickpeas (see page 8) or one 15-ounce (425 g) can, rinsed and drained

1 cup (200 g) chopped, steamed beets (see tip)

½ cup (125 ml) agave syrup or Happy Bee Honey (page 34)

½ cup (35 g) cocoa powder, plus extra for dusting, optional

1 teaspoon baking powder

1 teaspoon vanilla extract

¼ teaspoon salt

½ cup (90 g) chopped vegan dark chocolate

¼ cup (125 ml) coconut oil

A really good flourless chocolate cake is pretty much the epitome of decadence. A really, really good one can cause a brief moment of insanity. I mean, it's part cake, part fudge, and part magic! Usually, a ton of eggs are holding the cake together, but not in this baby. Even though the end result is rich and sumptuous, chickpeas and steamed beets actually work together as the binder for this cake, making it—*shhhh!*—secretly *a little healthy* (it's practically a salad, right?). It does take a while to bake, chill, and set, but the wait is absolutely worth it.

1. Preheat the oven to 350°F (175°C). Lightly spray a 7- to 8-inch-round springform pan with cooking spray and then line the bottom with parchment paper. You may use a larger pan, but decrease the cooking time if so (see tips).

2. In a food processor, combine the chickpeas, beets, agave syrup, cocoa powder, baking powder, vanilla, and salt. Process until smooth.

3. In a double boiler or large glass bowl over a pot of boiling water, melt the dark chocolate with the coconut oil. Remove from the heat. Add the mixture to the food processor. Process until combined.

4. Pour the batter into the prepared pan and even the top with a rubber spatula. Place the pan on a baking sheet. Bake for 45 minutes, or until the top looks dry and the outer edges have risen (the inside will not be fully cooked yet). Cover with aluminum foil and bake for 35 to 40 more minutes, until a toothpick comes out clean when inserted into the *outer* edge, and mostly clean when inserted into the center (a little wet is okay). It's okay if the sides are taller than the center. That's normal. Place the pan on a cooling rack to cool completely. (Don't even try it when it's still warm. It needs to cool completely to fully set.)

5. Refrigerate at least 2 to 3 hours or overnight. Remove from the refrigerator and run a knife around the outer edge to loosen the cake from the sides of the pan before removing the outer ring. Dust with cocoa powder, if desired. Slice and serve.

TIPS

- Follow the instructions on page 161 to steam the beets, or use store-bought steamed beets. Just be sure to measure them after steaming to make sure you have 1 cup (200 g).

- If using a wider spring-form pan, such as a 10-inch, bake for roughly 30 minutes (or until the top looks done and a toothpick inserted into the center comes out wet with crumbs), then cover with aluminum foil and bake for another 20 to 25 minutes, until a toothpick comes out clean when inserted into the outer edge, and mostly clean when inserted into the center (a little wet is okay).

PUMPKIN CHOCOLATE CHIP COOKIES

MAKES 2 DOZEN COOKIES

You may think that pumpkin is reserved for consumption between the months of October and November. That is true, except when that pumpkin is going into chocolate chip cookies. Then it is perfectly acceptable to eat it year round. The pumpkin acts as an egg replacer but also adds a lot of depth to the flavor. These cookies are a total crowd pleaser, so if you serve them to your omnivore friends, be prepared for the question, "*These are vegan?*"

1. Preheat the oven to 350°F (175°C). Line two baking sheets with parchment paper or silicone baking mats.

2. Whisk together the flour, flaxseed meal, baking soda, cinnamon, ginger, salt, nutmeg, and cardamom in a large bowl. Set aside.

3. Use a hand mixer (or whisk very quickly) to mix the pumpkin puree, vegan butter, maple syrup, coconut sugar, and almond butter. Add the wet ingredients to the dry and mix until just combined. Fold in the chocolate chips.

4. Use a tablespoon or ice cream scoop to scoop roughly 2 tablespoons of dough and place on the prepared baking sheets about 2 inches apart. Wet or lightly grease the bottom of a measuring cup and gently press down on each cookie to flatten. If you want them more evenly shaped, wet your fingers and gently form them into circles. Bake for 8 to 10 minutes, until firm with lightly browned edges. Cool on the baking sheet for 2 to 3 minutes before transferring to a cooling rack. Let cool completely before serving (or not—it would be a shame not to try at least one while they're hot!).

PREP TIME: 20 minutes
COOK TIME: 10 minutes

- 1¾ cups (220 g) unbleached all-purpose flour
- 1 tablespoon flaxseed meal
- 1 teaspoon baking soda
- 1 teaspoon ground cinnamon
- ½ teaspoon ground ginger
- ½ teaspoon salt
- ¼ teaspoon ground nutmeg
- ¼ teaspoon ground cardamom
- 1 cup (240 g) pumpkin puree (not pumpkin pie filling)
- ½ cup (70 g) vegan butter, melted
- ¼ cup (60 ml) maple syrup
- ⅓ cup (40 g) coconut sugar or vegan brown sugar
- 1 tablespoon unsalted smooth almond butter or whatever nut butter you have
- 1 cup (180 g) vegan chocolate chips

TIP

It is especially important with this recipe to measure the flour by shaking spoonfuls of flour into the measuring cup until full. If you scoop with the measuring cup, the flour will be too packed and will affect the texture of the cookies.

CHOCOLATE PEANUT BUTTER CUPS

MAKES 8 CUPS

The first time my husband tried one of these chocolate peanut butter cups, he exclaimed, "This is ridiculous. I mean, this is *stupid*!" I've made them several times since then, and the reaction is always similar, sometimes with more swearing. This is a very simple recipe and so good you will never crave a non-vegan or store-bought version again. The oat flour helps to thicken the peanut butter while adding a "cookie-ish" flavor to the filling. The chocolate exterior is thicker than what you get at the store (bonus!), and the salt sprinkled on top takes them to a whole new level.

1. In a medium bowl, use a fork to stir together the peanut butter, oat flour, powdered sugar, and salt (if using). Chill until ready to use.

2. Line a 12-cup muffin tin with 8 cupcake/muffin liners. Set aside.

3. In a double boiler or a glass dish on top of a pot of boiling water, melt the chocolate with the coconut oil, stirring, until completely smooth. Remove from the heat. Scoop 2 teaspoons of melted chocolate into each liner and use the spoon to spread it to cover the entire bottom.

4. Scoop 1 tablespoon of the peanut butter mixture into your hands and roll into a ball. Place the ball in one of the liners, on top of the chocolate, and use your fingers to gently press it down (not too much—just lightly flatten the top). Repeat with the other cups.

5. Scoop 1½ teaspoons of melted chocolate over each peanut butter ball and use the back of the spoon to spread the chocolate to meet the sides of the liner, making sure no peanut butter is visible. Repeat until all cups are covered in chocolate.

6. Sprinkle the tops with a tiny pinch of Himalayan salt (if using).

7. Place the pan in the refrigerator and chill for at least 30 minutes, preferably at least 2 to 3 hours. When firm, transfer them to an airtight container; keep them in the refrigerator for a couple weeks (if you don't eat them all before then).

PREP TIME: 30 minutes
DOWN TIME: 30 minutes

½ cup (130 g) natural-style peanut butter, smooth or crunchy

3 tablespoons oat flour (certified gluten-free if necessary)

2 tablespoons vegan powdered sugar or powdered xylitol

Pinch of salt (only if using unsalted peanut butter)

Water

1 cup (180 g) vegan chocolate chips or chopped chocolate

1 teaspoon coconut oil

Chunky Himalayan salt, optional

VARIATION

▶ To make mini cups, line a mini muffin pan with 12 mini cupcake/muffin liners. Coat the liners with 1½ teaspoons of melted chocolate. Scoop slightly heaping teaspoons of the peanut butter mixture into your hands, roll into balls, and place them in the lined cups. Top the cups with 1 teaspoon of the melted chocolate. Proceed with the directions from step 7.

MEXICAN HOT CHOCOLATE FUDGE

MAKES 16 BARS

page 271

Normally, fudge is a huge, unhealthy bomb of fat, powdered sugar, and calories. This vegan version is still an indulgence and should be consumed in moderation, but the fats are of the healthier variety. It is lightly sweetened with maple syrup, letting the bold chocolate flavor shine through. A few spices give this recipe its Mexican hot chocolate flair, which hits when you've already swallowed your bite and definitely keeps you coming back for more. If plain ol' fudge is what you're after, feel free to leave out the spices.

PREP TIME: 20 minutes
DOWN TIME: 75 minutes

Cooking spray

Water

1 cup (180 g) chopped dark chocolate

½ cup (80 g) raw cashews

½ cup (110 g) coconut butter (not oil), lightly melted or softened (e.g., by microwaving it for 10 to 15 seconds)

½ cup (40 g) cacao or cocoa powder

¼ cup (60 ml) maple syrup

½ teaspoon ancho chile powder

¼ teaspoon ground cinnamon

¼ teaspoon cayenne pepper

1. Lightly spray an 8 x 5-inch loaf pan with cooking spray and line with parchment paper, leaving some overhang at the edges. Set aside.

2. In a double boiler or a glass dish on top of a pot of boiling water, melt the chocolate, stirring, until it's completely smooth. Remove from the heat and set aside.

3. Combine the cashews and softened coconut butter in a food processor and process until smooth. Add the cacao, maple syrup, chile powder, cinnamon, and cayenne; process until smooth. Add the melted chocolate and process until combined.

4. Spread the mixture in the prepared loaf pan and refrigerate for at least 1 hour. Remove from the refrigerator and let sit for about 15 minutes. Use the parchment paper to lift the fudge out of the dish. Slice and serve. Leftovers can be stored in an airtight container for 7 to 10 days.

TIPS

- Coconut butter is a good investment. Softened, it can be used as a replacement for peanut butter or as a creamy spread for toast. If you want to make it yourself, place 2 cups of unsweetened dried coconut shreds in a high-speed blender or food processor and process for several minutes, until as smooth as (though slightly drier than) peanut butter. It will firm up when it sits for a while, but microwaving it for 10 to 15 seconds will make it smooth and pliable again.

- The fudge is slightly firm straight out of the refrigerator. It will still melt in your mouth, but if you like your fudge a little softer, resting is key.

BUT I SCREAM FOR ICE CREAM!

Vegan Ice Cream Recipes That Will Have You Screaming for More

What happens to ice cream when you don't use heavy cream? Well, when you replace it with equally creamy vegan counterparts, not much. Going vegan does not mean your days of melty ice cream cones, ice cream sundaes, ice cream sandwiches, and milkshakes have come to an end. It just means they're about to be guilt free!

DARK CHOCOLATE SORBET

MAKES 4 CUPS

GF SF NF 📷 page 285

During our honeymoon in Greece, my husband and I finished each day with a walk around town while eating chocolate sorbet (the only non-dairy choice at the local gelato shop). We weren't completely vegan yet, but we were trying to limit the amount of dairy we consumed, and *oh heavens!* That chocolate sorbet certainly showed us that being dairy-free was not a concession. This recipe is based on those late-night indulgences, and let me tell you, if you love chocolate, this sorbet will be your new BFF (Best Frozen Friend). Sorbets are naturally dairy-free, so if you're nervous about trying coconut milk or cashew cream ice creams, this is a great place to start.

PREP TIME: 20 minutes
COOK TIME: 5 minutes
DOWN TIME: 5 to 6 hours

2½ cups (625 ml) water

¾ cup (115 g) coconut sugar or vegan brown sugar

½ cup (125 ml) agave syrup or maple syrup

½ cup (20 g) cacao or cocoa powder

1 cup (180 g) chopped vegan dark chocolate

1 teaspoon vanilla extract or chocolate extract

1 teaspoon ground espresso, optional

¼ teaspoon salt

1. Combine the water, coconut sugar, agave syrup, and cacao powder in a medium pot and bring to a boil, stirring continuously. Reduce the heat and simmer for 1 minute. Remove from the heat. Add the dark chocolate and stir until it is melted and smooth. Stir in the vanilla, espresso (if using), and salt. Transfer to a blender and blend for 10 to 15 seconds. Cool completely before transferring to the refrigerator to chill for 1 hour.

2. Process the mixture in an ice cream maker according to the manufacturer's instructions. When the sorbet reaches the consistency of a thick soft serve, transfer it to a glass bowl. Place a sheet of parchment paper over the ice cream to prevent contact with air (and thus reduce freezer burn). Cover and freeze at least 3 to 4 hours before serving.

TIPS

To prepare the ice cream for Ice Cream Sandwiches (page 292), line a 8 x 8-inch baking dish with parchment paper. When you take the ice cream out of the ice cream maker, transfer to the prepared baking dish. Cover and freeze at least 3 to 4 hours or overnight.

PEANUT BUTTER CHOCOLATE CHIP ICE CREAM

MAKES 6 CUPS

As a kid, I loved to drop chocolate chips into the jar of peanut butter and eat them with a spoon, naturally scooping up gobs of peanut butter in every bite. As a grown-up, I generally try to stick to healthier snacks, but I still love the sensation of scooping up creamy peanut butter filled with little chunks of chocolate. That's what this ice cream is for. It's the richest, creamiest, nuttiest peanut butter ice cream that, with the help of coconut milk, happens to be vegan! Plus, the chocolate chips are distributed throughout so we don't have to go fishing for that bite.

1. Combine the coconut milk, peanut butter, agave syrup, arrowroot powder, grapeseed oil, almond extract, and salt in a blender and blend until smooth. Chill for 1 hour.

2. Process the mixture in your ice cream maker according to the manufacturer's instructions. When the ice cream reaches the consistency of a thick soft serve, add the chocolate. When it is incorporated, transfer the ice cream to a glass bowl. Place a sheet of parchment paper over it to prevent contact with air (and thus reduce freezer burn). Cover and freeze at least 3 to 4 hours before serving. You may have to let it thaw for about 5 minutes before scooping.

PREP TIME: 20 minutes
DOWN TIME: 4 to 5 hours

One 13.5-ounce (800 ml) can + 1 cup (650 ml) full-fat canned coconut milk

¾ cup (195 g) unsalted smooth peanut butter

½ cup (125 ml) agave syrup

2 tablespoons arrowroot powder

2 tablespoons grapeseed oil, sunflower oil, or canola oil

1 teaspoon almond extract

¼ teaspoon salt

¾ cup (135 g) vegan chocolate chips or chunks

DULCE DE LECHE ICE CREAM

MAKES 5 CUPS

Dulce de leche is basically caramel sauce but creamy—a great addition to ice cream, right? For those of you craving a sweet, salty, caramelesque ice cream, this recipe is begging to be made. The creamy base is made from a combination of cashew cream and coconut milk for a velvety texture that isn't overwhelmed with coconut flavor. If you'd like, you can double the dulce de leche recipe to make extra sauce to drizzle on top. And if you bake the Chocolate Chip Brownies (page 273) in a skillet, it's a perfect little bed for this ice cream.

PREP TIME: 25 minutes
COOK TIME: 30 minutes
DOWN TIME: 5 to 6 hours

dulce de leche (double, if desired, for extra sauce)

One 13.5-ounce (400 ml) can full-fat coconut milk

¾ cup (115 g) coconut sugar or vegan brown sugar

¼ teaspoon salt

ice cream

½ cup (80 g) raw cashews, soaked in water for 3 to 4 hours, *water discarded*

½ cup (125 ml) non-dairy milk

One 13.5-ounce (400 ml) can full-fat coconut milk

2 tablespoons arrowroot powder

1 tablespoon grapeseed oil, sunflower oil, or canola oil

1 tablespoon maple syrup

1 teaspoon vanilla extract

1. To make the Dulce de Leche, combine the coconut milk and coconut sugar in a medium pot. Bring to a boil, then reduce the heat and simmer, stirring occasionally, for about 30 minutes, until the mixture is thick enough to coat the back of a spoon. Remove from the heat, stir in the salt, and cool completely.

2. When the Dulce de Leche is cool, make the ice cream. Combine the cashews and non-dairy milk in a blender and blend until smooth. Add the coconut milk, arrowroot powder, oil, maple syrup, vanilla, and the Dulce de Leche (half, if you doubled the recipe). Blend until smooth. Chill for 1 hour.

3. Process the mixture in your ice cream maker according to the manufacturer's instructions. When the ice cream reaches the consistency of a thick soft serve, transfer to a glass bowl. Place a sheet of parchment paper over the ice cream to prevent contact with air (and thus reduce freezer burn). Cover and freeze at least 3 to 4 hours before serving. You may have to let it thaw for about 5 minutes before scooping.

TIP

To prepare the ice cream for Ice Cream Sandwiches (page 292), line a 8 x 8-inch baking dish with parchment paper. When you take the ice cream out of the ice cream maker, transfer to the prepared baking dish. Cover and freeze at least 3 to 4 hours or overnight.

OATMEAL RAISIN ICE CREAM

MAKES 6 CUPS

Sometimes I have the craziest daydreams. What if panda bears weren't becoming extinct and lived in the trees outside my dining room window? What if I were actually a spy? Would people at the gym ever suspect? What if an oatmeal raisin cookie morphed itself into ice cream? Would it taste like dipping the cookies into milk? Not all my daydreams come true (probably for the best), but I'm so glad this Oatmeal Raisin Ice Cream did! Soaking oats in coconut milk with spices and maple syrup before blending gives it a strong oatmeal taste. You could probably eat it for breakfast! One can only dream . . .

1. In a large bowl, combine the coconut milk, oats, maple syrup, cinnamon, ginger, nutmeg, vanilla, and salt. Cover and chill at least 3 to 4 hours or overnight.

2. Remove the mixture from the refrigerator and add the arrowroot powder and oil. Pour into a blender and blend until completely smooth.

3. Process the mixture in your ice cream maker according to the manufacturer's instructions. While the mixture is churning, combine the raisins and coconut sugar in a small pot and cover with water. Bring to a boil, then reduce the heat and simmer for about 5 minutes. Drain off the water. When the ice cream has reached the consistency of a thick soft serve, add the raisins. Once the raisins are incorporated, transfer the ice cream to a glass bowl. Place a sheet of parchment paper over it to prevent contact with air (and thus reduce freezer burn). Cover and freeze the ice cream at least 3 to 4 hours before serving. You may have to let it thaw for about 5 minutes before scooping.

PREP TIME: 25 minutes
DOWN TIME: 6 to 8 hours or overnight

Two 13.5-ounce (800 ml) cans full-fat coconut milk
1 cup (100 g) rolled oats (certified gluten-free, if necessary)
⅓ cup (80 ml) maple syrup
1 tablespoon ground cinnamon
1½ teaspoons ground ginger
1 teaspoon ground nutmeg
1 teaspoon vanilla extract
¼ teaspoon salt
2 tablespoons arrowroot powder
2 tablespoons grapeseed oil, sunflower oil, or canola oil
1 cup (120 g) raisins
1 tablespoon coconut sugar
Water

TIP

To prepare the ice cream for Ice Cream Sandwiches (page 292), line an 8 x 8-inch baking dish with parchment paper. When you take the ice cream out of the ice cream maker, transfer to the prepared baking dish (you may have some left over; store as described in step 3). Cover and freeze at least 3 to 4 hours or overnight.

OATMEAL RAISIN ICE CREAM SANDWICHES

MAKES 6 TO 8 SANDWICHES

One of my most favorite lines from my most favorite television show (*Arrested Development*) is "I'm having a love affair with this ice cream sandwich." I can't eat an ice cream sandwich without saying it (or at least thinking it). Since I started making these oatmeal raisin ice cream sandwiches, I've been saying it *a lot* (much to the chagrin of my family). These adorable little sandwiches are chewy, creamy, sweet, spicy, wholesome, and absolutely addictive. Give them a try; I'm sure you'll have an ongoing love affair as well.

PREP TIME: 10 minutes (*not including time to prepare cookies and ice cream*)
DOWN TIME: 30 minutes

1 batch Iced Oatmeal Cookies without the icing (page 270)

1 batch Oatmeal Raisin Ice Cream (page 291, see tip)

Cooking spray

1. Line a baking sheet with parchment paper. Spread 6 to 8 oatmeal cookies on the sheet, bottom side up. Set aside 6 to 8 more cookies.

2. Remove the Oatmeal Raisin Ice Cream from the freezer. If it is hard, let it thaw for about 10 minutes. Use the parchment paper to lift the fully frozen ice cream from the baking dish and place the sheet on a cutting board.

3. Choose a biscuit cutter just smaller than the size of the cookies. Lightly spray the cutter with cooking spray. Press the cutter into the ice cream. Slide your fingers underneath the parchment paper to help push up the ice cream as you lift the cutter (the ice cream should stay inside the cutter). Place the cutter on one of the cookies and, while lifting the cutter, use your fingers to gently press the ice cream onto the cookie. Place one of the set-aside cookies on top of the ice cream, top up. Repeat with the remaining cookies.

4. Freeze the sandwiches at least 30 minutes before serving. After they've been frozen longer than a few hours, you may have to let them thaw for about 5 minutes before serving.

||||||||||||||||||||||||||
VARIATION

▶ Switch out the cookies for Pumpkin Chocolate Chip Cookies (page 281) and the ice cream for Dulce de Leche Ice Cream (page 288) or Dark Chocolate Sorbet (page 286).

MANGO LASSI ICE CREAM

MAKES 6 CUPS

Listen up! Everyone's favorite creamy mango Indian beverage is now remade as vegan ice cream! Shock? Utter disbelief? Dismiss your confusion and give this lightly spiced, rich, and fruity dessert a try. Though lush and decadent, it is remarkably light and refreshing. Mango, coconut milk, cardamom, and saffron create a harmonious combination of flavors that will leave you wondering why you've been sipping the dairy-laden version.

1. Combine the ingredients in a blender and blend until smooth. Chill for 1 hour.

2. Process the mixture in your ice cream maker according to the manufacturer's instructions. When the ice cream reaches the consistency of a thick soft serve, transfer to a glass bowl. Place a sheet of parchment paper over the ice cream to prevent contact with air (and thus reduce freezer burn). Cover and freeze at least 3 to 4 hours before serving. You may have to let it thaw for about 5 minutes before scooping.

PREP TIME: 25 minutes
DOWN TIME: 4 to 5 hours

3 cups (405 g) chopped frozen mango

3 cups (375 ml) full-fat canned coconut milk

2 tablespoons arrowroot powder

2 tablespoons grapeseed oil, sunflower oil, or canola oil

1 teaspoon vanilla extract

1 teaspoon crushed black cardamom seeds

5 to 6 saffron threads, optional

¼ teaspoon salt

CHOCOLATE PEANUT BUTTER MILKSHAKE

MAKES 1 LARGE OR 2 SMALL MILKSHAKES

This book would not be complete without a vegan version of one of the best ice cream inventions of all time: The Milkshake. I don't know who came up with the idea to blend ice cream and milk together, but I wish I could shake his or her hand. For my tribute to this wonder drink, I've gone all out in the decadence department. Vegan chocolate syrup lining the cup, a malty peanut butter milkshake with millions of chocolate flecks, and homemade Chocolate Peanut Butter Cups (page 282) on top—one sip will send you to a 1950s soda shop heaven! Be sure to have a couple straws on hand so you can share.

1. Place the chocolate chips in a medium bowl and set aside. Bring the coconut milk to a boil and immediately remove from the heat. Pour over the chocolate chips and let sit for about 2 minutes. Whisk the coconut milk and chocolate together into a smooth, fudgy sauce. Set aside and let cool to room temperature.

2. When the chocolate sauce is cooled, combine the ice cream, non-dairy milk, maca powder (if using), and vanilla in a blender and blend until just combined (don't let the chocolate chips/chunks in the ice cream get too small). If you do not have a blender or if you prefer a chunkier, thicker shake, combine the ingredients in a medium bowl and use a spoon to mix them until mostly combined (little chunks of ice cream are totally good). If you prefer a thinner milkshake, add milk by the tablespoon until you have your desired consistency.

3. Use a spoon to drizzle the chocolate sauce around the inside of one tall glass or two small glasses. Pour a spoonful of chocolate sauce into the bottom of the glass(es). Scoop about ½ cup (120 ml) of the shake into the glass (or ¼ cup/60 ml for smaller glasses). Add a small spoonful of chocolate sauce, then another ½ cup (or ¼ cup) of shake. Repeat until you've used it all. If desired, drizzle a tiny bit of syrup on top of the shake. Top with 1 to 2 Chocolate Peanut Butter Cups, or chop them up and sprinkle on top. Serve immediately with a straw (or two).

PREP TIME: 10 minutes
DOWN TIME: 30 minutes

- ½ cup (90 g) vegan dark chocolate chips
- ½ cup (125 ml) canned lite (not full-fat) coconut milk
- 2 cups (410 g) loosely packed Peanut Butter Chocolate Chip Ice Cream (page 287) or store-bought vegan ice cream
- ⅓ cup (60 ml) non-dairy milk, plus more to taste
- 2 teaspoons maca powder, optional (see tip)
- ½ teaspoon vanilla extract
- 1 to 2 Chocolate Peanut Butter Cups (page 282), optional

TIP

Maca powder is a superfood made from a Peruvian root and is super smart! It adapts to provide your body with what you need when you ingest it. If you're fatigued, it boosts your energy. If you're anxious, it calms you down. It provides endurance and stamina. In addition to countless essential vitamins and minerals, it is also packed with amino acids. I always throw a bit into my smoothies because it's good for me, but here I add it for that good ol' malty flavor.

SO, STILL THINK YOU CAN'T DO IT?

Why are you still here? You should be in the kitchen, soaking macadamia nuts to whip up some Macarella (page 49) and mashing bananas so you can have Salted Caramel Peanut Butter Bars (page 261) for dessert. What's holding you back?

If it's change that you're worried about, take baby steps. Prepare one vegan recipe per week (I just gave you 125, buddy) and go from there.

Are you afraid of having to give up your favorite foods? I totally get it, but think of all the new foods you've found in this book! I guarantee that you'll end up introducing much more to your diet than you leave behind.

Have your friends and family been less than excited for you so far? Share some BBQ Bacon Burgers (page 161) with them so they can see how delicious vegan food is. Once they see how happy and healthy you are, they should be happy too.

Really, guys, you have no more excuses! Go forth, be vegan, and prosper!

GRATITUDE

If you'd told me five years ago, when I was working as a cheesemonger, that someday I would author a vegan cookbook, I would've told you that you were drunk. This book never would've been written if it weren't for all the nonhuman animals of the world who inspired me to be a more compassionate person and gave me the drive to make the world a better place for them. I owe them all of the thanks in the world.

I need to thank the team at The Experiment for making this book happen. I owe extra-special thanks to Molly Cavanaugh for finding me, trusting me, and being patient and positive and encouraging with me through all my weird little questions and requests along the way. Molly, you really are the best, and I am so thankful you came into my life.

I owe so much to all the readers of *Keepin' It Kind*. Your comments and emails bring such joy to my day, and I never would've made it this far without your support. I just adore each and every one of you.

Many thanks to Randy Clemens. You've been my personal Mr. Miyagi in this whole journey and for that I am forever grateful.

Thank you to all my wonderful recipe testers (and cheerleaders and editors and tellers of hard, serious truths):

Leah Barnes

Tiffanie Beal

Laurie Beattie

Lola Block

Christine Boulanger & Chloé Vézina

Alexandra Caspero

Shannon Cebron & Jasper Stroud

Anna Close

Vanessa Connelly & Kurt Thoens

Bobbie Crew

Kristina Denton & JJ De La Rosa

Danielle Deskins

Claire Desroches

Kelli Estes

Kirsten Fjoser & Brian Killoran

Shari Hardin

Katie Hay

Rika Huang

Sünne Kayser

Karen & Dustin Kilmczak

Beth & Amerie Mickens

Beth Miller Erman

Cindy Muller

Gabby Ouimet

Dara Purvis & Jeffrey Watts

Sara Rose

Alison Scarlet

Nikki Schuenke

Sarah Schwass

Audrey Singaraju

Jessie Spraggins

Elizabeth & Colin Tatterson

Cassandra Teatro

Lauren & Nick Trenc

Emily Watson

Amy J. Yang

Thank you to my canine roommate, Samantha, for keeping my kitchen floor totally crumb-free.

Thank you to my parents, Don & Shirley; my grandparents, Tom & Irene; and the rest of my family for your constant love, support, and encouragement.

My heart is swollen with thanks for Maxwell & Sophia Miller. Thank you for always trying my dishes even when you don't like cornbread, beans, cauliflower, or whatever might be on the plate. Thank you for always telling me you like it and asking for seconds. Thank you for luring me out of the kitchen or away from my computer to play Tetris or watch *Dr. Who*. Thank you for always, always, always bringing a smile to my face.

All this wouldn't be possible if it weren't for my photographer and husband, Chris Miller. There are just no words that can describe how much gratitude I have in my heart for you. Thank you not only for coming home from a long, hard day's work to do a photo shoot at 8 or 9 pm, but also for singing and dancing with me to the Violent Femmes while we do it. For spending so many weekends standing behind your camera. For turning the meals I make into beautiful photographs. For being patient with me when I'm frustrated with myself or a recipe that just won't work and laughing at me when I get angry. For giving me shoulder massages while I write. For encouraging me when I think I can't do any more. For making everything *so fun*. For loving me and being my partner in this great adventure. Chris, there's monkeys upstairs.

INDEX